"Peter Jesperson's enthralling tale of his relentless pursuit of the perfect emotional feelings that can come from hearing just the right song; and all the different roles he played, from record store manager and club DJ, to his discovering and nurturing of the Replacements and his brief but exciting work with R.E.M.—so many engrossing tales of the trials and tribulations. I loved learning more about him and how he found / earned his way."

—Jody Stephens, Big Star

"Behind the visible music biz lie a few discerning individuals whose taste, connections, and sound judgment bring about the most unexpected artistic conjunctions. Jesperson is just such a man."

—John Perry, The Only Ones

"More than a witness to the birth of independent rock 'n' roll of the late twentieth and early twenty-first centuries, Peter Jesperson was a key player: a founder of the prestigious indie label Twin / Tone Records, producer and manager of the Replacements, a friend and road manager for R.E.M., and a top executive at New West Records. Along the way he's been a significant champion of some of the era's most influential indie artists including Big Star, Soul Asylum, Vic Chesnutt, Drive-By Truckers, and so many more. In *Euphoric Recall* Jesperson gives us an all-access pass to some of the most crucial moments in modern American music history, reminding us of how it felt to be young, ambitious, and too in love with rock 'n' roll to not risk it all, and too good to fail."

—Peter Ames Carlin, author of *Sonic Boom: The Impossible Rise of Warner Bros. Records*

"Peter Jesperson's *Euphoric Recall* traces the journey of an avid listener whose skills were honed doing the less-than-glamorous back-office gigs crucial to the music ecosystem. Working as a record-store clerk, club DJ, talent booker, indie-label partner, artist manager, and cool-hunter, Jesperson devoted decades to the pursuit of new audio sensations with the ardor of a true believer. From the start, his passion made its own kind of luck: He was the guy on the receiving end of the initial demo tape by Paul Westerberg and the Replacements, and he became the evangelical force that accelerated the band's development. The artists, famous and not, within these pages are true believers, too. In the course of telling their stories, Jesperson celebrates the glorious, scroungy, endlessly reformulating mythology of rock 'n' roll."

—Tom Moon, music reviewer for NPR's *All Things Considered* and
author of *1,000 Recordings to Hear Before You Die*

"For more than forty years Peter Jesperson has always been *the* biggest music fan I've ever known. In *Euphoric Recall*, he doubles down to permanently own the title with his soulfully honest memoir. Part ballad, blues lament, and loud fast chronicle, the book explains why sainthood (or knighthood) should be bestowed on his bad self, simply for crawling from the wreckage after his tumultuous years as he discovers, then manages the Replacements. But it's also Jesperson's other, always worthy trips inside the indie-music biz at labels from Twin/Tone to New West Records that really show you just how far a rock 'n' roll heart can take you, from passionate fandom to personal satisfaction, as long as you're true to yourself. Take the ride."

—Martin Keller, author of *Hijinx & Hearsay:*
Scenester Stories from Minnesota's Pop Life

Euphoric Recall

Peter Jesperson in his Minneapolis apartment, 1979

Euphoric Recall

A Half Century as a Music Fan, Producer,
DJ, Record Executive, and Tastemaker

PETER JESPERSON

Foreword by David Fricke

MINNESOTA
HISTORICAL
SOCIETY PRESS

See credit information for quoted lyrics on page 257.

mnhspress.org

The Minnesota Historical Society Press is a member of the Association of University Presses.

Manufactured in Canada

10 9 8 7 6 5 4 3 2 1

♾ The paper used in this publication meets the minimum requirements of the American National Standard for Information Sciences—Permanence for Printed Library Materials, ANSI z39.48–1984.

International Standard Book Number
ISBN: 978-1-68134-271-9 (hardcover)
ISBN: 978-1-68134-272-6 (e-book)

Library of Congress Control Number: 2023941614

Book design and typesetting by
BNTypographics West Ltd., Victoria, B.C. Canada

For my significant others,
JENNIFER and AUTRY

My work upheld me, for I had chosen to do
what I could do well, did better daily, and liked doing.

—EVELYN WAUGH, *Brideshead Revisited*

Contents

Foreword

The closest I ever came to working for a record company was in the late 1980s, early in my tenure as a staff writer at *Rolling Stone*. I got a phone call from an A&R executive at a major label who asked if I was interested in a possible opening in his department. My idea of the job was like rock journalism with benefits: finding new artists of worth and vision (as I did already), then nurturing them in the studio, to vinyl, and savoring the rave reviews and chart action.

A close friend who was a manager set me straight. "You would be miserable," he warned. "You won't get to sign the bands you want. If you do, you'll get none of the credit if the album is a hit—and all of the blame if it stiffs." I decided to stick with writing.

Peter Jesperson took the road I didn't. He would have made a great rock critic. A vigilant listener with an explorer's vigor, Peter would have come to my gig the way he writes here about the exhilarating challenges, serial frustrations, and hard-won highs of his life in music: with informed passions, an articulate, encouraging way with judgment, and no time for compromise.

Instead, Peter put all of that into the vital, treacherous business of getting the music he cared about onto records and stages, to the people he knew would love it as much as he did. But it's the same drive to discover and share that made me want to write about music as soon as I found out it was possible: my high school library's subscription to *Downbeat*; the brief, ecstatic liner notes by *Crawdaddy* founder Paul Williams for Procol Harum's 1968 LP, *Shine On Brightly*; the interviews, at the polar ends of celebrity, with Mick Jagger and Van Dyke Parks, in the first issue of *Rolling Stone* I ever bought in the fall of 1968. Either way, it's a great ride, as Peter declares in the title of this book—if you can hang on.

I've always suspected that Peter and I were destined to meet. For karma, you can't beat the fact that he worked at a Minneapolis record store, Oar Folkjokeopus, named after 1969 albums by two of my favorite rock 'n' roll eccentrics (Moby Grape's Skip Spence and the provocative British folk singer Roy Harper). And I was right on time when Twin/Tone Records, cofounded by Peter, issued its maiden-voyage wax: three red-vinyl EPs by local upstarts the Suburbs, Spooks (with singer–guitarist Curtiss A), and Fingerprints. I got all three on arrival, in the spring of 1978.

It's been a mutual crusade. Peter finds and fights for music that I have, in turn, championed in my way, in print and now on the radio. When we finally connected in person, on a cold and snowy day in 1986, it was—inevitably—because of the Replacements. I was in Minneapolis to interview their singing and songwriting captain, Paul Westerberg, for the band's debut feature in *Rolling Stone*, published with the cheeky headline, "The Gospel According to Paul." Peter—their original manager and first fan after Westerberg dropped by Oar Folkjokeopus with a now-legendary demo tape—picked me up at the airport. We stopped at the store (as hip as I hoped) and then went on to a bar called the CC Club, where I had a long-lunch appointment with Westerberg, who popped quarters into the jukebox as we talked.

At the end of our conversation, after two hours of tales about jubilantly unhinged shows and Westerberg's blunt expressions of contempt for rock 'n' roll fame in the MTV era, I asked the singer if he could ever imagine his brilliant, misfit band winning a Grammy. "Believe it or not, I've rehearsed this acceptance speech in my mind," Westerberg replied, grinning. "I'd say, 'Thanks—and blow it out your ass. Where were you when we needed you?'"

Peter, of course, was always there, not just for the Replacements—all down the line, even after they dropped him as their manager—but for Soul Asylum, who made their punk-rock bones at Twin/Tone before going off to a bigger deal; for R.E.M., as a lifelong friend and a short, brutally instructive spell as their tour manager; and for Jack Logan, a mechanic in rural Georgia and an extraordinarily prolific songwriter whose 1994 two-CD set of home demos, *Bulk*—Peter's brainstorm— got me raving in *Rolling Stone*. There's the southern-gothic firepower of Drive-By Truckers; Vic Chesnutt's profoundly confessional songs and singing; and the comebacks of country titans Billy Joe Shaver and Delbert McClinton, all from Peter's time at New West Records. And that's just the short list.

A lot goes wrong along the way. Good souls are lost. Bands don't survive, or they leave you behind. Record labels are like that too; jobs disappear overnight. In this business, the odds are never in your favor. But then there are all the reasons to keep the faith: when the right people, the great art, and the honest labor come together in a song that won't get out of your head, on an album that can change your life when you need it most.

That's why we still do it, Peter and I, each in our way. This is his story—so far.

David Fricke

Music journalist and host of *The Writer's Block* on Sirius XM Radio

One

The Why and the How

I don't recall ever making a conscious decision to work in music; I just always knew that was where I was heading. Sixty-some years later I still can't put my finger on exactly what it is about music that affects me so deeply, but something my son, Autry, said to me in 2013 comes as close as I can get. We were at a club in LA called the Echo watching one of our favorite bands, an art-pop-punk outfit from Tulsa called Broncho. I'd seen them many times but this all-ages show was Autry's first live encounter. The band was killing it onstage and we were both awestruck. About four or five songs in, Autry, then all of eleven years old, tugged excitedly on my sleeve. I leaned down, and he said, "Dad, sometimes I get a feeling from music that I don't get from anything else." Out of the mouths of babes.

I grew up in Minnetonka, a western suburb of Minneapolis, and was first struck by music on the radio in 1958. I was four years old. I was playing in a stream that ran through a neighbor's backyard, and there was a transistor radio within earshot. The culprit was "All I Have to Do Is Dream" by the Everly Brothers. Elvis Presley's "Hound Dog" and "Tom Dooley" by the Kingston Trio also made an unusual impression on me. Music gave me a pleasurable sensation, but certain songs almost seemed to cast a spell over me. I'd get lost in them. The first record I ever owned was a 45—"Wipe Out" by the Surfaris—which my parents gave me for Christmas 1963. Then in early 1964, I experienced the Big Bang!

I can remember the moment I first heard the Beatles. It was after school on a weekday in January 1964. I was at my best friend Jon Siegel's house. He was ten and I was nine. We were in the living room, building a fort out of couch cushions and watching *The Flintstones* on TV. His three sisters were sitting on the opposite side of the room, drinking sodas and switching back and forth between the two Top 40 stations of the day, KDWB and WDGY. Jon said, "Hey, listen to this, it's that song I was telling you about." It was "I Want to Hold Your Hand." When that Beatles' sound came through the airwaves, there was a freshness, a joy, and a positivity that made it stand out, as if it were leaping out of the speakers.

I instantly loved the Beatles when I heard them on the radio, but it wasn't until their first appearance on *The Ed Sullivan Show* on February 9 that my feelings for the band entered the stratosphere. I was having dinner with my mother, father, and big brother, and as was common on Sunday nights in our house, the TV was on while we ate. Everyone knew the Beatles were on *Sullivan* that night, and we tuned in too. About ten seconds into the Beatles' opening song, "All My Loving," I was drawn like a moth to a flame, right up to the TV. My mother reprimanded me—"Peter Louis Jesperson, get back to the table!"—but I couldn't move.

The next day I begged my dad to take me to the record store. He drove me to Record Lane in the Knollwood Shopping Center, and I bought *Meet the Beatles*. It was the first album I ever owned. From then on, I bought every Beatles record as they came out.

I played *Meet the Beatles* incessantly on the Magnavox high-fi radio-phonograph console in our living room. When I went to bed, I set the album up on my dresser and stared at it until I fell asleep. Some people claimed the Beatles' long hair was an affront to society, but I thought they were the coolest-looking human beings I had ever seen. The otherness that the Beatles represented has stayed with me all my life.

I have always filed my Beatles records first in my music collection, then the alphabet starts.

The Rolling Stones hit me next. I bought their first US album release, *England's Newest Hit Makers*, when it came out in May '64. I got my initial glimpse of them live on *The Hollywood Palace* TV show in June, and I thought they were sensational. The album and TV performance lifted the Stones into the pantheon alongside the Beatles for me. For a while, I believed that the Beatles and the Rolling Stones were the only artists consistent enough to be worthy of investing in an album. For everyone else, you bought singles or greatest hits compilations.

The next tier of British bands I fell for was Herman's Hermits, the Kinks, and the Yardbirds. There were plenty of American groups, too, like the Byrds, Paul Revere and the Raiders, and the Lovin' Spoonful. TV shows like *Shindig!*, *Hullabaloo*, and *Where the Action Is* fueled the flames of my fixation on music.

The release of *The Freewheelin' Bob Dylan* in May 1963 was another early revelation for me. My big brother Alan, a fledgling guitarist, wanted to learn the songs, and he played the album over and over again. Consequently, it was drilled into my consciousness. And I was fascinated by the conversational lyrics ("If'n you don't know by now," "That light I never knowed"), and in particular the songs "Don't Think Twice, It's All Right," "Talkin' World War III Blues," and "Corrina, Corrina." I was only nine years old, but I felt a pull from it nonetheless.

By the time I was eleven, my preoccupation with music was becoming a matter of concern to my mother. "You've taken something that was meant to be a hobby and blown it all out of proportion," she told me. But my young brain disagreed.

My music mania also caused some razzing from my schoolmates. When the "We Can Work It Out"/"Day Tripper" double A-side single came out in December 1965, I brought a copy to my sixth-grade class for show and tell. The teacher had to request a phonograph from the school's audio-visual department, and it was delivered to our class-room on a rolling cart. I was set to play the record when the most popular girl in the class, Robin Merry, came over. I got nervous because she normally didn't talk to me, and like every other boy in class, I had a huge crush on her. She looked at the single and said in a deprecatory tone, "You mean, you still like the Beatles?" I thought, *Are you kidding? Do I still like the Beatles?!* Suffice to say, the crush disappeared instantly.

The "We Can Work It Out" / "Day Tripper" single came out the same day as the new Beatles' album, *Rubber Soul*, but neither song was on the album. It was like getting a bonus—two new Beatle records at the same time! My dad drove me to the record store and loaned me the money to buy both. I have a vivid memory of first seeing the sprawling array of *Rubber Soul* covers filling an entire wall inside Record Lane. The band looked so fabulously cool and so strange, I was stunned and felt weak in the knees. The cover photo was very artistic with an almost fisheye-lens effect. This was also the first time their album cover didn't say "The Beatles." But why should it? They were among the most famous faces in the world.

I don't think there's any question that my brain was shaped by the music I was listening to. I was eleven years old in September 1965 when I heard "Positively 4th Street" by Bob Dylan. The line "I wish that for just one time you could stand inside my shoes / You'd know what a drag it is to see you" was like nothing I'd ever heard before. When I first heard the Stones' "Paint It Black" in May '66, I thought it was so weird it actually scared me, as did hearing "Tomorrow Never Knows" from the Beatles' *Revolver* album three months later. My heroes had taken a turn, and it was tantalizing in a way I couldn't exactly identify, but I could not stop listening to those songs.

The following July, Jon Siegel and I went to the Minneapolis Convention Hall to see a four-band event called "Happening '67." It was the first time either of us had gone to a show unchaperoned. The concert was general admission, so we got there early. When the doors opened, we ran in and got right in front of the stage.

The opening band was the Electric Prunes. Their first single, "I Had Too Much to Dream (Last Night)," was a smash hit a few months earlier, and they were riding high on their second hit, "Get Me to the World on Time." The next band was the Shadows of Knight, who had a top-ten hit with a version of Van Morrison's "Gloria." We were psyched to see them and loved their look, very much the British Carnaby Street style. Band number three was Buffalo Springfield. This was a big deal for me. Besides loving their single, "For What It's Worth," I had a teenage fixation on the lead guitarist, Neil Young, because of the way he looked: the buckskin jacket with the fringed sleeves, and the massive sideburns. Imagine my disappointment when the band walked on and someone else was in Neil's place! We later learned that Neil had briefly quit the group in May, but he returned in August. Damn!

After Buffalo Springfield finished, the anticipation really kicked in. When the curtain opened, there was Jefferson Airplane. Building off the two singles "Somebody to Love" and "White Rabbit," they were becoming one of the most popular groups in the country. The two lead singers, Marty Balin and Grace Slick, were like male and female counterparts, prowling the stage. I will also admit that Grace was one of my first serious crushes, and like every other person in the room, I could hardly take my eyes off of her. The power of the band's sound hit me hard.

Another vivid memory of that concert was a young man in the audience standing a few feet from Jon and me. He was smoking a thin, homemade-looking cigarette, grinning madly, and dancing by himself. It occurred to me he must be smoking that marijuana stuff we'd heard so much about. He looked like he was having fun. Not much of a deterrent for a thirteen-year-old.

My first personal experience working with a band came in 1968 when four of my junior high school friends formed a group called the Gross

Reality: Paul Sylvestre on vocals and keyboards, Kevin Glynn on drums, Tom Mohr on bass, and Sean "Sam" Mastro on lead guitar. I often tagged along to their rehearsals in Paul's basement. Paul's younger brother David also had a band, called Seth, that included Steve Almaas, who would go on to be a founding member of the Suicide Commandos, and Jeff Waryan, who would be in two different groups that I later worked with directly, Fingerprints and Figures.

The Gross Reality didn't write their own songs; they learned new skills and tried out equipment to match the sounds of our favorite bands, like Cream (where with "Tales of Brave Ulysses" Sam could implement his wah-wah pedal!) and the Steve Miller Band (particularly "Living in the USA").

They played high school dances, house parties, and golf course banquets. I helped carry and set up the gear. It was good preparation for my future career!

Making a career of music in some way became my goal. I discovered two things quite early on. First, when playing records for someone, the order I played the songs in was key to winning them over. And, second, relating a few details about the artists helped pique their interest. These revelations led me to my initial dream of becoming a disc jockey. That would come in time, but I had to go down some other roads first.

I'd long had a deal with my father that once I turned sixteen and got my driver's permit I'd get at least a part-time job. I suspected he thought there'd be an additional benefit in it for him. My hair was relatively long, which was a major bone of contention between my parents and me, and we'd had many heated disagreements about it. Even in 1970, long hair was still frowned upon by the establishment. Though we never discussed it, I'm pretty sure my dad assumed that for me to get a job I'd have to cut my hair. Unfortunately for my dad and fortunately for me, that did not happen. And it was all Leon Russell's fault.

On September 6, 1970, I attended a Russell concert at the Guthrie Theater in Minneapolis. As I sat waiting for the show to begin, I watched the ushers going up and down the aisles taking people to their seats. The girls wore turquoise floor-length jumpers with white blouses underneath and flat black shoes. The guys were dressed in dark blue Guthrie blazers, gray slacks, striped ties, and black shoes. Suddenly, it hit me: most of the male ushers also had long hair! Clearly the Guthrie was not concerned with such things. I thought, *This is where I should get a job!*

The Guthrie loomed large in my family. Opened in May 1963, it was a highly respected Shakespearean repertory theater, and my mother had been going there for years to see plays. I'd been there a few times myself, including annual school field trips to see the Guthrie's acclaimed productions of Dickens's *A Christmas Carol*. The adjacent Walker Art Center also hosted concerts in the theater, and I'd attended several of those—like the fabulous Leon Russell show. I was inspired by the Guthrie from the moment I first set foot in it.

A couple of days after my epiphany at the Russell concert, I slipped away from school after lunch and hitchhiked downtown to the Guthrie. I walked in the stage door, introduced myself to the man behind the desk, and asked if I could fill out a job application. He handed one to me, and I sat down in an area outside of some administrative offices and started to fill out the form. As I was completing it, a well-dressed man in his thirties stopped and said, "Are you looking for a job?" I replied yes, and proceeded to gush about how much I loved the Guthrie and how I would consider it a real privilege to work there. He looked over my application, told me his name was David Hawkinson, and said, "You're hired." This was such a pivotal moment in life. Had I not taken this leap, I believe I would have become quite a different person.

The Guthrie was an artistic oasis, and I felt like I belonged there. In addition to my being immersed in the culture of the theater, my sophisticated, private-school coworkers opened up new horizons for me. They introduced me to everything from foreign films, to Alfred Jarry's Père Ubu plays, to the works of poet/author Charles Bukowski.

I began at the Guthrie as an usher but was eager to do more. I took on cleaning the theater between the matinee and evening perform-ance on Saturdays with another usher, Rod Gordon. Rod and I became close friends and would later reconnect when he played keyboards with the New Psychenauts and the Wallets, who signed to a record label I later cofounded. I also helped out in the scene shop, where they built sets and props. Hawkinson asked me to drive the Guthrie Volkswagen van to take actors around for vignettes from upcoming plays in various public areas. By the time I was a senior in high school, I had an independent study schedule, which allowed me to work Wednesday matinees. I even got bit parts in two plays, moving sets in between acts. They were non-speaking parts, but I was in full costume: for *Cyrano de Bergerac*, I was dressed as a bakery boy, and in *Of Mice and Men*, as a ranch hand.

In late winter 1972, my father was a salesman for Gordon & Gotch, a publishing company based in Toronto. They distributed a number of foreign publications, and at one meeting they discussed importing the British music newspaper the *New Musical Express*, or the *NME*. At that time, at least four music weeklies were being produced in London, and *Melody Maker* was the only one available in the United States, and by the time it arrived, the issues were usually four or five weeks old. To compete with *Melody Maker*, Gordon & Gotch was considering having the *NME* flown in to arrive two days after the publication date. They polled the salespeople for opinions. My father said it wasn't his field of expertise, but he had a "rock music–crazy" son who could offer some feedback.

He brought home a few sample issues of the *NME*, and I eagerly browsed through them. I told my dad I thought it was an excellent magazine, even better than *Melody Maker* because it covered more of the current music movements. The quality and style of the writing was also better than most of the music journalism I was reading in the states. When my dad reported my enthusiasm back to the company heads, they said they were planning on test-marketing the *NME* in major cities like New York, LA, Boston, and Chicago; they asked my dad if his son would like to distribute the newspaper in the Twin Cities. I said yes immediately.

The deal was that they'd air-freight a thousand copies of the *NME* to me every Monday morning. I'd set up consignment accounts with any outlet I could—newsstands, bookstores, record stores, anyplace that would carry them. I would be paid a nickel for every copy distributed, and an additional dime for every copy sold.

The first shipment arrived Monday, May 1, 1972—making that my first official day working in music. It was so exciting to see an airport delivery truck back up to my parents' garage and unload several bundles of the paper. The issue was dated Saturday, April 29. This was a big deal, to have such current news and articles from one of the most important centers of contemporary rock music. And the *NME* didn't just cover bands from the UK; it authoritatively wrote about music from all around the world.

· I was still a month shy of graduating high school, but being on independent study again came in handy, and I could do my deliveries in the afternoons after spending the morning in school. Sometimes in the summer, my buddy Mike Owens would ride along, which made it more fun. Mike would go on to be a founding member of the band Fingerprints and a co-owner of Blackberry Way Recording Studios; we remain great friends to this day.

The first issue I distributed was a whopper! It came with a free flexi-disc containing snippets of songs from the Rolling Stones album *Exile on Main Street*, two weeks before the album came out. As it says on the flexi's label: "M. Jagger with piano accompaniment introduces excerpts from their forthcoming double album." In the intro, Mick sings a little blues piece that isn't on the LP: "Exile on Main Street, a strange street to walk down." I was sure stores and customers would be champing at the bit to get their hands on this magazine. Turns out, that was not the case. I distributed eighteen issues through mid-September, when Gordon & Gotch decided to pull the plug on the whole national *NME* experiment. Apparently, the other cities didn't do blockbuster numbers either.

There was another important benefit to the *NME* gig. One of the record stores I had serviced was in Coon Rapids, Minnesota, a suburb fifteen miles north of Minneapolis. It was called the Odd Merchants. I delivered twelve issues every week. When I came back the next Monday, there'd always be eleven copies left. The owner apologized for the lack of sales but tried to make me feel better by telling me there was this one guy who eagerly came in for it every week. I finally met him a few weeks later. His name was Steve Klemz, and we've been best friends ever since.

I was sad the *NME* hadn't sold better, but for me, it was a personal success. I'd done the best job I could, and it was a fantastic learning experience. All in all, it was a fine way to dip my toes into the water of working in music.

Cover of the first issue of the *NME* that I distributed in the Twin Cities, May 1972. It came with a flexi-disc of songs from the forthcoming Rolling Stones album, *Exile on Main Street. Author's collection*

Two

Oar Folkjokeopus:
Where It Began

"Do you want a job?" That was the first thing Vern Sanden ever said to me. It was April 1973 and Vern was the new owner of Oar Folkjokeopus, the freshly renamed record store on the corner of 26th Street and Lyndale Avenue in a tree-lined, mostly residential, bohemian-leaning neighborhood of south Minneapolis. I was a nineteen-year-old record hound and stopped in nearly every day on the way to my job at the Guthrie Theater. I'd been flipping through the used records when I noticed Vern approaching. He was some years older than I, was not a talkative man, and had a rather gruff demeanor. I found him quite intimidating. His offer of employment took me completely by surprise. I'd already been a regular customer at the store for nearly two years. Did I want a job? In that record store? You bet I did!

The store that became Oar Folkjokeopus opened in late 1970 as North Country Music (inspired by Bob Dylan's "Girl from the North Country"). It was the brainchild of eighteen-year-old St. Louis Park resident and self-described music junkie Wayne Klayman. To fund his dream of opening a record store, he assembled start-up capital from a variety of sources, including insurance money following the tragic death of his parents when Wayne was in high school, as well as Social Security benefit payments and profits he made from selling pot.

Fascinated by what was then a new idea—retail outlets dedicated to selling secondhand records—Wayne built up an inventory from his own substantial record collection and by running a classified ad in the *Minneapolis Star*. One especially fortuitous reply was all it took. "A former DJ really saved my butt," Wayne recalled. "He had a huge collection from his radio days and no longer wanted them. . . . Thanks to his 800 LPs and my collection, I was now in business."

But first, Wayne had to find a storefront, which proved to be slow going. He finally landed on an affordable converted house in the Uptown area of Minneapolis at the corner of James Avenue and Lake Street. With roughly 1,200 used records and 75 new releases obtained from local distributor Dart, North Country Music opened for business in December 1970.

I first crossed North Country's threshold in June 1971 after calling every record store in town in search of the new Procol Harum album, *Broken Barricades*. North Country had it before any other store in the Twin Cities. I instantly became a loyal customer.

Wayne shuttered the store after a robbery in late June, but by early September, North Country Music was reborn at a new location about a mile and a half away, at 2118 Lyndale Avenue. Thanks to deals with two regional distributors—Heilicher Brothers and Select-O-Rax—Wayne was able to build a broader inventory of new records.

Business boomed at the new location, and Wayne soon realized he needed to relocate, again, to a larger space. "We treated customers like family, as always, and we were rolling," Wayne recalled. "The store just got too small for us!" The following August, a larger site became available on the northeast corner of 26th and Lyndale. Wayne and company moved overnight and reopened in their new digs on September 1, 1972, without missing a day of business.

That fall into winter, North Country's third location was thriving, but Wayne was feeling burned-out after all the ups and downs of running the business. One of the regular customers, Vern Sanden, had been asking if Wayne was interested in selling the store. Wayne finally decided to take him up on it.

A lifelong music fan who had dreamed of owning a record store since he was a kid, Vern took over North Country Music on February 1, 1973, and in a daring move, he renamed it Oar Folkjokeopus. The name was a combination of the titles of two of Vern's favorite albums: *Oar* by Skip Spence and *Folkjokeopus* by Roy Harper. The store's unwieldy moniker raised many an eyebrow before it permanently entered the Twin Cities music lexicon.

To take the job at Oar Folk, I needed to rearrange my life a bit. First, I had to turn in my notice at the Guthrie. I'd worked there for two and a half years, ever since I was a junior in high school. I couldn't have loved it more, and leaving was sad. Second, career-wise, I had an eye on radio, and in February 1973 I started attending Brown Institute to study radio broadcasting and electronics. This meant I'd need to work nights at the record store, the 4:00–10:00 PM shift, which was fine by me.

I officially became an employee of Oar Folkjokeopus on Monday, April 30, 1973. It was less than a year since I'd graduated from high school. Of all the jobs I've ever had, working at Oar Folk was probably the one I was best suited for, and the one I liked the most. I felt empowered working there. My mother had scolded me for years about my fixation on music. Getting the job at Oar Folk was like saying, "See, Mom and Dad, music was more than a hobby—all that time spent poring over records had a purpose after all!"

My first day at Oar Folk felt like something out of a fairy tale. At the time, I still lived with my parents in Minnetonka, about ten miles west of downtown. My commute to the store took me right past the Heilicher Brothers warehouse. On my very first day, I was charged with stopping by the distributor to pick up a new album being released: *Red Rose Speedway*, the fourth post-Beatles album by Paul McCartney. The

Beatles, and McCartney specifically, had pretty much ruled my world since 1964, and I felt delirious to be carrying a box of his new album in the trunk of my car.

When I started there, the Oar Folk staff was Vern; store manager Barry Margolis, a record collector and walking musical encyclopedia; and Rick Dorn, the one holdover from North Country. Much as I loved North Country, I felt the essence of the place improved when Vern took over. He brought an air of deep music appreciation and a sharp eye for record collecting, as well as a slightly more businesslike manner.

My first task was to get acclimated to Oar Folk procedures; how to hand-write receipts with artist name, label, and catalog number; being educated in the purchase of used records; how to be on high alert for shoplifters; and how to close out the till at the end of the night. I was also given a key to the front door and a code for the alarm system.

Until I was able to handle the counter on my own, Vern worked with me. It allowed him to fill me in on how he wanted things done and enabled us to get to know each other. I found that being a record store clerk came naturally, and I settled in pretty quickly. I was good at dealing with customers and had no problem talking about music all day long.

I often worked alongside Barry, and he became a good friend and one of my musical mentors. He's an unusual person: intensely smart and very opinionated. I enjoyed working with Barry, but he and Vern had a dispute and he was let go. In Barry's place, we hired a steady customer from the neighborhood, Rich Blomme. Vern took over store management and he, Rick, Rich, and I split the counter duties and the ordering of records.

Things slowed down around 9:00 PM, and sometimes I'd pull out my homework and study for the last hour until closing. Other times I'd prop the front door open, pull a stool into the corner entryway, put a record on, and crank it up. I have a specific memory of playing the Miles Davis soundtrack for the documentary about boxer Jack

Johnson, which to me has a cool city vibe. I'd sit and watch the traffic go by, marveling at the fact that this kid from the suburbs was now working at the best record store in town.

Vern and I got along very well. We had quite different personalities, but we liked and respected one another. As I got more comfortable with him I became more outspoken. For example, I thought it was odd that Oar Folk didn't carry 45s. When I mentioned it, Vern said he'd outgrown them and become "an album guy." I pointed out that, at the time, there were still three Beatles' singles that had B-sides that weren't available on albums. I said, "Don't you think we should at least carry those?" He finally relented.

I ordered the singles and displayed them in a cardboard box on the counter: "Help" backed with a McCartney screamer called "I'm Down"; "Lady Madonna" with an eastern-influenced George Harrison song on the flip side entitled "The Inner Light"; and "Let It Be," which featured the B-side "You Know My Name (Look Up the Number)," a zany, 1930s-styled pastiche. Within a couple of years we had more than 10,000 singles in stock, and it became one of the store's biggest attractions.

An early bonding experience Vern and I had was over a then-obscure power-pop quartet from Memphis called Big Star. I first encountered the band in 1972. I was record shopping downtown one day and went into Music City on the corner of Seventh and Hennepin. As I was flipping through the discount section, I saw a black cover with a large white and yellow neon star on it. The jacket was laminated, so it had a striking glossy sheen that you might see on an import. When I turned it over, the photo of the four band members sitting on the ledge of a bay window—with their faces in half shadow—got my attention. The band's name was Big Star, the album title was *#1 Record*, and the band members included Alex Chilton, who had been the singer of the Box Tops. A bright orange sticker pasted on the shrink-wrap said 99¢. I thought, *At that price, I'll give it a try.* When I got it home, one listen was all it took. By song number four, "Thirteen," I was *gone*.

Vern had a similar experience. We weren't always the first guys on the block to discover new artists, but this was one time we were well ahead of the curve. We became like Big Star evangelists. This is a key example of how we gained so many people's trust at the record store. To turn a customer onto a group as monumental as Big Star couldn't help but breed long-term loyalty.

It was quite the year to start working in a record store. Besides the McCartney album, other landmark releases were David Bowie's *Aladdin Sane*, the Rolling Stones' *Goats Head Soup*, John Cale's *Paris 1919*, Roxy Music's *For Your Pleasure*, and *Mott* by Mott the Hoople.

In December 1973, I finished up at Brown Institute. The job placement director at Brown said he had high hopes for me. I'd done well there and graduated with a then-much-coveted certificate—a first-class radio/telephone operator's license. This gave me an advantage in the search for employment because it qualified me to take transmitter readings, which allowed me to work at a radio station without an engineer on duty, thereby saving money for whoever hired me.

In my mind, the first order of business was to apply for a job at KQRS. It was the most powerful FM rock station in the Cities, and that's where I thought I belonged. In fact, I had pretty much gone to broadcasting school specifically with the hope that it would lead to a job at KQ. Although the station had gotten gradually more conservative, I thought I could combat this unadventurous backslide. I quickly submitted my résumé and an air-check (demo) reel. I was just as quickly turned down. They didn't even invite me in for an interview. I was crushed.

In June 1974, a new opportunity came up at another station. The placement folks at Brown let me know about a job opening at KRSI–KFMX. It was an AM/FM station based in suburban Eden Prairie. The trade ads listed the stations as "Combo Country and Contemporary (Rock)" respectively. I called and was given an appointment to interview for the position. After not much more than a brief chat, I was hired.

I was given the graveyard shift—1:00 to 8:00 AM, Monday through Friday, plus a daytime slot from 2:00 to 8:00 PM on Sundays. Both stations were automated, meaning music and spoken song intros and outros were all on pre-programmed tapes. My job was to cue up and monitor the fourteen-inch reel-to-reel tapes, cut in with live hourly news and weather breaks, take transmitter readings every two hours, and handle light equipment maintenance. At 5:00 AM, the news director would come in and I'd assist him in preparing his morning broadcasts. No question it was a weird gig. It didn't allow me to actually be a DJ, but I made the best of it, and the work was challenging.

When my shift ended at 8:00 AM, I'd drive home, have breakfast, and sleep until 2:00 PM. Then I'd get up, eat lunch, and go to work at Oar Folk from 4:00 to 10:00 PM. From there it was go home, eat dinner, make a pot of coffee, and head back to the radio station. This would go on for the next fifteen months.

With Vern putting his stamp on the record store, Oar Folk began to establish a new identity, and a personal feel that our collective tastes created. One of the store's specialties became records imported from other countries, primarily England. At the top of that list was the UK pressings of the Beatles' albums on Parlophone. When the albums were first released, the band's US label, Capitol Records, made revisions for the American market. The first seven Beatles albums had been shortened, the song selections were altered, and in some cases the album covers were changed. To be fair, the American sequences were exciting in their own way, but what serious Beatles fan wouldn't prefer to hear the albums as the band had made them? Another crucial dividend of the British pressings was that they simply *sounded* better, because the production runs for each vinyl pressing master were smaller in the UK and thus were more consistent in quality. All this made the imports ultra-desirable, and we sold them by the ton. The enormous quantities we sold gave us cachet with our foreign distributors. For a while, we were the only game in town as far as offering a comprehensive selection of imported LPs, singles, and EPs.

In addition to its import specialty, Oar Folk aimed to be a full-service, all-styles-served record store. We built up a good selection of more than just rock. We were well stocked with blues, R&B, jazz, folk, country, world music, and classical. Disco was huge at the time, and we sold lots of that too. Several dance-music DJs shopped regularly at our place. And if a customer was looking for something we didn't have or didn't know about, we took it as a challenge to help them track it down.

At Oar Folk, we could move relatively large quantities of certain titles by non-mainstream artists that didn't sell much anywhere else. For the most part, record store rules of conduct had long been dictated by businesspeople rather than music fans, and the former naturally concentrated on the artists and albums that had the biggest sales potential. When we fell hard for something that we felt wasn't getting its fair share of attention, we believed it was our duty to promote it, with gusto.

Maybe the best example of this was our promotion of an album called *McGear*. Born Peter Michael McCartney, Mike McGear had changed his last name to avoid sponging off his famous big brother. In 1966, along with two friends, Mike had formed a group called the Scaffold that mixed poetry, music, and absurdist humor, with a few of their songs denting the charts. After releasing a UK–only solo album in 1972, Mike was signed to Warner Bros. Records in 1974. He released *McGear*— a collaboration with his brother—in September. Mike is unquestionably the star of the show, but Paul produced the album and cowrote most of the songs with Mike. Conspicuous in its absence is a credit for bass guitar, so one can only assume.

To my ears, the *McGear* album is Paul McCartney's best work, post Beatles. It's playful, smart, adventurous, imaginative, humorous, well written, and well played; the album rocks, and the melodies are to die for. We played the album incessantly in the store and raved about it ad infinitum. I ordered 100 empty album jackets from Warner Bros. and covered one entire wall of the store with them. We kept the album on the new release rack for months. In the year following its release, we sold nearly 500 copies of the album. In the big picture, that might not seem like a lot, but I'd be willing to wager that no other single store in the world, with the possible exception of a store in Liverpool, sold that many.

The first artist we consistently sold notable amounts of over multiple releases was David Bowie. The whole staff was completely gaga over his music, but until *Young Americans* (released in March 1975), he received virtually no airplay on local radio.

Most of the local representatives from the major labels thought our store was too oddball to warrant their attention. On occasion, the ones that did have us on their radar would bring in promotional display materials by mainstream artists that we just couldn't get behind. When we'd decline one of their promotional displays, they weren't nice about it. A rep once told me we'd never get promo service from their company ever again and stormed out.

In the plus column, however, was Bob Heatherly, a regional sales and marketing man for RCA Records, which was Bowie's label. Heatherly was not so judgmental and believed we could be a strong ally. He was very generous, getting us prerelease copies of Bowie albums, showering us with promo and display material of all kinds.

In April 1975, we hosted Oar Folk's first artist in-store appearance. In those days, in-stores by artists were meet-and-greet autograph sessions only, with no live performance. We decided to kick off this new kind of promotional event with (drum roll, please): Ian Hunter and Mick Ronson! The duo was performing at the St. Paul Civic Center Theatre on April 22. Hunter's five-year tenure as lead singer and pianist with Mott the Hoople had come to an end the year before. Ronson had been David Bowie's right-hand man and lead guitarist (and genius arranger) since 1970, but had been squeezed out after Bowie's *Pin Ups* album in 1973, at which point he embarked on a solo career and a brief stint with Mott the Hoople.

Oar Folk was almost uncomfortably crowded for Hunter and Ronson, but everyone was excited to have them in the house. A favorite memory is standing behind the counter with Ian to my right and Mick on my left. The phone rang. I answered, and an overseas operator said, "I have a person-to-person call for a Mr. Mick Ronson." It felt so strange to be able to say, "Yes, he's here. Mick, it's for you."

In August, a couple of months into my second year at KRSI–KFMX, I approached management about a raise. I'd worked hard and been completely reliable, and I didn't think it would be a problem. I was told simply, "No." The manager wasn't even particularly compassionate or apologetic about it. I didn't expect this. It felt like a slap in the face. I remembered when I was hired I'd been told that after a year I'd be entitled to a two-week paid vacation. I brought this up. It was begrudgingly agreed to, and I took the time off.

During this vacation, Vern and his wife, Donna, invited me over to their house for dinner. As we talked, my frustrations about the radio job came up. Vern listened and then said, "Well, I've been thinking. I'd like to bring you in full-time to manage the store." I had not seen this coming, but it sure brightened my spirits quickly! I told him I loved the idea, but between working full time at the station and part time at the store, I was making pretty good money, and it would be hard for me to take a pay cut. Without hesitation, Vern said, "I'll match it."

I wasn't too broken up about quitting the radio gig. I had learned a lot and really did love the autonomy of the night shift, but it had become clear that that particular job was a dead end. During my time at KRSI–KFMX I'd ruminated on my career choice and come to the conclusion that, unless I could find a dream radio gig with the freedom to choose the records I played, radio wasn't the right thing for me. Managing Oar Folk was exactly what I wanted to do.

On my first day back at the radio station after my vacation, I turned in my two weeks' notice. My last day at KRSI–KFMX would be Sunday, September 21. Normally on Sundays I worked until 8 PM, but on this particular night I left early because I had a ticket to see Bruce Springsteen's Twin Cities debut at the Guthrie, centered around his new album, *Born to Run*. The show was nothing short of cathartic.

The next day, Monday, September 22, was my first day as the manager of Oar Folkjokeopus, and boy, did that ever feel good, like I was starting a new chapter in my life. I'd done the morning/afternoon shift a few times in between broadcasting school and the radio gig, but now that I'd be ordering the records and taking care of other assorted business matters, my new regular work slot was 10:00 AM to 6:00 PM. Coming off a year and a half of working overnights, I felt like I was rejoining the real world.

Our next hire at Oar Folk was Andy Schwartz, a New Yorker who'd moved to Minneapolis to attend the University of Minnesota. Andy was a music historian who had been writing features and record reviews for the arts and entertainment section of the *Minnesota Daily*. He'd been a regular customer at Oar Folk for months and was a perfect addition to the staff. He was with us for only two years, but he brought a lot to the table.

Later that fall we hired Dan Fults, also a dedicated customer. Dan's taste in music was eclectic and idiosyncratic. We were both devoted to the store and always had a ball together. Dan and I have been best friends for nearly fifty years now.

I had Oar Folk procedure down by then, and Vern, who didn't love working the counter, started coming in less often. He'd still work shifts as needed and hang around some. He just preferred to work at home, where he did the bookkeeping and banking, as well as running a robust mail-order business in collectible records. Dan, Andy, and I handled things at the store. It felt like we—the inmates—had been given the keys to the asylum.

By this point, Oar Folkjokeopus had attracted a wide-ranging clientele and was becoming more than just a record store. It had gradually grown into a clubhouse for music fanatics, a watering hole of sorts where people gathered to hear the hottest new releases, to talk about older things they'd missed, to browse through used records, to scour the music magazines and books, or to find out where the most exciting live music was happening that week. It was a place where, in a fun informal way, the staff educated the customers and vice-versa. But it wasn't just about fun. At Oar Folk, we were dead serious about what we were doing. We lived and breathed music. Dare I say, we were experts in our field. People actually moved into the neighborhood to be near Oar Folk, and the CC Club, which was located kitty-corner from the store. The CC Club, like Oar Folk, had also become a preferred spot for music folks. I remember someone saying that 26th and Lyndale was like the Haight-Ashbury of the Twin Cities.

The mid-'70s brought significant change to rock 'n' roll. Some music historians would have you believe that the freshness and excitement of what were eventually labeled "punk" and "new wave" saved the music world from the major-label/singer-songwriter/progressive-rock/disco doldrums of the early part of the decade. I don't mean to downplay the importance of this shift, but in reality, both periods produced lots of fantastic records and oodles of dreadful ones. The real difference was that much of the emerging music was on independent labels run by the artists themselves or their friends. DIY was the order of the day. In some instances, the records were so indie, we bought them directly from the artist. Case in point: I ordered the first Pere Ubu 45, "30 Seconds Over Tokyo," directly from singer David Thomas (aka Crocus Behemoth) after reading a rave review in the *New York Rocker*. Pere Ubu would later sign with Blank Records on their way to becoming one of the definitive art rock bands of the era.

Clearly, something big was happening. The savviest of the distributors we'd been dealing with for imports quickly started bringing in domestic indie releases as well, so we didn't miss a beat. Some of the earliest and most significant harbingers of the "new guard" for us at Oar Folk were:

The New York Dolls, self-titled, LP, Mercury Records, July 1973
The New York Dolls, *Too Much Too Soon*, LP, Mercury Records,
    May 1974

Patti Smith, "Piss Factory," single, Mer Records, November 1974

Various Artists, *Beserkley Chartbusters, Volume 1*, LP, Beserkley Records,
    July 1975

Television, "Little Johnny Jewel," single, Ork Records, October 1975

Pere Ubu, "30 Seconds Over Tokyo," single, Hearthan Records,
    December 1975

The Modern Lovers, self-titled, LP, Home of the Hits / Beserkley
    Records, July 1976

Significantly, the *Chartbusters* compilation introduced the world to Jonathan Richman and "Roadrunner," surely one of rock 'n' roll's greatest songs.

On April 23, 1976, the self-titled debut by the Ramones was released, and the reverberations were seismic. Arguably, the Ramones inspired more bands to form than anyone since the Beatles. Andy Schwartz, in his role as music journalist, received an advance promo of the Ramones debut album. As soon as he put it on the turntable at Oar Folk, we all quickly came to attention. The simplicity, the energy, the buzz saw guitar, and the kooky words grabbed us, as did the similarity to what our own Suicide Commandos had been doing.

All this new music felt fresh—part natural progression, part stylistic and cultural explosion. To some extent, we'd been warned. We'd heard elements of punk sporadically before, as far back as the Kingsmen's "Louie, Louie" (1963), the Seeds' "Pushin' Too Hard" ('65), and "Hey Little Girl" by the Syndicate of Sound ('66), and then in groups like the Velvet Underground ('67), the Stooges ('69), and the New York Dolls ('73). But this time it was a full-on, global movement. New wave (originally an umbrella term that included punk) was basically what would later be called "alternative music." It was a landslide of new groups that took on a catchy, artful, quirky, and sometimes deliberately amateur sound. For the next twenty months, a deluge of records were released that would define the era:

The Ramones, self-titled, LP, April 1976

The Suicide Commandos, "Emission Control," single, September 1976

The Damned, "New Rose," UK single, October 1976

Richard Hell and the Voidoids, "Another World" / "Blank
  Generation" / "You Gotta Lose," EP, November 1976

The Sex Pistols, "Anarchy in the UK," UK single, November 1976

The Ramones, *Leave Home*, LP, January 1977

Willie Alexander, "Kerouac" / "Mass Ave.," single, January 1977

The Damned, *Damned Damned Damned*, UK LP, February 1977

Talking Heads, "Love Goes to Building on Fire," single, February 1977

The Clash, "White Riot," UK single, March 1977

Elvis Costello, "Less Than Zero," UK single, March 1977

The Clash, self-titled, UK LP, April 1977

Graham Parker & The Rumour, *Howlin' Wind*, LP, April 1977

The Suicide Commandos, "Mark He's a Terror," single, April 1977

The Sex Pistols, "God Save the Queen," UK single, May 1977

The Clash, "Remote Control," UK single, May 1977

Elvis Costello, "Alison," UK single, May 1977

Elvis Costello, *My Aim Is True*, UK LP, July 1977 (US release November
  1977)

The Only Ones, "Lovers of Today," UK single, July 1977

The Sex Pistols, "Pretty Vacant," UK single, July 1977

Richard Hell and the Voidoids, *Blank Generation*, LP, September 1977

Talking Heads, *Talking Heads: 77*, LP, September 1977

The Heartbreakers, *L.A.M.F.*, LP, October 1977

The Sex Pistols, "Holidays in the Sun," UK single, and *Never Mind the
  Bollocks, Here's the Sex Pistols*, LP, both October 1977

The Ramones, *Rocket to Russia*, LP, November 1977

This international influx of new bands fed into a significant development in our local scene and the history of Minnesota music. On June 1,
1977, a new rock club called Jay's Longhorn opened in downtown

Minneapolis. At that time if you weren't mainstream, roots-oriented, or a cover band, it was hard to find a place to play. Right out of the gate, the Longhorn supported the left-of-center bands that focused on original material. Hallelujah! In addition, I was hired to put my DJ skills to work there in July, a complete gas of a gig that would last me for the next four years.

That June, I moved into the Modesto apartment building one block behind the record store, on the corner of 26th and Garfield. Over the next few years, more and more music people moved into the building, and it became a sort of rock 'n' roll dormitory.

It was shaping up to be a very happening summer. On July 1 and 2, the Ramones hit town for two nights at Kelly's Pub in St. Paul. The Suicide Commandos as well as Berlin were the openers both nights. Berlin seemed an odd choice for the bill, but the Ramones and the Commandos were perfectly paired. The two bands shared attitudes and musical influences—'50s rock, garage, pop, bubblegum. They played fast and loud, with a patent sense of humor. This hybrid was radical, ultramodern, brand new.

Memories are foggy on this, but we did two, possibly three, in-stores with the Ramones at Oar Folk. I believe the first one was the day after the opening night at Kelly's, on the afternoon of Saturday, July 2. We were downright giddy to have the Ramones in our humble digs. The Ramones came back to the store in January and November of '78. By their last visit, so many fans came—spilling out of the store onto the sidewalk and lining up all the way down the block—that the police showed up, just to make sure everything was under control.

In September 1977, Andy gave his notice at Oar Folk. He decided to move back to New York. Andy had been a good friend, integral to the development of the local music community, and an asset to the store. In his place, we hired yet another regular, a cool, bookish gent named Reid Matko. Reid started with a bang. His first shift at Oar Folk was on October 22, the day of the in-store appearance by that season's

most-talked-about new band, Talking Heads. They'd played the Longhorn the night before to an ecstatic sold-out audience and would do so
again that night.

In the early months of 1978, the local scene was really cookin', and Oar
Folk was too. We hired Terry Katzman, a music journalist and record
nut with vast musical knowledge who'd been a customer at our store
for a number of years. He was a perfect fit to work at Oar Folk; I don't
know why we didn't hire him sooner. Terry and I would become the
best of friends.

The Suicide Commandos' major label debut, *Make a Record*, was released on Valentine's Day 1978. As with their previous two 45s, Paul
Stark, a local recording studio owner and live soundman, was the engineer and producer of the LP. They used the most professional studio
in town, Sound 80 (where, among other things, half of Dylan's *Blood
on the Tracks* was recorded). We celebrated the album's release with an
in-store at Oar Folk that drew an overflowing crowd, followed by a
packed release party at the Longhorn.

On April 16 we hosted an in-store with one of our faves, Brit band
Ian Dury and the Blockheads. They were in town for two shows at
the State Theatre opening for Lou Reed. The band and crew were a
cool, ragtag bunch, resembling a gang of street-kid pirates. It ended
up being one of our most successful in-stores. We had so many people
turn out for it, not only did a local TV crew show up, but so did the
Minneapolis police, again.

We were all massive New York Dolls fans at Oar Folk, so we were
super psyched to host their former lead singer, David Johansen, for an
autograph session in July. David had released his first solo album in
the spring and was playing two shows that evening at the Longhorn. It
was a Sunday so there was a bigger crowd than our weekday events.

Blondie's Twin Cities debut was happening later that month as well,
and the anticipation was sky-high. Blondie had already released two
albums and had a third coming in September. They were doing two

shows at the Longhorn, and although their label hadn't committed to an in-store appearance, we were told it was highly likely the band would stop in. We kept that possibility fairly close to the vest, but of course word got out, and again the place was packed. The band did come by and received a rapturous welcome. They happily hung out, signed records, and chatted with fans.

One of Oar Folk's most successful promotions took place on October 1 and 2, 1979. The British band the Only Ones was coming to the states for the first time. Most everyone I knew felt the Only Ones was one of the best bands on the planet at the time. They were purveyors of a gripping kind of dark, majestic rock. Front man Peter Perrett's writing had echoes of Bob Dylan and Lou Reed.

My girlfriend, Linda, and I couldn't wait, and we took the train to Chicago to see the band play there before they got to Minneapolis for two nights at the Longhorn. The band hung around Oar Folk a good deal while they were in town, and they ended up coming over to my apartment after the first night's show. Perret walked in and immediately asked where my Dylan records were. He thumbed through until he found the album *Street Legal* and played "Where Are You Tonight" two or three times in a row, eyes closed, singing quietly along. It was a terrific night of conversation and listening to records. Lead guitarist John Perry and I liked lots of the same music, and we would trade records by mail off and on over the years. In the early 2000s, John became a regular guest at my house in Los Angeles, often spending two to three weeks in January or February. John is a gifted guitarist, an autodidact, and one of the most intelligent people I have ever known. I'm proud to count him as one of my very best friends.

In general, 1980 was a great year for the store. Big records for us were David Bowie's *Scary Monsters*, the Only Ones' *Baby's Got a Gun*, Captain Beefheart and the Magic Band's *Doc at the Radar Station*, and the third Peter Gabriel album.

It was also an unusually busy year for me. By this time, I was helping to build the embryonic Twin/Tone Records label and was working with an up-and-coming local band called the Replacements (both topics discussed at length in subsequent chapters); along with my ongoing responsibilities at Oar Folk and the Longhorn, I was working practically 24–7. Over the next year as things ramped up for the Replacements, I became the band's manager and often had to rearrange my schedule at the store to accommodate. Thankfully, Vern and my coworkers were supportive and happy to cover for me whenever needed.

In the spring of '83, when the band R.E.M. offered me a temporary gig as road manager (another topic for a later chapter), it finally hit me: My time at the record store was coming to an end. I loved Oar Folk, but I'd been there a decade, and it was time for me to move on.

When it came to telling Vern, it wasn't as hard as I'd expected. I explained why I was leaving, and he understood. He said he'd known the time would come eventually but was glad I'd stayed as long as I did. No question, there was sadness on both sides.

Reflecting back, Vern offering me a job at that record store was a providential moment in my life. It was my entrance, my "big break," into the music business. It helped me build the confidence to follow my instincts to promote music I believed in and allowed me to develop strong relationships with the many musicians who frequented the store. All of this was hugely beneficial to my later work as a talent scout and record-label liaison. I also got to work with some amazing people who were great influences in my career and, in many cases, lifelong friends, among them Vern Sanden, Dan Fults, Terry Katzman, Barry Margolis, Andy Schwartz, Jim Peterson, Bill Melton, and Mitch Griffin.

I treasure my ten years at Oar Folk more than words can say.

Three

Jay's Longhorn:
On with the Shows

I wish that I remembered the first time I walked into Jay's Longhorn and what band I went to see. It must've been sometime in June 1977. Little did I know then how much time I'd be spending there over the next four years, as both an employee and a music fan. What I do know is that I saw some of the best live music of my life in that club.

As a breeding ground for local Twin Cities bands, and as a destination for alternative-rock touring acts during the musical explosion of the late '70s and early '80s, the Longhorn had one of the most important stages in the United States. Comparisons to the venerated New York City club are apt; you could say it was the Twin Cities' own CBGB.

The club was located in a one-and-a-half-story building under a parking garage in downtown Minneapolis, just south of the corner of Fifth Street and Hennepin Avenue, the city's main drag. This part of downtown was a little questionable, especially at night. A precursor, of sorts, had been located across the street from the Longhorn, downstairs from one of many strip joints in the neighborhood. The short-lived Blitz Bar reflected the same open-minded music policy as the Longhorn and had booked some of the same bands that would be headlining across the street a year or so later. It was fun while it lasted, but truth be told, the Blitz had never really promoted the fledgling underground rock scene. Plus, it was a real dive. The toilets often over-flowed, and it didn't always smell very good.

The Longhorn was much more hygienic. In fact, it was a relatively classy place. Back in the 1940s it had operated under the name Curly's. In the '50s, it became the Starlite Club but closed after a fire in 1959. More recently it had been a Sweden House Smorgasbord, a Nino's Steakhouse, and then a jazz club. Coming in the front door, you hung a left and went down a few steps below street level into a sprawling, low-ceilinged, wood-paneled space with a huge kitchen, two bars, and another bar in a partial second-story area. The décor, originally installed in the Nino's days, had a Western motif: cow heads in the carpet design, steer horns on the walls, and wagon-wheel light fixtures hanging from the ceiling. The Blumenthal family, led by a father-son venue management team, turned the place into a jazz club and reinforced the design theme by naming it the Longhorn. When young entrepreneur and former auto-speed-shop owner Jay Berine bought the business and the liquor license in early 1977, he simply had a friend paint "Jay's" in front of "Longhorn" on the sign outside. He didn't have enough money to remodel and was impatient to get the place open. Suffice to say, it had an incongruous ambience for an underground rock club, but we all got over that real fast.

In its typical setup, the music room featured a dance floor in front of a roughly 14-by-25-foot, 20-inch-high stage, with small tables and chairs around the perimeter. In the back, abutting the kitchen, a larger over-flow area had additional seating and could be curtained off on less busy nights. Along that rear portion was a long enclosed hallway that served as a dressing room. Behind that was the office. Off the lobby was what everyone called the front bar, with red vinyl booths and velvet wall-covering. Conversation was more easily heard in the front bar, and it was where, for a short time, strippers performed during lunch and happy hour. The second level also had a bar and a stage. Before Jay took over, the upstairs was where the jazz bands played. Then it was rock bands. Then a game room. And later, rock bands played up there again.

In November 1977, the fire marshal deemed the Longhorn's official capacity to be 300, but the actual number of attendees could more than double that, as happened when Elvis Costello and the Attractions played on Valentine's Day '78 in the thick of their rising fame. That November, the Suicide Commandos played three farewell shows, the last of which allegedly had a headcount approaching a thousand, with bodies crammed into every nook and cranny of the building. Iggy Pop, Blondie, and the Police also played over-capacity shows at the Longhorn, but the Commandos attendance was never beaten.

The advent of the Longhorn was a crucial development for Minnesota music, because it welcomed bands that primarily did original material. In the early '70s, we had been lucky to have three main venues with broad booking policies: Walker Art Center, which put on shows in its own auditorium as well as the adjacent Guthrie Theater, and two now-defunct but no-less-legendary rooms, the Labor Temple and the Depot. By 1977, apart from the Walker/Guthrie, most of the bands we saw who performed their own songs were touring acts who played big places like the St. Paul Civic Center, the Minneapolis Auditorium, or theaters like the State or Orpheum. That's not to say original material was prohibited in other venues, but bands knew that the bottom line for most establishments was not a musical one. The clubs wanted to hire bands that would attract crowds that spent money on alcohol and food. Most venues in the metropolitan area preferred the groups that played recognizable hit songs. Conversely, the Longhorn's bottom line was always the music.

Jay's Longhorn opened on Wednesday, June 1, 1977. The first shows were in the upstairs bar. Jay had wisely brought in his good friend, ace musician, and music aficionado Al Wodtke to book the bands. It all began with a five-night stand by a dynamite straight-ahead rock 'n' roll band called Flamingo. I'd known of Flamingo but had never seen them live. When I did—yowsa! The band had personnel changes over the years, but this was the classic lineup: Robert Wilkinson (lead vocals/ guitar), Johnny Rey (lead guitar/vocals), Joseph Behrend (keyboards), Jody Ray (bass), and Bob Meide (drums). They were tight and exuberant, playing a mix of covers and originals. They came off like a young, modern take on the classic '60s rock sound.

The second and third bookings were bands I was already very familiar with. Week #2 featured an outfit that was especially significant for me: Thumbs Up, featuring Curt Almsted (aka Curtiss A), a man with a voice as big as a house and a scream that could rattle windows. Curt and his longtime sidekick and guitarist, Bob Dunlap, were the frontline of this remarkable band, which also included Roger Nash (bass) and Doc Young (drums).

Hitting the Longhorn stage the third week was the Suicide Commandos, featuring Chris Osgood (guitar/vocals), Steve Almaas (bass/vocals), and Dave Ahl (drums/vocals). The groundbreaking trio kickstarted the whole damn scene with their brainy, short, loud, fast, and often funny songs. This was punk rock for sure, but not the angry kind; it was the fun kind. These three bands—the Suicide Commandos, Flamingo, and Thumbs Up—were the triptych that launched the Longhorn and most of what came after in the local music scene.

By the end of June, attendance was already so strong that Jay and Al decided to move the bands downstairs, into a larger area where the pool tables and pinball machines had been. They did it overnight, hiring the gaming company to come down in the wee hours to move their equipment upstairs. Christening this new downstairs room was Thumbs Up.

A potpourri of local talent started filling up the calendar and kept the joint jumpin': Fingerprints, the Hypstrz, Fine Art, Riff Raff, the Dads, Wilma & the Wilburs, the Overtones, Safety Last (with future Jayhawk Gary Louris), Smart Alex, Urban Guerillas, the Phones, the MORs, Doggs, and Ben Day Dots. Down the road came the Suburbs, Kurt Nelson, Hüsker Dü, the Replacements, the Wallets, Johnny Quest, and the Schitz (with an underage Dave Pirner on drums).

Mink DeVille was the first national act to play the Longhorn, on July 29. They were a stylish R&B–flavored rock 'n' roll outfit from San

Francisco by way of New York. The lead vocalist was Willy DeVille, tall and thin, with a pompadour and a pencil mustache, well-dressed in a colorful, fitted jacket and pointy Italian shoes. They were one of the house bands at CBGB at the time and had been signed to a major label (Capitol).

Once the Longhorn hit the radar of the national booking agencies, the floodgates opened. Over the next few years, the club hosted shows with Talking Heads, the Dead Boys, Robert Gordon and Link Wray, the Only Ones, Elvis Costello and the Attractions, Iggy Pop, Willie Alexander and the Boom Boom Band, Pere Ubu, Destroy All Monsters, the Stranglers, David Johansen, Blondie, Shoes, the Dictators, Sonic's Rendezvous Band (featuring Fred "Sonic" Smith from the MC5), the B-52s (four nights!), Nick Lowe and Dave Edmunds, Peter Hammill, Lydia Lunch, Ultravox, the Fleshtones, Robin Lane and the Chartbusters, Gary Myrick and the Figures, the Boomtown Rats, the Police, the Beat, 20/20, the Buzzcocks, Gang of Four, Mitch Ryder, John Cale, Magazine, the Tom Robinson Band, the Plasmatics, Squeeze, the Cramps, and Grace Jones (with Sly and Robbie as her rhythm section). Our little underground joint was earning a revered place in music history.

By the mid-'70s, disco and the broader dance-music movement had spawned a proliferation of nightclub disc jockeys. We'd heard about a few adventurous venues in New York that borrowed the idea from the dance clubs and brought DJs into underground rock joints. Jay Berine decided to give it a go at the Longhorn. Andy Schwartz and I were the first DJs there. We worked alternating nights, and we always brought in our own records. Andy was an excellent DJ. Unfortunately, he quit after a couple of weeks. Finding another DJ was difficult, and I ended up working almost every night for a while there. Not sustainable! Fortunately, Roy Freid, aka Roy Freedom, came on board for a few months before decamping to a dance club down the street called Uncle Sam's. Over the years, other DJs who worked at the Longhorn included Oar Folk staffer Terry Katzman; Peter Davis, who published the hardcore/

punk fanzine *Your Flesh* and ran Creature Booking; Erik Hansen, now a visual artist in NYC; and Jim Fenn, a former member of Flamingo's road crew.

We rented a mobile unit with two turntables, a mixing console, and flashing disco lights (which we never used), all housed in a cabinet on wheels, with a squishy, sparkling, pink, Naugahyde covering. We positioned it to the left of the stage, next to the sound system's monitor board. It wasn't exactly a sturdy construction, and too often people bumped into it and made the records skip, which drove me crazy. But relief was just around the corner. Paul Stark implemented several invaluable improvements to the club, including building a sturdier stage, installing a house PA and monitor system, and bringing in higher quality lights. A few months later, he built a proper DJ booth in the rear left corner of the room.

I was in hog heaven. For years I had thought my calling was to be a disc jockey. Since I was a little kid I'd gotten a real buzz from playing my favorite records for people. As previously mentioned, I'd gone to broadcasting school and worked in radio, so I had some practical experience. I loved the radio work, but it wore thin fast. Spinning records for a roomful of music fanatics suited me much better.

The Longhorn music room opened at 9:00 PM every night. The typical schedule went like this:

9:00–9:30—DJ
9:30–10:15—opening band
10:15–10:30—DJ
10:30–11:15—headliner first set
11:15–11:30—DJ
11:30–12:30—headliner second set and encore
12:30–1:00 AM closing time—DJ

Pay for the DJs was fifteen dollars a night plus free drinks. I worked there for more than four years, and I never asked for a raise. It never occurred to me. In all honesty, it was so much fun, I might've paid Jay to let me do it. My role at the club expanded as time went on. I also became a booking advisor and produced all the radio ads for the club.

As far as what music we played, the DJs had complete free rein. The only requirement was to play records plugging upcoming shows. Though I often knew in advance some of the songs I wanted to play on any given night, I still needed to bring a reasonable selection to pull from. I always carried two boxes—one with thirty to forty albums and the other with fifty to sixty singles. Being carless at the time, I schlepped it all back and forth by bus.

I had a sizeable record collection going back many years, so older music was no problem. As for current and upcoming stuff, I got tons of that through Oar Folk's record distributors. Another source was the local reps of the major labels who serviced the store with promotional copies, frequently ahead of release. It was always good to have a scoop for the Longhorn audience. For example, Elvis Costello's first album, which we got as an import three months ahead of its US release; or the first four Sex Pistols singles, well before the album release. One of the more dramatic scoops was, in May of '79, when Jim Grady, another local RCA Records rep, called to say he'd just gotten an advance cassette of David Bowie's new album *Lodger* and would bring it to me at the Longhorn that night. It killed me to have to wait all day, but I brought my cassette deck to the club and patched it into the sound system in the DJ booth. Jim ran a little late so it was quite the nail-biter. He came through, though, skidding up to the booth just before midnight with the goods in hand. I cued up the opening song, "Fantastic Voyage." When the band onstage finished their set, I introduced the song and hit play. The crowd responded with a roaring ovation!

There was a flipside to the fun I had spinning records at the Longhorn. I saw it as my job to play a broad selection of music, old and new. Whatever it was, it just had to be something I considered great. But some of the clientele thought I should be focusing more on the punk and new wave records of the day. I disagreed with that, but I took it as a challenge, to try to win them over and maybe push their bound-aries a bit. I recall one occasion when a couple of unfriendly looking characters approached the booth to complain about what I was play-ing. "Play the Damned," they said, "Play Black Flag." I told them that I frequently played both, that I'd be doing it again, but at the moment I was playing Marvin Gaye or Randy Newman or the Everly Brothers or whatever it was, and maybe they should give it a fair listen.

On October 21 and 22, the most exciting new group of the moment played the club for two nights: Talking Heads. Released in February, their first single, "Love Goes to a Building on Fire," sounded like noth-ing we'd ever heard before and had enraptured everyone. The arrival of their debut album, *Talking Heads: 77*, in September was a highly antici-pated event. To have the band in our town, in our club, was almost too much to fathom. It was a completely sold-out Friday–Saturday book-ing, and we'd also arranged an in-store with them at Oar Folk for Sat-urday afternoon. The shows and the in-store went spectacularly well.

It turned out to be a noteworthy five-day run at the Longhorn. After Talking Heads, we had the Dead Boys on Sunday and Monday, and Robert Gordon, with guitar legend Link Wray, on Tuesday.

One night, not long after the Talking Heads shows, Jay walked up to the DJ booth, handed me a 45, and asked me to play it and announce an upcoming three-night stand he had just booked for December with a band from Lincoln, Nebraska. The group was Charlie Burton & Rock Therapy, and I was a little wary at first. Three nights for a band I'd never even heard of before? The A-side of the single was called "Rock And Roll Behavior." It was in a paper sleeve, the label said WILD in crude hand-lettering, and a xeroxed insert had a low-quality photo of the band, looking like they were vomiting into buckets. But when I auditioned the single in my headphones, I was instantly won over. The next day, I ordered copies to stock at Oar Folk, and over the next few weeks we played the hell out of the single at the club. By the time the band hit town, a groundswell of anticipation had built up. When they took the stage on Friday, December 9, a good crowd was on hand, in spite of a nasty blizzard, and the band blew everyone away. Charlie and the band became staples at the Longhorn, playing multiple-night stands and packing the joint several times a year.

Among the more adventurous of the early Longhorn bookings was in April 1978 with the Chicago band Skafish—a group so outlandish, it's hard to imagine another venue in the Twin Cities booking them. Skafish was an art-rock group that had been signed to IRS Records and featured a very unusual lead singer, Jim Skafish. I'd describe it as performance art with dramatic, topical, talk-sung songs. I DJ-ed the show. We were still using the mobile turntable unit parked next to the stage, so Skafish's monitor man and I were in close quarters. He and I chatted off and on all evening. His name was Jim too. He was complimentary about the records I was playing and at one point asked if I had anything by the Shadows of Knight. I was a huge fan of that band and often had a thing or two of theirs with me. As I was searching through my records, I said, "I assume you're a fan?" Jim replied, "I was the singer." You could've knocked me over with a feather. I was floored to realize that, for the last couple of hours, I'd been working next to Jim Sohns, a vocalist I'd listened to, seen live, and sung along with hundreds of times! From my record stash, I pulled out a copy of the *Nuggets* compilation, which has the Shadows' cover of Bo Diddley's "Oh Yeah." I showed it to Jim, he nodded his approval, and the song was soon blasting out of the speakers. He signed the record for me: "It's nice of you to remember!!! Jimmy Sohns."

Another memorable night was when Bob Geldof and Johnny Fingers of the Boomtown Rats stopped by the Longhorn in January 1978. Through Oar Folk, I'd gotten an invitation from Buddy, the local Columbia Records rep, to attend a happy hour meet-and-greet with members of the Rats in advance of their upcoming album release, *A Tonic for the Troops*. The six band members were split up and sent to different cities to do PR. We were fortunate to get Bob and Johnny, the lead singer and the keyboard player. My pal Steve Klemz and I went, and as was usual at these sorts of functions, we felt awkward. We watched as the label execs paraded the musicians around the room to talk to distributor sales reps, radio folks, and mainstream journalists, most of whom didn't appear to know much about the band and likely were there more for the free drinks and hors d'oeuvres.

When Steve and I were finally introduced to Bob and Johnny, we hit it off right away. I think they picked up on the fact that we were real fans who had all their records and were music nuts, period. I had to leave early because I was DJ-ing, and I mentioned to Bob and Johnny that I worked at a club downtown and a great local band called the Suburbs was playing that night. I invited them to stop by if they could. Bob waved Buddy over and told him what I'd said. Buddy gave me a hairy eyeball, looked at Bob, and firmly told him, "I've got a Johnny Paycheck show later tonight, and you guys are coming with me." Bob shrugged his shoulders and smiled. Steve and I left, figuring that was the end of that.

I got to the Longhorn and started spinning records at 9:00 PM, like always. Around 9:15 or so, Bob and Johnny walked in, spotted me in the booth, and came right over. I was excited but surprised. Bob said, "We told Buddy to give Paycheck a rain check!" and we all had a laugh. They loved the club and the Suburbs. They spent a lot of time looking through my records and requesting songs. Many, many drinks were drunk. If memory serves, Bob was legless by the end of the night and may have actually been carried out.

One of my favorite Longhorn encounters involves the notorious British manager and label man Jake Riviera. Jake came to town with Dave Edmunds and Nick Lowe and their band Rockpile in November 1978. To me, Jake was about as cool as you could get. He was a cofounder of Stiff Records and managed Elvis Costello, Nick Lowe, and later, Squeeze, among others. Before the club opened that night, I was sitting at a table chatting with Dave and Nick while Jake was in the office doing business with Jay. Out of the corner of my eye, I saw the local Atlantic Records rep, Kevin St. John, walk into the room. I didn't know Kevin well, but I knew him to be a kind and gentle man. Atlantic was the parent company to Rockpile's label, Swan Song. I'd never seen Kevin at the Longhorn but guessed that he'd come down to the club to show his support. The problem was, the powers that be at Atlantic had done nothing to promote the show. I intuited that Kevin was there to extend an olive branch. Suddenly, I saw Jake walk out of the office and directly toward Kevin. Kevin started to introduce himself, and I'm pretty sure all he got out was, "Hello, I'm Kevin from Atlantic," before Jake started kicking him and shouting, "Why don't I just give you a fucking shovel and you can fucking bury them right here?!" It's funny looking back on it now, but at the time I found it quite shocking.

Another one of the most memorable and emotional nights at the Longhorn was in the late fall of 1978. That September, the Suicide Commandos' label, Blank Records, unexpectedly shut down, and the band was released from its contract. The Commandos were shattered and decided to call it a day. The decision to break up was extremely difficult for the band members, and it was hard for us fans too. The Commandos had led the charge for Twin Cities punk before the genre even had a name. They carved a path and opened doors for many other bands. They were local heroes. A farewell performance or two was in order. Make that three.

The shows were booked for the Wednesday, Thursday, and Friday of Thanksgiving week under the banner: "The Commandos Commit Suicide Dance Concert." All three performances were sensational. The electricity in the room was overwhelming. The crowd size, especially on the third night, far exceeded what the fire marshal had deemed "capacity"—it was a miracle the authorities didn't shut it down. I'll never forget looking out from the DJ booth at the massive audience. After the farewell shows—the third of which was captured on the live album, *The Commandos Commit Suicide Dance Concert*—the three ex-Commandos launched new musical endeavors. Guitarist Chris Osgood and drummer Dave Ahl stayed local and formed various bands, including Boy's Life, L7-3, and 55401, all of which frequented the Longhorn stage. Bassist Steve Almaas formed a combo called the Crackers and moved to New York City.

As devastating as it was when the Commandos broke up, the Suburbs were there to carry the torch and became the next big Twin Cities band. They were loaded with talent, funny as hell, snappy dressers, and genuinely good human beings. Notably, they did almost exclusively original material. I was smitten with the Suburbs' zany art-rock, but not everyone shared my enthusiasm. Some thought they were amateurs, including Jay Berine, who said to me, "I don't know what you see in these guys. They sound like they stepped right off the playground and onto the stage."

The Longhorn was also drawing good crowds with regional bands like the Jonny III from Littleton, Colorado; Milwaukee's Yipes; New York's Marbles; and the aforementioned Charlie Burton & Rock Therapy from Lincoln. The Commandos had played in Denver on their way home from a West Coast tour, and the Jonny III opened for them. It was love at first sight for both bands.

A few months later, at the Commandos' recommendation, the Jonny III were booked at the Longhorn for three nights. They were electrifying. Not only was their blend of surf and rockabilly a big hit on the Longhorn dance floor, they were visually striking. The drummer, Leroy X, had a wild look in his eye and played with great physicality while half standing behind his kit. Guitarist/singer Kenny Vaughan was a Fender man, and boy, could he play guitar. He wore jeans tucked into cowboy boots, and the day after their first Longhorn show, I swear I saw several locals walking around town sporting the same look. Over the course of those three nights, every guitar player in town worth their salt was front and center, watching every move of Kenny's fingers. I thought both Charlie Burton and the Jonny III would have been perfect for the Twin/Tone label, but we didn't have enough of a track record yet and both bands politely declined my offer. For me, these were the two that got away.

In a dreadful occurrence in early 1979, Jay Berine was busted for illegal substances and went to jail. Recreational drugs were everywhere at the time, but sadly Jay was one of the ones who got caught. As for the future of the Longhorn, in what initially seemed like a serendipitous move, Jay's cousin, Hartley Frank, swooped in to run the club. Jay had made him a partner in late '78 because Hartley's catering business could make use of the well-equipped kitchen at the Longhorn, which in turn helped cover the club's overhead.

After Jay's arrest, Hartley was like a hero who had come to save the day. But that wouldn't last long. He knew nothing about rock 'n' roll, and with Jay gone, Al Wodtke left too. It didn't take long for the booking agents, who'd had strong professional relationships with Al and Jay, to realize Hartley was not a real music guy. As time went on, Hartley's business practices became more and more unscrupulous and self-serving. He was sloppy too. For example, when Gang of Four came to town, he advertised them in the calendar ads as "Bag of Four." Hartley also had a temper, and I witnessed many serious tantrums. Hartley was an older gay man, and his penchant for hitting on all the boys didn't win him many friends, either. Though Hartley and I were respectful to each other, from the beginning I made it clear that I worked for the Longhorn and not for him.

The atmosphere around the Longhorn was changing, but the club still hosted tons of fantastic shows. The Stranglers were the first of the bona fide British punk bands to play the Longhorn, and they stated their case by putting on an intense show with a decidedly dangerous edge. The band had a surly stage presence, and at one point during the show the bassist, Jean-Jacques Burnel, jabbed an overzealous kid in the head with his guitar.

NNB, an arty and dark local rock band that featured astounding twin-guitar interplay, had a wildly exciting live debut at the Longhorn in June. And in July, everyone's favorite, Blondie, came in for two shows.

In the Oar Folk chapter I discussed the monumental event of the Only Ones coming to town in October '79. I will never forget Hartley ringing me at Oar Folk to tell me he had booked the band. He said he'd heard us talk about them so much, he booked them for two nights. Then he asked me: "That was the right thing to do, wasn't it?" Barely able to contain my enthusiasm, I replied, "yes!"—even though one night probably would have been sufficient. But I knew that if we pulled out all the promotional stops at the store, we could entice enough people to buy tickets to justify the two nights. A good crowd showed up for the first night, and the band was so stupendous, most everyone who was there came back for the second night.

While continuing to bring in these amazing rock bands, the Longhorn took a bit of a left turn in the fall of 1978, introducing the "Sometimes Jazz" series. Kicking off with local ensemble the Wolverines, the series continued into 1979 with shows by Flora Purim, Carmen McRae, Dexter Gordon, and Spyro Gyra. Even though I was not particularly well versed in jazz, I loved DJ-ing those shows.

Other developments beyond the walls of the Longhorn also affected the club's business. In July 1979, a new club in south Minneapolis called Duffy's opened and started booking the same types of alternative bands that played at the Longhorn. Later that year, Uncle Sam's launched itself into the alternative music fray, booking the Ramones, with Longhorn favorites the Hypstrz opening. In early 1980, Uncle Sam's became Sam's, and on March 21, they opened a small side room, the 7th Street Entry. Now there were four clubs booking alternative music in the Twin Cities.

Another significant change came in the fall of 1980 when local businessman Zelmar Shrell bought the Longhorn. Keeping Hartley on as manager, Shrell decided to put his own stamp on the club and changed the name to Zoogie's. Rock bands continued to play, as did jazz musicians. Hartley also began putting on gay-oriented dance events in the downstairs room, so on some nights the rock music was moved upstairs.

The end of my DJ-ing at the Longhorn/Zoogie's happened unexpectedly in late October 1981. The Flamin' Ohs (formerly Flamingo) were headlining that night. By this time I'd been working with the Replacements for over a year, and the bassist, Tommy Stinson, was hanging out with me at the club. He was only fourteen years old, but Hartley and I had made a deal. It was okay for Tommy to be at the club, but when he wasn't performing, he had to stay near the DJ booth with me. On this particular night, I'd run out front to check something at the ticket booth, and on my way back I bumped into a friend. As we were chatting, Hartley walked up and interrupted: "Peter, you told me when Tommy wasn't performing, he'd leave the bar." I was surprised, as that wasn't what we'd agreed on, and I reminded Hartley of that. He got in my face and shouted, "Peter, you're a fucking liar!" The whole lobby went quiet, and everyone turned and looked at us. Startled, I stood there for a few seconds collecting myself. Then I calmly turned around and walked away, back into the music room. I played my last set of records for the night, took all my posters down from the walls of the booth, and packed up my records, and Tommy and I left. Hartley called me the next day and said, "Peter, I hope I can still consider you our DJ." I said, "No, I'm done." And that was that.

DJ-ing at the Longhorn was a tremendous gift. Playing a variety of the best music I could each night was the most important thing, but so was surprising the audience or turning them onto a song they'd never heard before, or making them laugh. "Drunk" by Jimmy Liggins was one song that always did that. As was "Rover's Return" by the Korgis. But my favorite, especially as the last record of the night, was "Always Look on the Bright Side of Life" from the Monty Python film *Life of Brian*. I can still conjure the scene now—maybe it's Curtiss A who has just left the stage. It's the calm after the storm, the band is tearing down, the lights are turned up. The room is full of smoke, beer bottles are clinking around the floor, bar patrons are singing along with Python's Eric Idle, some likely inebriated, most of them sweaty and a little spent, everyone happy. That's how I like to remember the Longhorn.

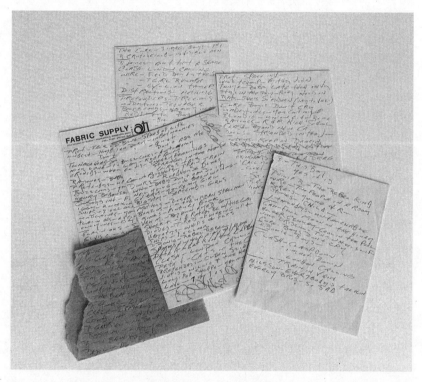

A sampling of my DJ set lists from the Longhorn, 1978–79. *Author's collection*

Four

Twin/Tone Records:
Flyin' by the Seat of Our Pants

In the early months of 1978, everything was moving along well with a new record label I started with two associates. The first three groups we signed—Thumbs Up, Fingerprints, and the Suburbs—were finishing up tracks for their debut EPs. My label partner, Paul Stark, oversaw the sessions. Third partner Charley Hallman and I frequently popped by the studio to listen.

Paul, Charley, and I had formed a partnership and were now in the process of incorporating. The funny thing was, we didn't have a name for the label yet. We'd kicked around dozens of ideas but hadn't landed on anything we all felt strongly about. The one that Charley kept coming back to was Red Records, because we had decided to have the EPs pressed on red vinyl. Paul was ambivalent. I was opposed. We were really getting down to the wire, though, and we needed a moniker, fast.

Then one morning, I woke up in my bedroom at the Modesto and saw a matchbook that was flipped open on my nightstand. On the inside, in my handwriting, it said "Twin Tone Records." I didn't remember writing it, but I must've done it in a dream state. I immediately thought, *Yeah, that's it, there's the label name!* "Twin" referenced the Twin Cities, and "Tone" had a musical connotation. I couldn't wait to run it by Paul and Charley. And when I did, they loved it too. We had a graphic designer friend, Cindy Allen (sister of Bruce from the Suburbs), draw up a logo. She added a slash between Twin and Tone— and Twin/Tone Records we were! Over the next twenty years, Twin/ Tone would establish itself as a leading independent label, releasing some 300 titles, including the first recordings by the Replacements and Soul Asylum and the sophomore effort by the Jayhawks.

The corporate major record labels were pretty much running the show in the rock 'n' roll business in the late '70s, but the pendulum was ready to swing back the other way. Working in a left-of-center record store gave me a bird's-eye view of the approaching onslaught, and it was a beautiful thing! We were entering a period of David giving Goliath a run for his money. The number of independent labels that were cropping up all over the world was astounding. It was inevitable that Minnesota would join in.

In the fall of 1977, three Twin Citians began discussing this possibility: Charley Hallman, music enthusiast and sportswriter for the *St. Paul Pioneer Press*; Chris Osgood, de facto leader of the seminal punk rock band the Suicide Commandos; and Paul Stark, recording engineer and live sound man. Paul operated P. David Studios, a recording facility he'd built in a house he owned near the University of Minnesota. There, among a variety of projects, he'd recorded the first two Suicide Commandos singles.

Charley was a music connoisseur, and besides his main gig at the newspaper, he frequently moonlighted writing record and concert reviews for the paper. After he caught a Commandos live show one night, he thought he'd glimpsed the future of rock 'n' roll. Charley introduced himself to the band. After seeing another gig or two, he was convinced they were contenders for the local rock music throne. He told Chris the Commandos should get an album out ASAP, and he offered to help. Chris agreed and said it would make sense to bring Paul into the conversation. The three of them met, one thing led to another, and they expanded on the idea. Maybe forming a local label to release music by the Commandos and others was in order.

On Monday, October 24, fate intervened. Talent scouts from Phonogram's newly formed punk/new wave imprint Dip Records (soon renamed Blank Records) had come to see the Commandos at the Longhorn. The Commandos, who regularly headlined there, were doing an underplay for fun, opening for Cleveland's Dead Boys. The label execs were so impressed they offered the Commandos a record deal on the spot. After the smoke of excitement cleared, Chris realized he was going to be too busy being a full-time Commando to be involved in starting a record label. He recommended that Paul and Charley talk to me to see if I'd be interested in taking his place.

Paul Stark called me in late October. I didn't know him well, but we'd crossed paths a few times on the underground music scene. Paul gave me the lowdown on what he, Chris, and Charley had been talking about and asked if I'd like to meet for lunch to discuss the possibility of getting involved. I was all for it, and we made a date to get together a few days later. The four of us met at Williams Pub uptown. It felt like a strong brain trust to me, and Paul, Charley, and I soon became a formal partnership.

For me, there was a feeling of pride that came with starting a record label. The idea that I might be able to help guide the direction of music in our little corner of the world was exhilarating. Through the holidays and the first weeks of the new year, the three of us met every Tuesday for lunch at the CC Club to brainstorm and put together a plan for the label.

In January 1978, Paul offered up office space in the basement of his house on the western edge of downtown. It was a comfortable spot with a room for desks, a lounge where Paul had his audio and visual equipment set up, and an area for storing our record inventory. Charley would handle PR and talent scouting. Paul would oversee the recording and manufacturing. I would focus on talent scouting and distribution. But as with any small company, we all did whatever needed to be done.

I quickly found Paul and Charley to be excellent partners. Paul was very "Spock-like," intensely smart, ruled by logic, and, on the surface, seemingly unsullied by emotion. Underneath it all, he was a kind and funny man. Charley was rotund, always dapper-looking with his newsboy cap, thin mustache, and ubiquitous Camel Straight cigarettes, and he had a boundless enthusiasm for our cause.

After many lengthy discussions about which groups we should be considering for our first releases, we assembled our thoughts into a plan. We started by looking at the three most popular bands at the Longhorn, the only place that consistently booked the type of artists we were interested in. The Suicide Commandos were spoken for. Much as we loved Flamingo, everyone felt they could be the next band to get a national recording contract, and were probably out of our reach. The third band was Thumbs Up, which I was especially partial to.

Thumbs Up was a quartet I'd first heard in 1974 at the CC Tap (before the name was changed to the CC Club). At that time, the band had two lead singers: Gary Rue and Curt Almsted. Gary was a natural front man with a gorgeous, pure pop voice. Curt could sing pretty, and he could do Wilson Pickett–style, raspy-throated soul, very similar to Detroit's Mitch Ryder. He was a tall man with an imposing stage presence. Drummer Tilly Thielges was an excellent harmony singer. On the bass was Mike Burt. For me, seeing Thumbs Up felt like a revelation. They were the first local rock band I heard that affected me as much as the records I loved. They had that all-important "X factor." Their sound was a blend of British Invasion and American soul. They mostly did cover songs but put their own stamp on each one. In 1976, Bob Dunlap joined the band. His guitar playing was a mix of traditional and unconventional. He played with a thumb pick and didn't sound like any guitarist I'd ever heard before. Bob brought a new level of artistry to the band. He would become Curt's musical director and foil for many years to come. When Curt and Bob introduced their own original songs to the mix, Thumbs Up was even more appealing. Paul and

Charley were 100 percent in agreement with me that this was a band we should approach for our label.

Fingerprints was a band of seasoned musicians who had taken the Longhorn by storm. They were a full-tilt rock 'n' roll band with elements of prog and glam, and they were terrific songwriters as well. Lead singer Mark Throne was a flamboyant master of ceremonies with a voice that could be hard one minute, crooning the next. He also played saxophone and rhythm guitar. Guitarists Mike Owens and Robb Henry were precision players, with Robb the primary lead guitar man. The lockstep rhythm section of Steve Fjelstad (bass) and Kevin Glynn (drums) drove the band well. One bonus for me was that Robb and I had been friends since third grade, and I'd been buddies with Kevin and Mike since junior high.

Chris Osgood was the person who had first tipped me off to a band called the Suburbs. They'd played a few parties on the outskirts of town, but the first time I saw them was at their downtown debut, opening for the Commandos on New Year's Eve '77 at a bar/disco called Sutton's. It was primarily a gay bar that had experimented with booking the new breed of rock bands on a few occasions and done well. The Suburbs' Sutton's show was a knockout. They were such a tantalizing mix of ideas: accomplished and arty on one hand, silly and spontaneous on the other. Piano player Chan Poling was erudite and classically trained. Rhythm guitarist Blaine "Beej" Chaney was like Iggy Pop with a guitar—he was self-taught and so wild, I was sure he was going to hurt himself when he played. Chan and Beej were also the lead singers. On lead guitar was Bruce Allen, a guy who had loads of musical style and a cool manner of dress. The rhythm section of Michael Halliday (bass) and Hugo Klaers (drums and occasional vocals) had a bottomless energy. Hugo and I became especially close friends.

I saw the band again at a party in their rehearsal space a short time after the Sutton's show and was further convinced they were worth pursuing. It reinforced my feeling that musicianship and professionalism weren't the only criteria to consider. That's not to say the Suburbs weren't good musicians; they just had a lot of rough edges and hadn't completely gelled as a band yet. But my gut said these guys had something special. After some cajoling, my partners agreed the Suburbs should be in the mix as well.

Paul, Charley, and I decided to invite the bands into the studio to record a few songs. It would be an audition of sorts, where we could hear how the groups responded to a recording session, and to see how we got along.

We scheduled an all-day session at P. David Studios for Tuesday, January 31, 1978, and recorded five bands: Thumbs Up, Fingerprints, and the Suburbs, along with two other outfits we were interested in, Riff Raff and Muscle Pump. The air was full of genuine excitement, and everyone seemed to put their best foot forward. It was a long but successful day. I don't think I left the studio until after midnight.

Paul, Charley, and I reviewed the tapes over the next few days, and we all felt that the performances by Thumbs, Fingerprints, and the Suburbs were the strongest. We decided to record one 7-inch EP with each of the three bands. Although we did not include Riff Raff and Muscle Pump in our first releases, members of both bands would appear in different guises on Twin/Tone in the future.

A fastidious bunch, Fingerprints had laid down six tracks that January day, including their signature song, "(Now I Wanna Be a) Spacegirl." The Suburbs cut twelve songs, including seven of the nine that would ultimately make up their debut EP.

Thumbs Up also knocked out six numbers—three original songs and three covers. By the time we were preparing the artwork for the EP sleeves, Thumbs Up had changed their name to Spooks, which seemed to signify a new phase for the band. Old-schoolers that Curt and Bob were, I was initially startled when they introduced two Clash songs to their repertoire at the Longhorn, but their forceful renditions soon blew away any trepidation I had. Their style was being influenced by the new, edgier music that was circulating, and their original songs were beginning to reflect that as well. Over the course of additional sessions, the three covers they recorded at the demo session were replaced by three new originals.

With the increasingly busy schedule at P. David Studios, Paul often needed assistance. Mike, Kevin, and Steve from Fingerprints were operating a small studio out of a basement in Minnetonka, and they were happy to do some work downtown. They began bringing in their own equipment to augment Paul's. Finally Paul asked if they wanted to move all their gear in and run the studio for him. As an added incentive, they could live in the three upstairs bedrooms. Mike, Kevin, and Steve moved in and brought their studio name with them. P. David became Blackberry Way (named after a 1968 single by the Move).

The first Twin/Tone EPs were issued in the spring of 1978 and were well received locally and beyond. Next up were singles by Fingerprints (with new lead guitarist Jeff Waryan replacing the departing Robb Henry) and the Jets (new Longhorn favorites from Pekin, Illinois). We began planning another batch of EPs, but when we made a list of all the artists we thought worth considering, we came to the conclusion that a full-length LP was in order. I had been inspired by indie label Beserkley and their *Chartbusters* compilation from 1975. Most of Beserkley's artists were based in the Bay Area, and I suggested we take a crack at doing something similar to spotlight artists from our neck of the woods.

But first, an event of considerable magnitude required documentation: the farewell concerts of the Suicide Commandos at the Longhorn in November '78. The band talked to Paul about recording the final night, and collectively we decided that Twin/Tone would put out a limited-edition LP. *The Commandos Commit Suicide Dance Concert* was released in April '79. It's a joyful keepsake of a landmark band and a memorable night, and we sold hundreds of copies at Oar Folk alone.

As the various artists compilation was coming together, we soon realized that a single LP wouldn't be enough. We thought some of the

groups warranted two songs, and since the Commandos were disband-
ing, we wanted to give them three, so each member would have a lead
vocal. The comp would have to be expanded to a double album.

A preview of sorts took place on February 3 at Walker Art Center,
with a concert called Twin/Tone Tunes, featuring Spooks, Fingerprints,
and NNB. Getting "our" bands into that prestigious institution gave
the underground scene some well-deserved aboveground attention.

Big Hits of Mid-America Volume Three was finally released in the spring
of 1979. (The title was an homage to two revered local compilations from
the '60s.) Bruce Allen, lead guitarist of the Suburbs, was a gifted graphic
designer by day and the go-to guy for Twin/Tone's artwork. He put
together a whimsical, retro-looking design package for the record. Bruce
had all the musicians take photo booth pictures, and he lined the inside
of the album's gatefold with them. Chris Osgood wrote the liner notes.

The double album contained twenty-two songs. It featured eleven
Twin Cities acts: Curtiss A, the Commandos, the Suburbs, Fingerprints,
the Pistons, the Hypstrz, NNB, Robert Ivers & Ice Stars, the Wad, Buzz
Barker and the Atomic Burns, and the Swan Lake Six—those last three
groups each featuring at least one former Commando. Four additional
songs were contributed by bands from neighboring cities: Yipes (from
Milwaukee), the Swingers (Erie, Pennsylvania), and the aforementioned
Jets (Pekin, Illinois). The album was a perfect snapshot of what was
going on in local rock 'n' roll at that time—with one regrettable exception. Flamingo wasn't on it. Their management had larger aspirations
and decided against it, which broke my heart.

In the fall of '79, we released an album by a friend of Chris Osgood's
from Hampshire College, Robert Carey. It was an experimental project
that used bits of dialog recorded off TV and other clips of "found
sounds" edited together to create montage-like compositions. For this
album project, Robert went under the name Orchid Spangiafora, and
the album was titled *Flee Past's Ape Elf* (a palindrome). It wasn't a big
seller, but I'm proud of it being one of our first releases.

With the Suburbs' popularity on the rise, the January '80 release of their debut full-length album, *In Combo*, was highly anticipated and well received, even in the more conventional media. The local press was unanimously positive, and the album earned significant accolades nationally as well. *Village Voice* music critic Robert Christgau gave the album an A-minus. And the influential *Trouser Press* wrote: "The Suburbs are like an American analogue to Wire, though more crazed than angry or bleak." From my point of view as a fan, *In Combo* was everything I'd hoped it would be: full of the Suburbs' quirky but smart well-written songs, spirited performances displaying their sense of humor with the songs "Cows" ("I like cows / And they like me") and "Chemistry Set" (containing as its only lyric, "I'm into chemistry and that's about it"). Even the classy album cover photo, showing the band members stylishly dressed with blurred heads, was a home run. It was Twin/Tone's first taste of mainstream recognition.

One of the new groups that had been gaining a serious following at the Longhorn was Hüsker Dü. They were a powerful live band that played regularly at the club, and we'd gotten to be friends. One day drummer Grant Hart gave me a cassette with two songs they'd recorded and asked if I'd give it a listen for possible release on Twin/Tone. The band's music was intense and fast and the overall sound was unique. I liked the punk element of what they did but not the more hardcore side. I also knew their music would not appeal to Charley, who was a little older and less open to this new hybrid. I told Grant I was sorry, but I didn't think it would work for Twin/Tone.

Two years in, the Twin/Tone roster was five bands strong: Fingerprints, the Suburbs, the Jets, the Pistons, and Spooks—or whatever Curt was calling his group that particular week! The Pistons and Fingerprints had new singles out. We'd just signed the Overtones, a surf-rock band led by hot young guitarist Danny Amis, and released their debut three-song maxi-single in May.

In September, Twin/Tone issued its fifth long player and the first from Curtiss A, called *Courtesy*. I had seen Curt perform live more than

I had seen any other band, and I knew every song by heart. Curt's colossal voice and presence are best experienced in a live setting, but *Courtesy* got as close as any recording machine could to capturing it. It's hard for me to put into words how much I love the guy, or to describe the impact his music has had on me over the years.

Earlier that year, in the spring of 1980, I was working the counter at Oar Folk when a young guy I didn't know walked up and handed me a demo tape. His name was Paul Westerberg, and the demo was my first exposure to a band called the Replacements. The story of my introduction to and long-lasting relationship with the band is told in detail in later chapters. But suffice to say, the Replacements would require a significant piece of Twin/Tone's focus, and mine, over the next several years.

As my involvement with the Replacements was increasing, Paul Stark was assisting the Suburbs with both studio work and business decisions. So, both Paul and I were handling quasi-management responsibilities for a band while continuing our roles at Twin/Tone and the recording studio.

As we got into the spring of 1981, Twin/Tone had many balls in the air. The Replacements' first album, *Sorry Ma, Forgot to Take Out the Trash*, was ready to go, the second Suburbs LP was getting last-minute tweaks, as was the debut by new signing the Pistons. Stark, Hallman, and I looked at our release schedule and did a little practical analysis. Releasing all three at the same time would give us a number of price-breaks. We could cut a deal with the people we used for manufacturing, advertising, and publicity. It wasn't exactly "three for the price of one," but it would save us a significant amount of money. So, we decided to wait until all three albums were done. College radio play at that time was crucial, and so it made strategic sense to release the records in late August, right before school was back in session. The release date for all three albums was set for August 25.

The Pistons were building a solid following, and their first album, *Flight 581*, took them even further. Led by Spooks alumnus Frank Berry, the Pistons had a Rolling Stones–like sound that allowed them to get into more mainstream, suburban venues. Their song "She Got Sex" opened the *Big Hits* compilation and received a fair amount of late-night radio play, which gained them a lot of attention. As did Charley Hallman's stewardship in helping the band choose the strongest material for the album and using his press contacts from his newspaper work.

The Suburbs, meanwhile, came up with so many incredible songs during the recording sessions for their new record that it became clear it had to be a double album. Tying it all up with a beautiful cover design by painter and visual artist Duncan Hannah, *Credit in Heaven* is the Suburbs' masterpiece.

It felt fitting to return to a three-pronged attack, like our initial releases in '78. We'd gone from three EPs to three LPs, one of them a double. Twin/Tone was learning its trade, improving the sound quality and package design with each release. These three albums, so varied in style, hitting the racks together was a defining day for Twin/Tone.

The label took on several new recording projects beginning in mid-1981. We signed a fantastic rockabilly group, Safety Last, led by bassist/singer Rusty Jones and including guitarist/singer Tim Mauseth and drummer Jim Tollefsrud, later augmented by guitarist Sprague Hollander. They recorded an EP during the summer, but when Tim and Sprague left the band, we decided to hold the EP release until a full band was in place again. Enter Gary Louris and Lianne Smith, both of whom played guitar and sang. The eponymous EP hit the stores May 7, and the four-piece band went on the road.

Riding high on the release of *Credit in Heaven*, the Suburbs were touring heavily and gaining ground on the West Coast, especially. Though the Suburbs were a madly creative and punky bunch, much of their new music had a danceable element to it, and the rise of post-disco dance pop in the early '80s opened a door for them. One song in particular from *Credit*, "Music for Boys," seemed ripe for the picking, and they enlisted "Funkytown" mastermind Steve Greenberg to do an extended remix. Stark engineered and coproduced, and a 12-inch 45 of the remix was in stores on June 24, 1982. That same day, *The Replacements Stink*, an eight-song EP we'd recorded in secret, was released and took everyone by surprise.

The major labels were noticing the Suburbs' rising profile in dance clubs and on tour. The band was aware of it too, and played their cards well. The Suburbs opted to be thrifty with their material, effectively saving songs for the national recording contract that we all felt was imminent. They recorded a four-song EP for Twin/Tone called *Dream Hog*, featuring another track well suited for the dance floor, "Waiting." Greenberg and Stark produced once again. A 12-inch 45 remix of "Waiting" was released shortly before the EP. Both came out in November.

At this point, Polygram came knocking. The label signed the Suburbs and bought their entire back catalog from Twin/Tone, immediately rereleasing *Dream Hog* under the Mercury imprint. The label also put the band right back into the studio to record a full-length. Their major label debut, *Love Is the Law*, came out in March 1983. As a small, regional indie label with limited resources, Twin/Tone was happy in its role as a "farm system" for major labels. It was the first time we'd helped one of our bands step up to the next level, and we were mighty proud.

Twin/Tone was a beehive of activity in 1983. Curtiss A's second album, *The Damage Is Done*, was out on Valentine's Day. It signaled a solid leap forward for Curt, with the songs being more sophisticated, the singing more intricate and harmony-laden. The guitar playing was remarkable once again, with Bob Dunlap's maverick work sharing space with the finesse of new recruit Jeff Waryan.

The Replacements' third album, *Hootenanny*, arrived in April, and the band did its first full tour to the East Coast, which took me out of the Twin/Tone office and away from Oar Folk for over two weeks. We'd be gone again for most of July and August, which led to my difficult decision to finally leave Oar Folk. I also did a short run touring with R.E.M. as an interim road manager, which meant even more time away from the label.

In July 1983, Twin/Tone hired its first full-time employee. Blake Gumprecht moved up from Lawrence, Kansas, where he'd been a terrific Twin/Tone ally as music director at KJHK radio. His meticulous organizational faculties with media mailing lists and advertising were instrumental in Twin/Tone's growth, and his relentless work ethic kept the rest of us on our toes. Although he was hired primarily to handle publicity and radio, Blake brought in some interesting A&R ideas as well. One was East Coast power-popper Tommy Keene. When Blake played me a few songs, I was knocked out. After several conversations with Keene's management, we sent them a contract draft.

Early that summer of '83, a band called the Phones brought us a finished album and asked if we'd give it a listen. We loved what we heard and offered them a deal. We thought the record had great potential, with a more commercial sound than anything we'd done to that point. They were also a hard-touring bunch, which was a real asset for Twin/Tone in selling records. The band met at college in Moorhead, Minnesota, and shortly thereafter were touring the Midwest and East Coast, performing five or six nights a week. Front man Jeff Cerise had a magnetic stage presence. Bassist Jim Riley and lead guitarist Steve Brantseg were the primary writers, while Cerise and rhythm guitarist Rick Taves provided some co-writes. The album title was *Changing Minds*, and we released it in August. Getting introduced to Steve Brantseg was a major perk of signing the Phones. Steve would go on to play with Figures, Bash & Pop, Curtiss A, and the Suburbs, among many others. Steve and his wife, Merrie, have been dear friends of mine for forty years.

Also that summer, Jeff Waryan made his first album for us, entitled *Figures*, which then became the name of his band. Blackberry engineer Steve Fjelstad played bass, Jay Peck was on drums, and Brantseg joined as second guitarist after leaving the Phones. Away from Fingerprints, Jeff's music still rocked plenty, but it also had a warmer, gentler side. His guitar playing was distinctive and powerful. To me, his sound had something in common with Richard Thompson's folk-inflected rock.

Things got complicated for me in the fall of '83. At the same time that the Replacements were embarking on their first West Coast tour, I had a previous commitment to road manage a short series of dates with Figures on the East Coast. This meant I had to miss the first three Replacements shows in California. The Figures shows included an opening slot for Tommy Keene at the renowned 9:30 Club in DC. I had a bad reaction to Tommy's set. It felt way too slick to me, and I hastily decided to halt the contract talks. I regret that deeply; Tommy went on to become one of my favorite artists, as well as a great pal.

The Figures tour finished up in Ann Arbor, Michigan. It was a successful run and a real joy for me to get to see several shows. I loved Jeff's writing and guitar playing, and he'd put together a formidable band. Bassist Steve Fjelstad rarely went on the road, and I enjoyed getting the chance to spend time with him away from his hectic studio schedule at Blackberry Way.

Following the Ann Arbor show, Figures and I drove back to Minneapolis. The next day, I jumped on a plane and flew to California to meet the Replacements for their first LA date, at Club Lingerie, on November 19.

By 1984, Twin/Tone was outgrowing its basement office. Although Charley was in the office less—being busy at the newspaper and doing a lot of traveling with the North Stars hockey team—Paul, Blake, and I were there on a daily basis. We'd also recruited Grady Linehan from Twin Cities Imports, a distributor in St. Paul, to help with sales. Paul was interested in finding a building that could house both a larger office for the label and a recording studio.

That summer, Paul swung a deal to purchase a building near the corner of 26th Street and Nicollet Avenue. Originally opening as a movie theater in 1914, the building had housed a recording studio since the '50s. It was the site of historic recordings by the Trashmen ("Surfin' Bird"), Dave Dudley ("Six Days on the Road"), and the Fendermen ("Mule Skinner Blues"), among many others. We moved there in July, and Paul renamed it Nicollet Studios. It had three recording studios and a reception area on the first floor, with room for offices and master-tape storage upstairs. We hired a full-time receptionist, the friendly and unflappable Roz Ferguson, and rented out extra office space to Hüsker Dü. The feeling of community within those walls was inspiring. We'd worked our asses off and come a long way in six years. We felt like we'd earned nicer digs, and having such impressive new quarters certainly upped the company's profile.

At this time, Twin/Tone was working on a few new albums, including the debut release from Soul Asylum. I had gotten to know the band when they were called Loud Fast Rules. Back in October '82, they opened for the Replacements at Merlyn's in Madison. When they took the stage, there were maybe twelve or fifteen people in the room, but the band was tearing it up, playing like they were in an arena full of screaming fans. Replacements' bassist Tommy Stinson was watching with me, and we looked at each other with our jaws hanging open. Thinking back on it now, I still get goose bumps. After the set, we marched into the dressing room, where the band was all sweaty, sprawled on chairs and couches, and I blurted out, "We gotta talk about you guys making a record for Twin/Tone!" There was absolutely zero question in my mind: Loud Fast Rules had to be on the label. The band and my Twin/Tone partners agreed.

Loud Fast Rules continued to make quite a splash on club stages around the Twin Cities, and in March '83 they changed their name to Soul Asylum. It took a bit to figure out who should produce the album. Hüsker Dü's Bob Mould had become a big fan of the band, so when he expressed interest in working with them, everyone agreed he was the right choice. By January, they were finishing a nine-song mini-album at Blackberry Way.

On August 24, 1984, three new Twin/Tone records hit the stores: Soul Asylum's *Say What You Will . . . Everything Can Happen*; the Phones' second album, *Blind Impulse*; and the Replacements' 12-inch "I Will Dare." All three bands had plenty of tour dates to promote the records, which is always good for business. The Replacements full-length *Let It Be* was released October 2. Within two years it sold nearly 50,000 copies, and it would go on to be the best-selling album in Twin/Tone history.

By this point, I had gotten so busy with the Replacements, and was out of town so much, that I was no longer able to keep up with my other duties at Twin/Tone. There was no telling when or if that might change. Much as I loved the label, I knew I'd be sticking with the Replacements as long as they needed me. So, Stark and I decided to hire a couple of people to help with A&R and distribution.

Local journalist Dave Ayers had long been a supporter of the label. He also was a regular at Oar Folk and was working the counter there part-time. We thought he'd be the right person to bring in for A&R. And in a fitting full-circle development, Chris Osgood came in to handle distribution and retail marketing—becoming an employee at the label he'd had a hand in birthing eight years before.

Part of Paul's expansion plan was to bring more labels into the fold. Wide Angle, which did dance-oriented music, was first, in January 1985. Stylistically, Wide Angle may have seemed an odd fit to folks on the outside, but artists like Insoc and Viola Willis had aesthetic and commercial appeal that Paul thought was worth exploring. Next came Coyote Records, cofounded by our friend Steve Fallon, owner of the club Maxwell's in Hoboken, New Jersey. The label was home to several favorites of ours, among them Chris Stamey, the Feelies, and Beat Rodeo, Steve Almaas's new band. Twin/Tone proper had new releases from Figures and from new recruits the Slickee Boys, David Thomas, and Jonathan Richman. And, in big news, the Replacements signed with Sire/Warner Bros. Records. They would have one final release on Twin/Tone: a limited edition (of 10,000), cassette-only, live project entitled *The Shit Hits the Fans*.

Soul Asylum was also staying busy. In 1986, they made two albums, *Made To Be Broken* and *While You Were Out*, as well as a cassette-only compilation of rare tracks, *Time's Incinerator*. Dave Ayers became their manager, and the next year, they signed with A&M Records.

My last direct involvement with the label for the decade was on *Big Hits of Mid-America Volume IV*, a new various-artists compilation that Chris and Dave were producing. I suggested a singer I was working with named Dave Postlethwaite. We cut the track "Hank Slumped" at Nicollet Studios with Tommy Stinson on bass and Chris Mars on drums. It was a beautiful recording that sat nicely among a fantastic collection of songs by artists including Bob Dunlap, the Mofos, the Magnolias, and new group the Jayhawks, among others.

I didn't have an official departure date at Twin/Tone. I just gradually phased out of the day-to-day work over the course of late 1985 and early '86. Otherwise, things were pretty solid at the label. Paul was his usual visionary, multitasking self. Blake, Dave, and Chris had things well under control in their departments, as did Roz and new office manager Abbie Kane. A fifteen-year-old intern, Jake Wisely, came in over the summer of '86 loaded with ambition; it wasn't long before he'd be running a label of his own in the same building.

Things were in full swing at the label. My leaving was temporary. I had some things to sort out in my life, but I'd be back.

Flyer for the Twin/Tone release party for the Replacements, Suburbs, and Pistons albums at the CC Club in Minneapolis, 1981. *Author's collection*

Five

The Replacements, Part I:
When It Began

One day in May 1980, a young man walked up to the counter at Oar Folkjokeopus, handed me a cassette tape with "The Replacements" written on it, and asked if I'd give it a listen. I could never have predicted how much of an impact that moment would have not only on my life but on the lives of so many other music fans. I'm eternally grateful I received that tape, and then had the privilege to work with this extraordinary group for years to come.

At that time, between my work at Twin/Tone and the Longhorn, I was inundated with submissions from bands, some hoping for a booking at the club, others for a record deal. About a week or so after I received the Replacements demo, I gathered up a pile of cassettes, a boom box, and a stack of Oar Folk paperwork and shut myself away in the back office. I put in one tape after another while I worked. As usual, it was a mix of styles and quality. But when I popped the Replacements' four-song demo tape in, it was like something out of a storybook.

From the very first listen, I could tell the recordings were head and shoulders above any new submission I'd gotten in a long while. The band's performance was downright startling. Just twenty or thirty seconds into track number one, "Raised in the City," I could barely believe my ears. When I caught the lyric, "I got a honey with a nice tight rear/ She gets rubber in all four gears," I rewound the tape to the beginning and listened again, just to be sure I heard it correctly. I thought, *Holy crap, this is like some kinda X-rated Chuck Berry song!* The other three songs—"Shutup," "Don't Turn Me Down," and "Shape Up"—knocked me out too.

As soon as I finished listening to the tape, I called my two best pals—Linda Hultquist and Steve Klemz—and said, "You gotta come down here right now and hear this demo I got. Either I've lost my mind or it's the best thing I've heard in ages." When they arrived and I played the tape, Linda and Steve reacted much like I had. Their corroboration reassured me that I wasn't crazy and this was indeed something special. Still, I needed to listen a few more times and think about it before I got back to the band.

I played the four songs repeatedly over the next few days. I grew more convinced that this band was uncommonly good. So, one afternoon I pulled out the piece of paper I'd gotten with the tape. There was a name on it—Paul Westerberg—and a phone number. I called and reintroduced myself to Paul, told him I loved the demo, and asked if the band was hoping to record a single or a full album. After a pause, Paul replied, "You mean you think this shit is worth recording?" I suddenly realized he'd given me the tape in hopes of getting a gig at the Longhorn, not as a pitch to Twin/Tone. I said I did think the songs were worth recording, and I was sure I could help the band get a show at the club as well. In the meantime, I said, I'd love to see them live as soon as possible and asked when they were playing next. Paul said they didn't have anything booked at the moment, but he'd let me know.

Paul called back a few days later and told me they had a show in a couple of weeks at the Bataclan, a sober club at a church in south Minneapolis. In the interim, I practically memorized the demos and played them for a handful of my closest music buddies. I liked the recordings so much I was having a hard time thinking about anything else. Could the band really be as great as I thought they were? Was there a catch?

The church gig was on 26th Street, about twenty blocks east of Oar Folk. I was on needles and pins and wasn't sure what to expect, so I went alone. As I approached the front door, I saw a dark-haired teen-ager sitting on the steps looking dejected. When I started up the stair-way, the kid said, "You must be Pete. I'm Chris, the drummer. We ain't gonna play; we just got kicked out." A minute later, two of the other band members sheepishly wandered out. I recognized Paul from the store. He introduced me to Bob Stinson, the lead guitarist. Apparently, the bass player couldn't make it. He'd been climbing a tree earlier that day, fell, and tore a muscle in his arm. I was disappointed not to see them play, but I was glad my first live experience wasn't one with a missing band member.

It turned out the guys had been caught with pills and booze. The manager of the Bataclan was in a rage and told them to get out. The band was worried they'd blown an opportunity with me as well, but I assured them it wasn't an issue, and that I'd get back to them soon about a date at the Longhorn. As I walked back to my car, I chuckled a little at what had just happened.

The Replacements' first appearance at the Longhorn was Tuesday, July 1, 1980. I'd been raving about them for weeks and had played the demo in the record store, so when they took the stage at 9:30, the room was filling up nicely. I was hoping the band would be great, but what I saw and heard that night was something else. They didn't have their shit together onstage—they had crappy equipment, took too long be-tween songs, and didn't tune their instruments often enough—but they were a revelation, embodying nearly everything I loved about rock 'n' roll music.

The ingredients for greatness were there from the beginning. The songs were crude but impressive; the band members had an undeni-able chemistry and an uncontrived irreverence; they were smart, wildly entertaining, and really funny. Bob in particular could be positively clownish, all the while doing these searing leads that seemed to come from a different universe than any guitar player I'd heard before. I was shocked when I met the bass player, Bob's half-brother, Tommy Stinson. He was only thirteen years old. But he played well, despite

being airborne for most of the set—grounded just long enough to periodically yell "fuck!" into the mic. Chris Mars was the anchor, hunched
over the drums, always ready for whatever the other three threw at him.
And then there was Paul, who looked like a square peg in a round hole.
Though he played spot-on rhythm guitar, he seemed uncomfortable—
teeth clenched as if he was trying to will himself into the front man role
right before our eyes. And yet somehow he pulled it off, with panache.

There is no recording of that night, but I remember the song selection was a mix of covers and the Replacements' own songs. Some great
originals, like "More Cigarettes" and "Raised in the City"; others, like
"Get on the Stick" and "Off Your Pants," were acceptable placeholders
until better songs came along. The covers included the Syndicate of
Sound's "Hey Little Girl," "So Long" by Slade, and the Kinks' "All Day
and All of the Night." And they did three Johnny Thunders songs. When
I first encountered the Replacements, it was like they wanted to *be*
Johnny Thunders's Heartbreakers.

The show was raw, but it blew Stark, Hallman, and me away. A
record deal was inevitable in our minds, and the band was all for it
too. The next move was to bring them into a proper studio. Our go-
to recording spot, Blackberry Way, had an open day on July 21, and I
snatched it up. I also spoke to the band and Hartley about arranging a
return booking at the Longhorn, and a date was set for July 17.

My excitement over the band's first show was so intense, I relished
being able to see them again in a calmer frame of mind where I could be
more analytical. We did record the show this time. It was an eighteen-
song set, kicking off with a smokin' version of Johnny Thunders's "I
Wanna Be Loved." They also did the Ramones' "I Don't Want You."
That song has a fantastic hook, and the Replacements did it so well,
I'm amazed it didn't become a regular part of their sets. The closing
song that night was an inspired cover of Dave Edmunds's "Trouble
Boys," which would be in their repertoire for years.

July 17 also marked the Replacements' first photo shoot. We were surprised when, after only one gig, the Twin Cities weekly *Trax Magazine*

wanted to do a story on the band. They hired Jean Pieri to take photos in and around the club. The accompanying article by Christopher Farrell was the first ever written about the band. In his words, "The talent is unmistakably there in the raw, as everyone in the room senses. They simply have the feel."

For the session on the twenty-first, Paul Stark and I schlepped the band and their gear over to Blackberry in Stark's van. We picked up Westerberg first and met the other three at the Stinson house. The six of us driving to the studio in the van that day was a wee bit awkward. From the beginning, Paul Stark and the Replacements were strange bedfellows. Maybe it came down to Stark being very adult, while the band was mostly anything but.

Paul Stark and I had different expectations about what might transpire in the studio. I had no doubt that we'd get some great performances on tape, and I was already certain we'd be making a full-length album. Stark was less convinced they'd respond well to the studio environment and thought we'd be starting with a single.

In the studio that day, the band totally rose to the occasion. They did everything they needed to do to prove my point to Stark. They knocked out twelve songs in what felt like twelve minutes. Stark and I were sitting at the console in the control room, and I kept looking at him out of the corner of my eye to gauge his reaction. By song seven or eight I could see him trying to stifle a grin, and I knew I'd won the debate. Eight of the twelve songs they recorded that day made the Replacements' debut album, two of them straight off this July session tape.

September brought a handful of firsts for the Replacements. The weekend of the fifth and sixth, they were invited to play out of town for the first time, opening for the Suburbs at the St. Croix Boom Company in Stillwater, Minnesota. The club's advertising said: "With guest performance by the new Twin/Tone Band—The Replacements." Stillwater is only twenty-five miles east of the Twin Cities, but apart from a few city folks that made the trek, it was a completely different audience. This seemed to have a positive effect on the band's performance.

On the seventeenth and eighteenth, they made their debut in the prestigious Sam's Danceteria complex, playing in the 250-capacity 7th Street Entry. I thought it was time to make a flyer for the band, and I included the descriptor "rock 'n' roll." Westerberg objected. After fishing for something he deemed acceptable, I finally said, "How about "Low Class Rock"? That, he approved.

The last first of that month was a big one. The Replacements headed into Blackberry Way to begin recording their debut album. Steve Fjelstad was the engineer, and his relaxed manner and patience served the band well. We worked in clusters of days—two here, three there—between September and November. Some of the sessions were productive, some weren't.

All the songs so far were rockers. Then one day Paul started running down a slow one he'd written after seeing Gang War, a short-lived band that included the Heartbreakers' Johnny Thunders and the MC5's Wayne Kramer. It was a biographical song about Thunders called "Johnny's Gonna Die." A watershed composition, it was the Replacements' first ballad.

In early December we decided to shake things up and record them in their "natural habitat"—on a stage. Nobody wanted to do an actual live album with an audience, but what if we tried capturing them on the Longhorn and/or the Sam's mainroom stage, without people in the audience? We could certainly pull favors at those venues and do daytime recordings when the clubs were closed. Paul Stark had a twenty-four-track mobile recording unit that we could use. Since the group had gotten comfortable with Steve Fjelstad (or "Feljy," as we called him) engineering at Blackberry Way, we wanted to stick with that formula.

So, with Fjelstad and Stark working as a team, we spent a day laying down some tracks at the Longhorn (now renamed Zoogies) in December. Then in early January, we tried the same thing at Sam's. Long story short, we didn't get anything usable either day. The band gave it their best shot, but they just didn't click in the faux-live setting. After further discussion, we moved the operation back into Blackberry

Way, and things quickly turned around. My guess is that simply show-ing the band we were willing to bend over backward to get the sound they liked is what made the difference.

About this same time, the band and I had a major confrontation with Hartley. Hartley had a habit of not always tending to the Zoogies calendar very well. He'd often have to fill holes in the schedule at the last minute, leaning on bands to come to his rescue. When he started to make eleventh-hour offers to the Replacements, I spoke up against it, and Hartley blew a gasket. We'd started the conversation in the club, but then Hartley said, "Let's go outside, where we can talk privately." The six of us walked out of the club and stopped at a marble bench in front of the Northern States Power Plaza. All four Replacements sat down, awkwardly staring at their feet like they'd just been called into the principal's office. Hartley started yelling. "What's the problem here? I'm offering you guys great opportunities! It's good exposure for you! You'll make more money!" Keeping my voice down, I explained that I thought he was doing the bands a disservice by offering them dates that neither they nor Zoogies had time to properly promote—no time to put up flyers, put ads in the weeklies, contact the daily papers' calendar sec-tions, or even let people know by word of mouth. Then, pointing at me, Hartley shouted to the band, "Do I have to talk to this guy every time I want to book you?" Westerberg glanced at me with an *Okay if I say yes?* look on his face. I nodded. He turned to Hartley and said, "Yes, you do."

I had never aspired to become the Replacements' manager, but that's how I fell into it. I had little choice. Their reputation as a "band to watch" was rapidly growing, but they were still relative novices in the music game, and they needed protection from the Hartleys of the world. So, I ran interference for them. I assumed I'd do that until they could attract a real manager who could properly represent them. But in the meantime, in addition to being their A&R man, I fended off bad guys and handled logistics so they could focus on the music: writing it, rehearsing it, recording it, performing it. Between Twin/Tone and myself, we gave the band our concerted support.

By this time, I'd gone so far past the deep end about the Replacements, I was getting a lot of flak about it, especially from other acts who were hoping to get a deal with Twin/Tone. Some were really pissed off. They felt like they'd paid their dues and the Replacements hadn't. The Replacements didn't give a shit about paying dues, of course. But I was taken aback by the resistance from the other musicians. Had these people really *listened* to the Replacements' songs? How could they not think the band was enthralling onstage? I remember wagging my finger at one of the more caustic protestors and saying, "Just you wait—someday, people are gonna be writing books about these guys!" At the time that may have sounded like hyperbole even to me, but deep down I genuinely believed it was a possibility.

Beyond working together, the band and I were developing a real friendship. We all lived near one another, and my apartment at the Modesto essentially became the Replacements office. Chris frequently popped by. Tommy and Bob hung out there and at Oar Folk all the time. Paul and I grew especially close. We spent hours and hours together, listening to music, talking, smoking, drinking. In one odd little coincidence, Paul and I smoked the same, very unpopular brand of cigarettes, True Blues. He used to joke that smoking Trues was the equivalent of spitting in your Coke—no one ever asked you to share.

The Replacements got into a steady groove of studio sessions and live shows over the next few months. In late November, I was surprised when we got an opening slot with the Suburbs at the Cabooze, the bastion of blues 'n' boogie music in the West Bank neighborhood of Minneapolis. Leave it to the Suburbs and their immense local following to break through the wall. The booker at the Cabooze knew that if he booked them, the place would be full, even if the regulars at the club would look down their noses at these interlopers on their stage. The funny thing was, the Replacements played consistently well there. I've always believed part of the reason was the club's powerful PA system. Over the coming months, they played several dates there and rocked it every time; I have some fantastic tapes of those shows.

At one of the early Zoogies gigs, just before kicking into the first song, Westerberg said to the audience, in an offhand manner, "We are the Placemats. Don't ask why." So, devotees took to calling the band "The Placemats," eventually abbreviating it to "The 'Mats." Little did we know that would stick.

In early December 1980, the band took its first real road trip: 150 miles north to Duluth, where they once again opened for the Suburbs. The venue was a roller rink. I borrowed Paul Stark's van, we packed up the gear, and off we went, the five of us and our first roadie, Lou Santacroce. Lou was a musician and musicologist from upstate New York who'd relocated to Minneapolis and found sanctuary at Oar Folk. Lou and I became great friends. Like me, Lou fell hard for the Replacements the first time he heard the demo, and he never missed a show. He offered to help and worked cheap, which was good because the Replacements sure weren't making any money yet. He and Westerberg really hit it off too. Lou had a vast knowledge of rock, old blues, folk, free jazz, and opera. I think Paul was genuinely flattered that someone like Lou was so taken with him and his music.

There were two people in those early days who I believe had this effect on Paul: Lou, and my girlfriend, Linda Hultquist. She and I had gone to the same high school but didn't meet until later, when she expertly did lights for the Commandos and helped to haul gear. (She was considered the fourth Commando.) Linda was whip-smart and didn't suffer fools gladly. And she had no problem putting Paul in his place, with retorts like "Oh, color me impressed, Paul" (a phrase Westerberg filed away for future use). I believe these two highly intelligent people thinking he was something special made a huge impression on Paul, giving him confidence at a crucial time in his development as an artist.

As for the Duluth show, the Suburbs were becoming well known outside of the Twin Cities, but no one there had a clue who the Replacements were. The Replacements were giving it their all while most of the people skated in circles and paid little attention. One unforgettable moment was when the band blasted into a new song called "I Hate Music." Westerberg grabbed the mic stand forcefully and pulled it toward him, accidentally snapping the neck of his guitar and somehow managing to cut his forehead. Blood was running down his face as they finished the song, at which point Westerberg completely demolished what was left of the guitar, smashing it on the stage. I don't know how many of the skaters even noticed, but for me, it was a true rock 'n' roll moment.

For these out-of-town gigs, it was always a trip picking Tommy up from school. He was still only fourteen and in ninth grade, and the other kids would look at him wide-eyed as he climbed into the van. In the early days, Tommy's age had been more of a novelty than a hindrance, but over time, the more we branched out in our gigs and went on the road, the more we faced resistance from bar owners who were wary of having an underage kid on the premises. Early in 1982, as we were doing more touring, Anita Stinson, Tommy and Bob's mom, said she'd be happy to sign a document stating that I was Tommy's guardian for touring purposes. I always got along with Anita, and she trusted me. I typed up some formal-sounding language on Twin/Tone stationery. She signed it, and we had it notarized. It probably wouldn't have stood up in court, but it looked official and did the trick.

Sometime in late '80 or early '81, an important development took place between Paul and me. He confided in me that he had been recording solo guitar and piano demos in his parents' basement, and asked if I'd give them a listen. Of course I said I'd love to. He started sneaking them to me in strict confidence, usually one or two at a time. He asked me not to mention it to the band, especially Bob. He knew Bob had a fixed idea about what the Replacements should and shouldn't be, and tender, introspective ballads fell into the latter category. The first things Paul gave me varied from rough sketches to more finished songs, and I was gobsmacked. One of the first was called "Bad Worker." The chorus alone blew my mind:

I'm a bad worker
My father would be ashamed
I'm a bad, bad worker
I give ya minimum effort for a minimum wage

Another one that impressed me was called "Gas Station Attendant" (still to this day unreleased). He'd never worked at a gas station, and yet the words were so clever and funny:

You were fixin' your hair while I was checkin' your air
You caught me smokin' at the pump

Westerberg's method of delivering these songs to me was interesting too. The Modesto apartment building where I lived had a security system to buzz people in. Paul used a particular buzzing pattern so I'd know when it was him. Late one night, he called to say he'd just recorded a song that he sang mostly in falsetto and had to get the tape out of his house fast, before he had second thoughts and erased it. I was surprised how quickly he got to my place after the phone call; he must've run the whole sixteen blocks. When I heard his buzz, I cracked my door open like always, but when he got to my apartment, just his arm came through the gap, tape in hand. I grabbed it, and he turned and ran back down the stairs.

I played the cassette right away. The song was spellbinding, and though his high-pitched singing was a little ragged, it worked. From the lyric, I guessed the title might be "You Hold Me in Suspension." It's a beautiful song that has one of my all-time favorite Westerberg lyrics: "All paint chips, and all love fades" (also still unreleased).

Being on the receiving end of these private solo recordings was a privilege I didn't take lightly. I couldn't wait for the next installment!

Over the next few months, the band and I continued with an active schedule, bouncing back and forth between rehearsals, the studio, and live shows. For another gig at the Cabooze with the Suburbs, Lou cooked up a surprise for Paul. The band had been doing Chuck Berry's

"Maybellene" and knocking it out of the park, but Paul had a bad habit of not learning all the lyrics to the covers they did. Lou gave him endless shit about that, especially when it came to songs by wordsmiths like Berry or Hank Williams. During the Replacements' set at the Cabooze, Lou was hovering near the stage with a smirk on his face and what looked like a rolled-up poster sticking out of his back pocket. As soon as Bob Stinson hit the signature lick that opens "Maybellene," Lou rushed to the front, unfurled the large roll of paper, and held it up in Paul's direct line of sight. It had the lyrics for "Maybellene" printed out large in black magic marker. Paul cracked up but quickly regained his composure and sang the song correctly for the first and maybe only time!

The Replacements got a nice confidence boost when *Sweet Potato*, the top weekly in the Cities, did a feature on the band and put them on the cover in February 1981—a full six months before they even had a record out. Music editor Marty Keller had enlisted scribe PD Larson to write an article about the most impressive up-and-coming band he could find.

We finished laying down basic tracks for the 'Mats' debut album by early 1981. The sound was unpolished, but it wasn't all first takes knocked out live in the studio. It took time to get the results the band wanted. . Overdubs and mixing took place in February, and by March the album was complete: eighteen songs, only two of them breaking the three-minute mark. All in, the album was just shy of thirty-seven minutes long.

Album titles were being tossed around, and for a while the consensus was *Power Trash*. Then one night, as we were driving to a gig at Zoogies, Paul announced he had a new idea for the title: *Sorry Ma, Forgot to Take Out the Trash*. Everyone erupted with laughter and agreement. Could there be a more perfect moniker for it?!

We'd also been kicking around a lot of ideas for the album artwork, and we tapped Bruce Allen to handle the execution. In addition to his skills on guitar for the Suburbs, Bruce had done a masterful job on the design for *Big Hits of Mid-America, Volume Three* and other Twin/Tone releases.

Meanwhile, I'd become good friends with Oar Folk customer Greg Helgeson. Greg was a professional photographer who started out as a staffer for *City Pages* and occasional freelancer for the *Minneapolis Star-Tribune* before adding the Minnesota Orchestra and publications like the *New York Times*, *Rolling Stone*, and *Mojo* to his résumé. In August 1980, I had asked him if he'd take some photos of the Replacements. One afternoon, at Greg's suggestion, we converged on the Walker Art Center in Minneapolis. Greg liked the Walker's stark white lobby walls for a backdrop. He shot several rolls of film over the course of an hour or so. It was only the second photo shoot the Replacements had ever done. Although those Walker photographs were good and we used them for early flyers and on the back of the first single, they weren't what we wanted for the album. In early 1981, for LP package purposes, Greg took photos of the band onstage at the 7th Street Entry, as did Laurie Allen, Bruce's wife.

Bruce selected one of Greg's photos for the album cover: a close-up live-action shot of Westerberg and Tommy Stinson. It made me a little uncomfortable not having all four band members represented, but I had to agree that it was a striking image. I also felt uneasy when Bruce took the gorgeous 14-by-11-inch print Greg had made and ripped it in half. He'd created a graphic for the band's name and colored "The Replacements" in *Never Mind the Bollocks*–style Day-Glo pink over a bright cyan background. He placed the graphic vertically between the two torn sections of the photo, and when he added in the album title, *Sorry Ma, Forgot to Take Out the Trash*, alongside it—voila!—there was the album cover. Four of Laurie's shots were used on the back. Bruce also did a sleeve design for the "I'm in Trouble" single. I'm generally a good speller, but if you check the credits on the back of an original copy of the single, you'll see I blew it on "rythm" guitar.

In all, it had taken roughly seven months to make the album. Westerberg was the most bothered by how long it took. In retrospect, it does

seem like a long time to make a punky rock 'n' roll record by a rowdy
bunch of teenagers. But not rushing things was beneficial. This was
early in their evolution, and the Replacements were still in the process
of becoming a band. And the songs were getting better by the day. As
journalist and author Bob Mehr wrote in his liner notes for the *Sorry
Ma* fortieth-anniversary set, "In reality, *Sorry Ma* was a major undertaking, recorded in multiple locations, and completed with purpose
over many months. Like the band itself, it was the product of considerable—if often well-hidden—hard work, refinement, and intention."

There were other hurdles to getting the album done too. Tommy
was still in junior high, and Bob was a cook on the lunch shift at Mama
Rosa's, so we couldn't record on weekdays. And because Paul Stark
owned the building the studio was in, the sessions were often paid
for with rent deductions for the Fingerprints boys, who were running
the studio while living upstairs, which in turn meant they had to hustle
for actual cash-paying customers. This kept the studio very busy, and
the 'Mats had to squeeze in when time allowed.

The long haul getting the record done was made a little longer after
Stark, Hallman, and I decided to coordinate the Replacements' album
with those by the Suburbs and the Pistons (as mentioned in an earlier
chapter) and to maximize the college radio impact by releasing the
records in late August. It's also important to remember that the Suburbs were the most popular group in town at the time, and being in
their slipstream would greatly benefit the Replacements. The Suburbs'
coattails were well worn.

There was one more element we needed for the Replacements' first
album: pick a song from the LP to release as a single, with a non-LP
B-side, and put it in a cool picture sleeve. The song we kept coming
back to for the top side was "I'm in Trouble." For the B-side, I thought
about the solo songs Paul had been giving me. The juxtaposition of a
rocker and an acoustic, singer-songwriter type of song would be provocative and show that the band was no one-trick pony. I ran the idea
by Paul. His first reaction was, "Nah, that ain't the Replacements." It

was a battle I didn't think I'd win, but I kept at it. My argument was that it would set the 'Mats apart from the strictly loud-fast brigade.

One day toward the end of the album mixing sessions, Paul called me at Oar Folk. I was going to pick him up in a couple of hours to go to the studio, and he asked me to come a little early so he could play me a song he thought might be good for the B-side. When I got to his house, Paul played a cassette of a fragment he'd been working on. Then he played me another piece of the song on his acoustic guitar. I loved what I heard and told Paul we should record it right away. He packed up his guitar and we were off. On the way to Blackberry, Paul was scribbling intently in a notebook. I thought, *I'll be damned, he's finishing the song as we drive!*

When we got to the studio, Feljy saw Paul with an acoustic guitar case and asked, "What's that for? I thought we were mixing." I told him Paul had a solo song we wanted to record for a possible B-side. Feljy set up two mics, one for the guitar, one for the vocal. We rolled tape, and Paul did the song in one take. Then he wanted to add a bit of additional guitar after the second chorus, so we rolled tape one more time and—done! Probably took fifteen minutes in all. It was as thrilling a studio experience as I've ever had. The song was called "If Only You Were Lonely." When the rest of the band heard it, they were all in favor of it for a B-side too.

At last, the big day arrived. On August 25, 1981, the Replacements album *Sorry Ma, Forgot to Take Out the Trash* and the single "I'm in Trouble" backed with "If Only You Were Lonely" were released. The response locally was tremendous. Our bundling the release with the Suburbs and Pistons albums worked well for all the bands, and we landed good reviews in the *Village Voice*, the *Boston Phoenix*, the *New York Rocker*, *Trouser Press*, and others.

Two or so years into their existence, the Replacements dusted off a classic rock 'n' roll number for their live show and gave it new life. The song was "Rock Around the Clock," and they played it as if possessed. Marveling at their performance, I thought, *I can't imagine there's a better rock 'n' roll band on planet Earth at this moment in time.* Of course, that's a fanciful and immeasurable notion, but it illustrates just how convincing the band could be when they were on. And I was noticing a strange phenomenon in their live shows: They'd introduce a new cover to their repertoire, and for the next few shows it would be the highlight of the set. In the case of "Rock Around the Clock," the Replacements didn't just cover the song; they commandeered it. All due respect to Bill Haley and the Comets, who did it first and did it well, but it's a bit like comparing Pat Boone's and Little Richard's recordings of "Tutti Frutti"—one was well mannered, while the other disregarded manners altogether.

Just after the first of the year, we took our longest trip yet. Hüsker Dü invited us to open a show for them in Chicago at a place called O'Banion's on January 16, 1982. As we pulled into the city, I saw a flashing temperature sign that read "-20." When we arrived at the club, the heat wasn't working. It didn't seem to faze the locals, though. Everyone kept their coats on until there were enough people in the room to generate sufficient body heat to make it tolerable.

That night, the 'Mats did a monster performance of a new-ish song called "Kids Don't Follow." It wasn't the first time they'd done the song, but it was the first time they *killed* it. As we drove back home through snowy Wisconsin the next day, we listened to a boom box recording I'd made of the show. Hearing the song again, I had a revelation: *This song is an anthem, and we must record it immediately!*

At the next Twin/Tone meeting, I laid it on thick for Charley and Paul. I told them I was convinced the Replacements had a game-changer of a song, and it was crucial that we put it out on record as soon as possible. Paul and Charley reminded me that *Sorry Ma* was not even six months old yet, and because Twin/Tone was still promoting it on the radio, for retail, and in the press, it was premature to talk about a new release. But I kept pushing. I admitted the band didn't have a full album's worth of material ready but said we could pull together seven or eight songs, and we could do it fast and cheap. I told them to keep costs down for the artwork, "I'll fucking hand-stamp jackets if I have to." Damn, if they didn't take me up on it!

In mid-March, we recorded and mixed "Kids Don't Follow" and seven other songs. The tracks were blistering ("Gimme Noise," "Fuck School"), topical ("God Damn Job"), raunchy ("White and Lazy"), funny ("Dope Smokin Moron," "Stuck in the Middle"), and gut-wrenching ("Go"). Initially, Paul wanted to call the EP *Too Poor to Tour*. He changed his mind when the record was done. It was to be called *The Replacements Stink*.

When the audio was wrapped up, Bruce Allen and I had rubber stamps made with all the credits. We had jacket-stamping gatherings with friends pitching in and everything was sent off to be manufactured. With no advance fanfare, *The Replacements Stink* was released in June. We managed to surprise everyone. *City Pages* journalist Marty Keller wrote that "Kids Don't Follow" "may rank with some of the best rock songs to come out of the land of 10,000 guitars," and he gave the record an A+.

Around this time, Paul slipped me two new solo recordings. "It's Hard to Wave in Handcuffs" was a piano song referencing an incident Chris and Paul had with the police. It's unique and weird and fascinating. The second song, "You're Getting Married," knocked me for a loop. He played this one on electric guitar, moving back and forth between delicate and forceful. The words were so tender and poetic:

You're like a guitar in the hands of a man that just can't play
You're like an inmate, counting off the days
You're like a student on vacation, waiting for school to resume
You're like a flower in the dark, ain't never gonna bloom
You're getting married

Well, you say you'll both be real happy
You forget to tell your eyes
You're like a bird in a cage, watching the flock fly on by
You're like a student on vacation, waiting for school to start
I don't know what's in it for you but it ain't, it ain't your heart
You're getting married

The desperation in his voice at the end is jarring. I'd be shocked if the song wasn't autobiographical (I've never asked). I had a hard time wrapping my head around the fact that a twenty-one-year-old had written it. It's hard for me to explain my reaction to hearing this song without sounding like a lunatic, but honestly, it frightened me. It was a watershed moment in my personal Replacements history, and I felt like I had grossly underestimated Paul. I thought the song was so good that it made me doubt my ability to work with a talent of this magnitude. I can't think of another musician of this era who was simultaneously writing punk-ish electric rock and folky acoustic balladry of this quality.

It had been clear for some time that Paul Stark's van was not a reliable option for road trips and touring. For the Chicago run in January '82, I rented a van from the Suburbs' Beej Chaney because I knew the journey would've been more than Paul's van could handle. With out-of-town shows becoming more frequent, the Replacements needed their own vehicle. Tom Carlson to the rescue!

Tom was a mad fan of the band. He'd been coming to 'Mats shows almost since the beginning. One night when we were packing up after a Zoogies gig, Tom approached me and gushed, "The Replacements are my favorite band since the Sex Pistols and Wire. If you ever need help, let me know." I kept this in the back of my mind, and when Lou's day job made him unavailable for regular roadie work, I asked Tom to take over the position. He was a terrific addition to our entourage, and he was a great help to me in taking care of the band, on and off the road.

When we began exploring how to go about purchasing a van for the band, Tom offered to help. He'd been in a minor accident on his motorcycle, and thanks to his insurance settlement, he was able to loan us $6,000. We signed a promissory note with him on June 23, 1982, but it would take us a month or two to find an acceptable vehicle.

That summer, the 'Mats opened a couple of shows for the Suburbs at a venue called Grandma's in Duluth. Carlson—or "Carton," as he became known—borrowed a friend's pickup truck and drove up with Bob, Tommy, and the band gear. Chris, Paul, and I drove in Tom's car. As the three of us walked into the venue, Paul pulled me aside and said under his breath, "I just came up with the best line I've ever written." I said I was all ears, and he recited the following: "I can live without your touch if I can die within your reach."

I was stunned by the simple beauty of the line, and I told him so. I can't deny I felt incredibly honored that he would share this with me.

In July, the Replacements were invited to Lawrence, Kansas, for a one-off show at the Off the Wall Hall on the twenty-second. The gig was organized by Blake Gumprecht, the music director at college station KJHK. The 'Mats were much revered in Lawrence thanks to the heavy airplay they'd gotten on the station.

The venue looked like an old airplane hangar, and we had some unexpected drama during sound check. Walking onstage holding the neck of his guitar, Bob reached out to grab one of the mic stands. There must've been a bad ground somewhere in the sound system, and electricity started coursing through his body. He couldn't let go. His body was spasming so violently that he snapped the neck of his guitar in two places. Chris was sitting behind the drums, and he vaulted over the kit and kicked the mic stand out of Bob's hand, cutting off the electrical current and probably saving Bob's life. The burn marks left on Bob's hand by the strings were horrifying. Everyone was so shaken that we finished a simple line-check to make sure the PA was working and promptly left the building. We'd been invited to someone's house for dinner and got a ride there in a station wagon. It was a somber and quiet drive. Bob and Tommy were sitting in the rear-facing back row, and I believe some tears were shed.

Later that summer, we had another gig at the St. Croix Boom Company in Stillwater. We still hadn't found a van, and once again Bob, Tommy, and Carlson rode with the gear in a borrowed pickup truck while I drove Tom's car with Chris and Paul. It was a fairly uneventful evening. The show was good, and I wasn't aware of any excessive partying by any of the guys. It was after midnight when we headed back to Minneapolis.

I was driving and Chris was in the front passenger seat when Paul started making retching noises in the back. At first I thought he was kidding, but I soon sensed something was seriously wrong. Paul was doubled up, clutching his stomach or chest, and clearly in pain. I thought he was having a heart attack, and I stepped on the gas. A minute or two later, I felt Paul's hand on my shoulder. He said, "Pete, if I die, don't let Bob sing." I can't recall if Chris or I laughed. As we got to downtown, I was running red lights while trying to remember where the Hennepin County Medical Center emergency room was. We pulled up in front of the Medical Center, and Chris and I carried Paul to the doors. They were locked; I'd gone to the wrong entrance. We lugged Paul back to the car, I drove around the block to the actual emergency room entrance, and we took him inside. Paul was quickly put on a gurney and taken into the hospital's inner sanctum and out of our sight.

Chris and I stayed until one of the paramedics told us Paul had been stabilized, but they were still doing tests and would need to keep him overnight. We went home, shaken.

The next day, after his parents had fetched him, Paul called me. He'd been diagnosed with pleurisy, an inflammation in the lining of the lungs that can cause serious breathing difficulty. The episode likely had been brought on by a combination of Paul's intense vocal performance and amphetamines he'd taken. The doctor recommended that, in the future, Paul apply Ben-Gay (a topical pain reliever) to his chest before singing. That salve became as essential to our band accessories as duct tape or guitar strings. Paul also mentioned he'd written a new song, "Take Me Down to the Hospital."

That fall of '82, we started recording what would become the *Hootenanny* album. The band didn't know what kind of record they wanted to make, but their stature had risen enough by this time that we could justify experimenting a bit, and we wanted to start recording new songs as soon as we could get studio time. We'd done the first two records at Blackberry Way with Steve Fjelstad but decided to try something different this time. I talked to Paul Stark about him engineering some sessions with his mobile truck. We cut tracks in two different warehouse spaces just north of Minneapolis over the following months. The 'Mats started with songs they'd road-tested live, like "Junior's Got a Gun," "Ain't No Crime," "Willpower," and "Staples in Her Stomach" (the latter a reference to a men's magazine centerfold).

At one point, just to mess with Stark, the band all switched instruments. Stark couldn't see them from the mobile truck and had no idea. They crashed into an improv jam. Paul was on drums and hollered into the mic, "It's a hootenanny!" It was a god-awful mess, but a funny god-awful mess. When the band finished, Stark's voice came through on the headphones: "Do you want to try that again, or do you want to come in and listen?" When the 'Mats realized Stark hadn't gotten the joke, they were all falling down laughing. That track became the title song and opened the album.

The tape kept a-rollin', and they revisited an old, rockabilly-style pre-Replacements song of Paul's, "Lookin' for Ya," but the band tracked it in a slowed-down, swing arrangement. When overdubbing the vocal, Westerberg improvised; instead of singing the original lyrics, he read from the *City Pages* classified ads. The song was retitled "Lovelines." They tossed off two songs they'd barely rehearsed, "Punk Poop" and "20 Proof"; did a throwaway romp through the Rolling Stones' "Jumpin' Jack Flash"; and took a go at two other cover songs they'd been doing live: Slade's "My Town" and Larry Williams's "Slow Down." They even attempted a version of "You're Getting Married," but Bob was uncooperative, saying, "Save it for your solo album, Paul." Then Paul whipped out a classic: "Color Me Impressed." The album was shaping up to be a great one—eclectic, yes, but in a freewheeling way that suited the band at this point in time. There would be one more song we'd pull from a secret recording session.

Late one night, shortly before we'd begun the warehouse recordings for the album, I was listening to all the solo material Paul had
given me. It hit me that if we didn't start capturing some of the songs
properly, he might forget them or just shove them aside, and they'd
be lost forever. The next morning I called Steve at Blackberry Way and
booked a solo session for Paul for a week or so later—swearing Feljy to
secrecy and paying for it myself to keep it off the band books. Then I
called Paul and explained my idea. He was caught off guard, but he
came around pretty quickly and agreed to do it.

On the day of the session, Paul met me at Oar Folk, guitar in hand.
We were about to head to the studio when Chris Mars happened to
pop in at the store and spotted the guitar case. The jig was up, so we
invited Chris to come along, emphasizing that mum's the word.

The three of us and Steve spent the evening at Blackberry recording three songs: "Warning Sound," Big Star's "September Gurls," and
"Within Your Reach," which included the lyric Paul had told me about
that afternoon in Duluth. The recording of "Warning Sound" was lost
somewhere along the way, but part of the song turned up later in
"We're Comin' Out." Paul made Steve erase "September Gurls" at the
end of the night (it wasn't a great version). Only "Within Your Reach"
survived the session. We tried adding Chris drumming on the studio kit,
but Paul didn't think the feel was right. Steve spoke up: "What if we try
a drum machine?" The Commandos drummer, Dave Ahl, had left one
at the studio, a Boss Dr. Rhythm. Paul played a flanged electric guitar
part and sang over the electronic percussion. He added a lead guitar, a
bass line, and later a synthesizer part, and it all worked like a charm.

Back in February, Hüsker Dü had invited the Replacements to open
for them at a show in Madison, Wisconsin. We were looking to expand
the 'Mats' regional reach, so it was a great opportunity. It also introduced us to a club that would be a favorite in the coming years, a second-
story venue called Merlyn's on State Street, Madison's main drag.

After *Stink* was released, the band was invited back to Merlyn's as
a headliner in September. The attendance for that gig and the 'Mats'

off-the-chart performance won them a quick return engagement, for two nights in late October. For most of the out-of-town shows, we relied on the kindness of strangers for gratis sleeping accommodations. In a new development for us, this two-night stand paid well enough that we could actually afford a hotel. I found one conveniently located walking distance from Merlyn's. We got into town, loaded into the venue, did sound check, and promptly retired to the luxury of semi-private relaxation in our hotel room before the show. This was the gig I wrote about earlier, where Loud Fast Rules was the opening act and blew me away to the point that I practically offered them a recording contract on the spot.

Merlyn's, and Madison in general, was incredibly important to the Replacements' growth as a band. That city was their Hamburg. They played for rabid audiences that hadn't watched them stumble through their early growing pains. This seemed to matter to Paul especially. Their performing prowess grew exponentially in Madison. Merlyn's owners, Serge and Lila Ledwith, deserve a boatload of credit for it. They recognized greatness in the band and treated us like family.

The Replacements kept busy through the end of the year with gigs at the 7th Street Entry, First Avenue's mainroom, and Duffy's, playing with Hüsker Dü, the Urban Guerillas, and our Lawrence friends, the Mortal Micronotz. They also had a heavy schedule in the studio finishing up album number three.

In early 1983 the 'Mats and I were at the warehouse with Stark, listening to a playback of all the recordings we'd amassed and deciding which tracks to include on the album. I'd told Charley Hallman about the switching-instruments prank the 'Mats had played on Stark, and he stopped by the session with an old Elektra Records folk compilation he'd found—it was called *Hootenanny*. The band loved the cover design and decided to "borrow" it. We enlisted Grant Hart from Hüsker Dü to do the layout, which he did under the pseudonym "Fakc Name Graphx."

A few weeks after we sent the album off for manufacturing, Westerberg called me at the Twin/Tone office. He said he'd just finished writing a new song that we needed to record right away and add to the album. I could tell he was excited, but he knew as well as I did that the new record was already in production. I explained that it would cost a fortune to halt the process and make the revisions, and it would delay the record's release. He wasn't happy, but he understood.

A couple of weeks later, the 'Mats had a show at Goofy's Upper Deck in downtown Minneapolis. They were five or six songs into the set when Paul began strumming a peppy rhythm guitar part I didn't recognize. The bass and drums kicked in with a bouncy tempo while Bob laid a hooky melodic line on top of it all. I instantly knew this was the song Paul had called me about. I thought it sounded like a hit record. As soon as they came off stage, I asked Paul what that new song was called. He said, "I Will Dare." Part of me was devastated that we would have to wait for the next album to release it, but if this song was an indication of where Paul was headed, songwriting-wise, the future looked very bright.

Back around the first of the year, with a third album nearly finished, the pressure was on me to get the band on the road nationally. I started making inquiries with people I thought could be helpful in setting up dates for the Replacements out east. The sales reps at the record distributors I dealt with for Oar Folk gave me some tips on the best venues in New York, Philadelphia, and Boston. I talked to Andy Schwartz, who was running the *New York Rocker* magazine, and he offered advice on clubs and promised to let his VIP contacts know about shows once they were booked. I rang up friend and Minneapolis ex-pat Danny Amis. Formerly a member of the Twin/Tone band the Overtones, Danny was living in Hoboken, New Jersey, and playing with an instrumental rock combo called the Raybeats. It was a fruitful call. Danny filled me in on what he thought were the best East Coast clubs, gave me some touring advice, and suggested I contact Julie Farman, who booked the Rathskeller in Boston. When I got Julie on the phone, she was ecstatic.

She loved the Replacements. She said she'd give them a date at "The Rat" and was happy to help in any way she could, and she even offered to put us up at her place.

Danny also took it upon himself to drop off his copy of *The Replacements Stink* with the Raybeats' booking agent, Frank Riley, at Singer-management in New York City. Frank was handling an A-list of bands on the indie rock scene. In addition to the Raybeats, he represented Television, the dB's, Meat Puppets, and the Violent Femmes.

In a striking bit of serendipity, reps from two separate NYC–area record distributors messengered copies of the Replacements' *Sorry Ma* to Frank the same week that Danny dropped off his copy. Apparently this got Frank's attention, and he called me at Oar Folk. He'd gotten my number from Steve McClellan at First Avenue. Frank said he knew that Steve often picked my brain regarding bookings and that I'd endorsed his bands. He wanted to reciprocate and offered to help get the Replacements out east. Remarkably, at a time when the Replacements were barely known outside of the Twin Cities area, we were in business with a reputable New York City booking agent.

Having Frank Riley in our corner completely changed the Replacements' trajectory. He became both facilitator and protector. He booked the band into the right rooms as they evolved through each phase of their career. When we experienced trouble, he was always there to help. In all my years working in music, I've never met a person I admire more.

The first tour Frank booked consisted of thirteen shows between April 8 and April 24, 1983, starting in Milwaukee, Wisconsin, and ending in Worcester, Massachusetts. Our entourage was originally going to be six: four band members, me, and our trusted friend and roadie of the last two years, Tom Carlson. In recent months, a friend of Tom's, Bill Sullivan, started lending a hand—moving equipment, helping set up the stage, and being a bodyguard of sorts when the crowds got too wild. Bill was not averse to being the tough guy when called for—something neither Tom nor I were built for, physically or in our demeanors. This and a number of other factors led us to decide to bring Bill on tour with us. Not only did we all like him, but from a practical point of view, having Bill along meant we'd have a third driver, and Tom wouldn't have to handle the gear by himself when I was tied up doing band business. Plus, Bill had bonded with Paul and could help appease him when Tom or I couldn't. And we knew Bill would be willing to accept whatever we could afford to pay him. So, six became seven, and with one Walkman to share among us, we headed out of town.

It became a kind of tradition that whenever we were leaving on a tour, Oar Folk would be our last stop before hitting the road. Everyone got a Coke, maybe bought a music mag, went to the bathroom, whatever. As we drove east out of Minneapolis for this first tour, we were all hopped up and cracking jokes. We'd been to Madison and Chicago and had made the drive before, but I remember Chris piping up from the back of the van: "Hey, are there any mountains in Wisconsin?" On our way to Detroit, we entered the Eastern time zone. I announced to the band that they should all set their watches ahead an hour—joking, of course, because none of them had watches. Bob was incredulous and asked, "Whaddaya mean?" I told him we had entered Eastern time and that it was now an hour later. Bob replied, "They can't do that!" I wasn't always sure when Bob was kidding.

The Detroit show was at City Club opening for the Neats. I was a fan of theirs and had been told they dug the Replacements too. The Neats's front man, Eric Martin, and lead guitarist, Phil Caruso, were very friendly when we loaded in. Since we weren't traveling with our own soundman, the Neats's roadie, Skip Welch, kindly offered to mix the Replacements' set at no charge. At sound check, he worked out the basic levels but told them they should turn down their amps for the set so that the vocals could be heard above the din.

When the Replacements went on at showtime, only a handful of people were in the club. The first song was so loud that the few people who were there went out to the lobby. Skip told me if they didn't turn it down, he'd have to leave too to protect his own ears. Between songs,

I walked to the side of the stage and told Paul their volume was a problem, gesturing toward the empty room, and said the soundman was on the verge of exiting too. Paul had a glass of whiskey on the floor next to his mic stand. He kicked it at me and the contents sprayed in my face. Then he turned around, walked over to his amp, turned it *up*, and launched into the next song. Skip vacated the soundboard, and I stormed out while the Replacements played to a completely empty room (apart from their roadies and one or two of the Neats). I'd seen Paul display irrational behavior toward others, but this was the first time I'd been on the receiving end. I walked to the first bar I could find and had a quick shot. I was pissed, but I decided to turn the other cheek and went back to the club. Paul and I never discussed the incident.

For most of the tour, we relied on friends' or fans' couches and floors for sleeping accommodations. Hotels or motels were considered only on an as-needed or as-could-be-afforded basis. In those instances, I'd typically get a room for four and we'd sneak in the other three. Our routine was to leave the amps and drums in the van and bring the guitars to the room. Sometimes one of us slept in the van to guard the gear or simply to get a little peace and quiet. In Detroit, we stayed in a relatively nice high-rise downtown hotel I'd found for a good deal. I chose this hotel specifically because it had advertised a secure parking lot, but when we got to the van the next morning, the gas had been siphoned out of our tank. So much for security. At least the gear wasn't stolen. We drove straight through to the next stop in New York.

We had arranged free places to stay in the New York area, but we arrived late at night, so I got a motel room in Jersey City, planning to check in with our hosts the next morning. None of us had ever been to New York before, and looking across the Hudson River at the skyline was awe inspiring.

During our weeklong stay, we split up into three different places, which served as our home bases for shows in the immediate area and the relatively short drives to Philadelphia, Albany, and Long Island. Paul and Tom were put up by a friend in Manhattan. In Hoboken,

Bill and Chris stayed with Bill's cousin, while Bob, Tommy, and I bunked with Danny Amis. Two of Danny's roommates were Ira Kaplan and Georgia Hubley, who were musicians starting a band of their own called Yo La Tengo.

The Replacements' New York City debut was on April 13, 1983, at Gerdes Folk City. This West Village establishment was the site of Bob Dylan's first professional gig in 1961. Even though it had since moved from its original location, walking into the place was still heavy. The club was hosting rock bands doing stripped-down midweek shows in a series called Music for Dozens, organized by Ira Kaplan and journalist Michael Hill. The Replacements were on a bill with the Del-Lords and the Del Fuegos, and all three bands were stellar that night. Once again, though, volume was a problem for the 'Mats. At sound check, the woman running the board told me that if the Replacements didn't turn down for their set, she was going to leave. I told her I'd do what I could. Surprise, surprise—they didn't turn down, the soundwoman left, and yours truly was left to do what I could to push the vocals up to some degree of audibility. The band played a blazing set, and sound issues aside, it was an auspicious NYC debut.

While the band was playing, I noticed a young man right in front of the stage watching them intently. I was thinking, *He's right in front of Bob's amp. He's not going to have any eardrums left!* When the band finished, I walked over and introduced myself. He said his name was Glenn Morrow. I knew of Glenn as the front man of Hoboken band the Individuals. He later became a partner in one of the best and longest-running indie labels in America, Bar/None Records. It was a chance meeting that bred a friendship that continues to this day.

The next two nights, Thursday and Friday, we had poorly attended shows in Philadelphia and Albany. A very different side of our NYC experience was at Danceteria on Saturday night—or, I should say, Sunday morning; the Replacements went on at 2:00 AM. The live music almost felt like an afterthought, as it was primarily a dance club occupying multiple floors. The dimly lit stairways were "anything goes," with drugs and sex in plain view. We shared the bill with the Violent Femmes, who went on at midnight. They had a fair crowd, most of whom didn't stick around for the Replacements.

The next night the 'Mats played with Hüsker Dü at Great Guildersleeves in the Bowery. My childhood fixation with *The Bowery Boys* TV show made the location extra special to me, and CBGB was just a few doors down the street. The dean of rock critics Robert Christgau was in attendance for the show, which was also exciting.

The test pressings of *Hootenanny* had arrived, and I knew my friend Jack Rabid was DJ-ing at the club that night, so I brought one with me. To get to the DJ booth at Guildersleeves, you had to climb up a ladder to a loft. Paul and I went up with the goods. Jack was genuinely thrilled about getting a sneak preview of the record and to meet Paul. He asked which cut we'd recommend he play. I was about to suggest "Color Me Impressed" when Paul beat me to it and said, "Side one, track one." Jack cued up the piss-take title song "Hootenanny" and hit play. After about thirty seconds, he asked us, "Does this ever get any better?" The crowd started booing and chucking stuff at the booth. He finally just faded the song out and cranked up F-Word's "Do the Nihil," which got the hardcore punks downstairs off his back. I asked Jack about the incident in 2022, and he told me that, in all his decades of spinning records in clubs, it was the only time he was ever booed by an audience. Jack says it was maddening at the time but he can laugh about it now. (Jack was the founder and publisher of the long-running, and still running, alternative music mag *The Big Takeover*.)

After midweek shows on Long Island (with Flipper) and New Haven, Connecticut, on Friday we landed at a club where we would become regulars in the coming years: Maxwell's in Hoboken. It's one of my favorite rock clubs ever. You couldn't find a homier-feeling, better-run place. The music room was about 200 capacity, situated in the back of a restaurant that had a killer jukebox. I have the utmost respect for the owner, Steve Fallon, and I crashed in his apartment upstairs from the club more times than I can count.

Leaving Hoboken and the New York area, we headed to the Rat in Boston. The club was in Kenmore Square, a happening section of town near Fenway Park with tons of bars and restaurants. The fabulous Hoodoo Barbeque was upstairs from the Rat, and it seemed like everyone in the Boston music scene worked there at one time or another.

On Sunday, April 24, we drove an hour east to Worcester for the last show of the tour. The band played to virtually no one, which was a disheartening finale for sure. After that, everybody just wanted to hit the road, so we did—1,300-plus miles and twenty-some hours later, we were back in Minneapolis. For the most part, the tour was a fun and successful time. The band did some truly great shows, we met a lot of cool people, and we got a brief taste of what it was like to tour. It was also good to find out that the seven of us could get along relatively well for that length of time on the road.

Back home, the Replacements played a show at First Avenue on May 8 with Man Sized Action and Figures. On the twenty-first, the 'Mats did a gig on Navy Island in St. Paul on a spectacular bill: the Suburbs, R.E.M., Let's Active, and the Phones. This show reconnected me with R.E.M., a band I had long known and admired, and within a couple of days, my career would shift dramatically when they asked me to be their temporary road manager.

Six

R.E.M.: *Princes Among Men*

In the summer of 1983, I found myself in a dream situation: I was working with what were then my two favorite bands on the planet, the Replacements and R.E.M. At this point, I'd been involved with the Replacements for three years, almost since their inception, and the five of us had become both a team and close friends. In the case of R.E.M., I had been a mad fan of their music since before I met them, and having the chance to work with the band was almost too hard to believe. Stories abound of fans meeting artists and being let down, but for me, getting to know and work with R.E.M. was quite the opposite. It was not only the music they made; I loved and admired them as people.

R.E.M. first came to my attention in the summer of 1981 with their debut record, the single of "Radio Free Europe"/"Sitting Still." It was the inaugural release on a new Atlanta-based indie label called Hib-Tone. I was placing an order for Oar Folk, and a longtime sales rep at one of our distributors gave the R.E.M. single a hearty endorsement. He told me the band hailed from Athens, Georgia. I knew Athens was the college town that three years prior had spawned another band we loved, the B-52s. With that and my rep's endorsement in mind, I took a chance and ordered a few more copies than I otherwise would have. When the single arrived at the store a few days later, it quickly landed on the turntable. *Eureka!* Both sides were super catchy, and the exuberance in the performances sucked me in right away. There was also an air of mystery surrounding the band—the blurry cover photo, the night-lit overhead shot of the band on the back, the barely perceptible words. The staff and I gobbled up all the copies, and I immediately ordered a box of twenty-five. By the time those landed, our regular customers were champing at the bit, and we sold out in an afternoon. I ordered fifty the next time. And on it went. We went through hundreds of copies over the course of a few months. This band was a bona fide phenomenon on the strength of one 45.

The singer's largely unintelligible mumbling made me listen closely to the songs. The music grabbed me too. R.E.M. played melodic indie rock infused with elements of folk and pop, with the distinctive ringing Rickenbacker guitar sound. As we learned more about the band over time, we found there was a special balance among the members—two relative beginners and two experienced musicians. But in that first flush of falling in love with R.E.M.'s music, what caught my ear was a high-spirited blend of four potent imaginations and, on their first few recordings, an endearingly unrefined feel. Ambition without arrogance. And it was so damn fresh!

Bassist Mike Mills and drummer Bill Berry had been in previous bands together; both sang and were multi-instrumentalists. Bill also had some music business experience, having worked with a booking agency in Macon before moving to Athens. Peter Buck was a guitarist, music nut, and bookworm who worked at Wuxtry Records in Athens. Singer Michael Stipe's musical awakening came later than the others. I remember him telling me that hearing Patti Smith was his true aha moment. His shy, enigmatic stage presence was a big part of what defined R.E.M. at the start. His confidence grew as time went on, and Michael eventually became a charismatic front man. R.E.M. had that one thing that all groups strive for: they didn't sound like anyone else.

The Twin Cities' first sighting of R.E.M. was Thanksgiving night 1981. They were originally booked to play the 7th Street Entry, the 250-capacity annex to the 1,500-capacity main room then known as Sam's.

Mother Nature intervened when a blizzard hit town, and the Sam's head-liner cancelled. (No one recalls now who that band was.) Club man-ager Steve McClellan decided to move R.E.M. into the larger room. Official attendance records show they played for an audience of eighty-eight, which was not a bad number for them at the time, especially in a city they'd never been to before. At that point, Minneapolis was the farthest they'd traveled from their southeastern homeland for a gig.

Unfazed by the weather, Tommy Stinson and I took a bus down-town. We went first to see Curtiss A perform at Goofy's Upper Deck and then hoofed it the two blocks to Sam's to catch R.E.M. Our good friend Chrissie Dunlap, who was the office manager at Sam's, did the same. She had caught R.E.M.'s sound check and told us it was mes-merizing. Like us, she decided to duck out of Goofy's early—even though her husband, Bob, was Curtiss A's lead guitarist. When R.E.M. took the stage, they looked a little intimidated by the big room with the small crowd, but the extreme weather had an unexpected positive effect. Because everyone had to struggle a bit to get there—both audi-ence and band—there was a warm sense of camaraderie among strang-ers. It was like having our own, private show. Jefferson Holt, R.E.M.'s original manager, summed it up well in a later interview with *Pitchfork*, saying, "Because of the enthusiasm of the people that came out, it was one of the best shows that they ever did." I had been dying to see these guys live, and they exceeded my expectations.

R.E.M. returned five months later, on April 26, 1982—this time for a show intended for the main room—and drew nearly 350 people. (By this time, Sam's had changed its name to First Avenue.) I chatted briefly with the band before and after the show. They were aware of Twin/ Tone, and Peter was a fan of the Replacements, which was gratifying to me. I was flattered when, just before they did a cover of the Velvet Underground's "There She Goes," Peter ran up to the mic and said, "This one goes out to Peter J." Peter later told me that was the first time he'd ever said anything into a microphone onstage. I still have the band's set list from the show, written on a napkin. This visit was also the first time the band came by Oar Folk and hung out. They had days off before and after the First Avenue show, which gave Peter and me the first of several opportunities to stay up until dawn listening to records. And he was not averse to crashing on my couch.

By the time of R.E.M.'s third Twin Cities show, in September 1982, the cat was out of the bag. Fueled by the August release of their EP *Chronic Town* on IRS Records, a thousand devotees turned out for the show, again at First Avenue. I thought it was R.E.M.'s best performance yet. This made three shows in Minneapolis in less than a year. These guys were working hard.

My next encounter with R.E.M. was on May 21, 1983, when they were part of a multi-band bill on St. Paul's Navy Island, roughly two acres of land in the middle of the Mississippi River. The Suburbs headlined, and the Replacements, Let's Active, and the Phones were also on the bill. The next two nights R.E.M. was playing Milwaukee and Madison, and Peter invited me to come along. One indelible memory from the Milwaukee set at the Palms is a performance of a new song, largely written by Bill, called "Perfect Circle"—possibly my favorite R.E.M. song ever. I have no idea what the lyrics mean ("Shoulders high in the room," indeed!), and it matters not. The music gets me every time. When I first saw it live, the performance began with Bill executing the lovely intro on a Casio keyboard. Michael then came in singing a heartrending vocal melody, with Mike playing spare bass notes, before Peter's guitar and Bill's drums joined in at the chorus. Positively magical!

After another killer show at Headliners the next night in Madison, the backstage area was mobbed with friends and fans. The dressing room was full to overflowing, so I plopped myself down on a road case in the hallway. I was feeling a little down. I'd just spent three days with R.E.M. and was witnessing up close how fast their star was rising. I had that conflicted feeling many music fans have about an artist they feel like they "discovered" before the masses—happy for their success but sad that they were being appropriated by a more general population, who couldn't possibly understand them like we, the early fans, did!

Peter came into the hallway and saw me sitting there by myself. He seemed to sense my mood and asked if everything was alright. I said, yeah, that I'd just seen three knockout shows in three days and was sad it was over. He replied, "Well, we've been talking. Would you be interested in tour managing us for a while?" A flood of thoughts ran through my head: *What??!! You must be joking! I am not worthy! Fuck yes!* It was immensely flattering, but it was also surprising. My road experience was quite limited; I'd only just returned from the Replacements' first tour the month before. I voiced this concern to Peter, but he laughed and said they were still beginners too. The Replacements were my first responsibility, though—how could I do both? Peter told me, if I accepted their offer, they would do it in a way that had the least impact on my work with the Replacements. We agreed I'd mull it over and get back to them ASAP.

I discussed R.E.M.'s proposition with two or three close friends. I weighed the pros and cons. My thought process boiled it down to two conclusions: First, more than just a dream come true for me personally, working with R.E.M. would be educational on a practical, professional level, allowing me to learn what the business was like a few rungs up the ladder, as well as exposing me to some advantageous contacts that could help the Replacements. Second, I'd been at Oar Folk for over a decade, and while I still loved it, I thought it was time to roll the dice and take a chance on something new.

Before I could make a final decision, though, I needed to talk to the Replacements. I called a band meeting. I explained the offer I'd gotten and my thoughts on it. I made it very clear: If they were uncomfortable about it for any reason, I'd turn it down. Our talk went better than I had expected. The 'Mats all seemed to agree with me; it was a great opportunity that could be beneficial for all of us. Tom Carlson could handle the road managing on whatever Replacements tour dates I had to miss. I perceived no hesitation or resistance from them. After a bit more discussion, it was decided. I accepted the offer, with the Replacements' approval.

Famous last words. Thinking back on it, I've often wondered how I ever thought that me working with R.E.M. was going to go smoothly with the ever-volatile Replacements.

For the next month and a half, it was business as usual, and business was busy! R.E.M. seemed to be permanently on the road and had released their first full-length album, *Murmur*. The Replacements had just finished their first national tour, and their third album, *Hootenanny*, was out. The Replacements' booking agent, Frank Riley, had been sketching out summer tour dates when R.E.M. offered them a slew of opening slots in July. This was a huge deal. The band would be playing bigger rooms in front of more people. The itinerary would begin July 2 in Indianapolis. The plan was that I'd leave Minneapolis with the Replacements, and we'd work our way east, opening for R.E.M. On the thirteenth, the two bands would do a show together at the Paradise in Boston, and at the end of the night, I'd leave with R.E.M.

As for the business of road managing, I'd already taken to it well, my inexperience notwithstanding. I credit some excellent mentors—Paul Stark, for one. He'd been on the road regionally with the Minneapolis band Straight Up, so he knew the ropes and gave me several pointers. Frank Riley schooled me well. And R.E.M.'s manager, Jefferson Holt, was a tremendous resource. The tutelage of these three people gave me a serious leg up on the mechanics of The Road. Advancing the dates by phone ahead of time with the various promoters, club managers, and sound technicians was something I found I was good at and enjoyed doing. The practical and technical aspects were important—like confirming how much the band would be paid, establishing set times, going over sound and hospitality requirements and preferences, getting directions to the venue—but simply a friendly introduction to a liaison at each venue on the itinerary paid dividends later when we arrived.

The Indianapolis show at the Chase was a nice kickoff to the tour. From there we went to Cleveland for a show at the Pirate's Cove, and then to Cincinnati on July 7. After a stop in Detroit at St. Andrew's Hall on the eighth, the two bands split up. R.E.M. went off to Toronto, and the Replacements headed east to Boston.

After the Paradise show on the thirteenth, I did the load out with the 'Mats as usual, we said our goodbyes, and then I left with R.E.M. No question, it was an odd feeling.

Not surprising to anyone, I'm sure, traveling with R.E.M. was quite different from traveling with the Replacements. On the one hand, I missed some of the madness. On the other, I discovered how civilized touring could be. I got along well with all the R.E.M. band members and crew, and I'll always be grateful to Bill Berry, who was especially welcoming to me.

R.E.M. traveled in two vans: a beige Dodge Ram, which they owned and had been customized with an equipment compartment built into the back; and a rented silver Ford van. We stayed in hotel rooms every night, two to a room. The R.E.M. entourage consisted of the four band members, manager Jefferson Holt, myself, and three crew—Billy Lindsay (soundman), Gevin Lindsey (guitar and drum tech), and Paul Lenz (lights). Jefferson handled hotel arrangements, and interestingly, he paired me with Michael Stipe. I had assumed I'd be sharing a room with Peter, but no complaints. I enjoyed bunking with Michael.

One of my responsibilities was getting paid at the end of the night, and it was quite an honor to log income and expenditures into a little black book that went all the way back to the very first paying gig R.E.M. had ever done.

The R.E.M./Replacements dates together wrapped up in Richmond. The 'Mats continued on the road for another month, stretching into the third week of August. R.E.M. had only one more date on this tour: July 23 at Baity's Backstreet Music Garden in Winston-Salem, North Carolina. Let's Active opened, and there was an after-show party at front man Mitch Easter's Drive-In Studios. It meant a lot to me to see the place where R.E.M. had recorded the "Radio Free Europe" single and *Chronic Town* EP, not to mention the site of other recordings by

Let's Active and the Bongos. As an interesting side note, the studio's very first client was Twin/Tone band the Crackers. The studio was in the garage of Mitch's parents' house, and I spent a fair bit of the soiree hanging out with his mom and their dog, O.D. (Old Dog).

The next day we drove to R.E.M.'s hometown, Athens, Georgia. Getting the play-by-play from the band as we got into town was hilarious. It was my first time there, and I was excited. I was such a fan of the music that sprung out of this little college town, and I had heard so much about its bohemian vibe. As we pulled into the city, the air was thick with heat and humidity, the landscape was green and dense with kudzu vines, and the antebellum architecture was stunning. I felt like I was in a Tennessee Williams play. First impressions did not disappoint. This was most definitely the deep South.

Peter and Jefferson shared a house on the northwest side of downtown. It was an old two-story yellow Victorian that had been sectioned off into apartments. It was an odd layout; you had to go through a closet in Jefferson's quarters to get to Peter's room, where I'd bed down in an alcove.

We arrived on a Sunday, a day you can't buy alcohol in Athens. So, after we got settled, Peter and I got back in the van and drove about fifteen miles to the small city of Arcade. We pulled up to a concrete block building with one window and one door. Peter tooted the horn. The window opened, and Peter asked the clerk if we could buy some beer. The transaction was quickly completed, and off we went. Apparently, the authorities in Arcade looked the other way when it came to alcohol sales on Sundays. We got back to Peter's and listened to records and drank beer well into the next morning. In those early, leaner days for the band, the house had no AC. I'll never forget how ungodly hot and humid it was in Athens during the summer, even at night. One afternoon Peter and I went downtown to see some terrible movie (*Octopussy? Porky's II?*), just for the air conditioning. The theater also served beer, a practice unheard of back in Minnesota. Two days later, I flew home until the next tour began in about two weeks.

The following run of dates was an exciting proposition; R.E.M. was opening for the Police in seven stadiums and arenas on the East Coast. This good fortune stemmed from Bill's long friendship with Ian Copeland, the brother of Police drummer Stewart Copeland. They had met before R.E.M. existed when Bill and Ian worked for the Paragon Agency, a concert booking outfit in Macon, Georgia.

Although this was certainly a remarkable opportunity for the band and for me, advancing the R.E.M. dates for the Police tour was quite intimidating. I was still new at this, and to be suddenly thrown in with the big dogs took some getting used to. The Police's British tour manager had been doing this kind of work for years, and it was all I could do to keep up with his instructions. Luckily, he took a liking to me. The entire experience was a real education. It's not the level of show business I'm much interested in—I prefer my rock 'n' roll in clubs—but I sure am glad I got to do it once.

The tour was set to start on August 12 in Hartford, Connecticut, and I flew back to Georgia a few days ahead of time. I knew Michael was picking me up from the Atlanta airport, so I cooked up a surprise for him. I knew how much he loved Patti Smith, and I had a large promotional poster for her first album, *Horses*, that she'd signed for me after a show at the Guthrie in 1976. I knew it would mean more to Michael than to me. I had it mounted on a solid foam-core backing and wrapped it in thick, brown paper and carried it carefully onto the plane. When I came off the jetway, Michael was there waiting and saw me carrying this bulky package and asked what it was. I said it was a gift for him but he couldn't open it until we got to Athens. When we arrived at his house an hour or so later, he excitedly tore it open and his jaw dropped. It was a touching moment.

Being in Athens more frequently, I was able to be a fly on the wall at R.E.M. band practices, which was quite a treat. I attended one at a house Bill and Mike were sharing on Barber Street. I was amused to see they'd assembled a shrine to Abba above the fireplace mantle. Peter recently reminded me that this rehearsal was when he first played his sketch for "So. Central Rain." It was also the first time I witnessed musicians preparing what were essentially music beds for a lyricist, in this case Michael. That's not to say Peter, Mike, and Bill didn't contribute to all aspects of the songwriting, but words and vocal melodies were more often than not Michael's domain.

On departure day for Hartford, the crew guys and I met at the band's rehearsal space, packed the gear, and headed up the eastern seaboard in a two-van convoy. The band and Jefferson would fly up two days later.

On the first day of the tour, I drove into the bowels of the Hartford Civic Center in the van that held all of R.E.M.'s gear. As I came down the ramp, I saw six semitrailer trucks and chuckled to myself while backing our little van up to the loading dock. The Police's seasoned, burly British road manager came out, probably expecting at least another van or two. When I told him that this was it, he said incredulously, "Wot? Is this all you got, mate?!" Once I realized he was a funny and bighearted man behind his bluster, everything was just fine.

We did two nights in Hartford, with R.E.M. getting thirty-minute slots that allowed for a nine- or ten-song set. They did a mix of material from *Chronic Town* and *Murmur*. Though there were still many empty seats when R.E.M. went on, the people who'd come early received them warmly, and the band held their own on the big stage. On the first night, Mick Jagger and two of his young daughters were in attendance and got the VIP side-stage treatment. I only saw them from afar, but it was still pretty damned cool.

In the wee hours after the second Hartford show, the two R.E.M. vans hightailed it out of town. We had the next day off and wanted to wake up in New York City. It was only a two-hour drive, and with so little traffic at that time of night, we made good time. I was driving in the Ford van with only Peter on board. At some point we realized we were out of beer. The Dodge van had left a little ahead of us, so Peter suggested I step on it and try to catch up to them. After a few miles, the other van came into view. I moved into the left lane and pulled up alongside them. Peter stuck half of his body out the passenger window, waving and shouting to get their attention. One of them noticed and rolled down the window. Peter cupped his hands around his mouth and hollered, "Do you guys have any beer left?" They did and proceeded to pass us several cans while driving sixty or seventy miles per hour on the highway. Yikes! We pulled into Manhattan sometime after 4:00 AM and checked in at the Mayflower Hotel right across from Central Park.

After our day off in New York, we made our way down to Norfolk, Virginia, for the third show of the tour on August 15. Post-gig, we went back to have some drinks at the hotel bar with some of the band and crew. A couple of us slipped outside to smoke pot, and with the combo of alcohol and weed, I was pretty high when I got back to the room. Michael had been reading and we chatted for a bit. Then he popped a cassette in a portable player and turned off the lights. I was expecting something calm and sleep-inducing. The volume was low, and it was a repetitive, crunching sound, not unpleasant but kind of weird. I finally asked, "What is this, anyway?" Michael quietly replied, "Rats." I think I bolted upright in bed. It turned out he was kidding, messing with my altered state, and we both had a laugh. I wish I could recall now what it actually was. I enjoyed getting to know Michael. He's a fairly introverted person, and getting past the protective armor even a little bit meant a lot to me. Sleep was slow in coming that night as I pondered where we were headed next: in two days R.E.M. was going to play Shea Stadium.

Naturally, being on the Police tour brought all kinds of new and bigger publicity opportunities to R.E.M. One of the most prestigious was Peter and Mike being invited to do the band's first television interview, with Nina Blackwood for NBC's "Live at Five" program in the famed 30 Rockefeller Plaza building. They looked a little intimidated on the air, but their down-to-earth demeanor was charming.

The day of the concert at Shea Stadium was a whirlwind. Our load-in time was 11:00 AM, and I took the gear out there by myself. It was about a twelve-mile ride from the hotel in Manhattan to the stadium in Queens, and I'll admit I was all aflutter. Being the Beatles devotee that I am, this was like a pilgrimage: to the site of their legendary July 15, 1965, performance. Getting into the Shea complex was tricky, but I soon found myself backing the van up to the stage. As I got out, I nearly opened the door into someone walking by. Turned out it was Sting, who was going up to the stage with a bass guitar slung over his shoulder and a baseball cap on backward. I checked in with the Police's road manager to let him know R.E.M.'s gear was on-site. The crew kindly unloaded the van and stacked the equipment in a holding area.

Joan Jett and the Blackhearts were also on the bill, playing the middle slot. Sound checks always go in reverse order from the show, which meant R.E.M.'s was last, so I had some time to kill. I checked out our luxurious trailer–dressing room and wandered the grounds for a while. The whole experience felt totally surreal to me. Could this actually be happening? Was I really working a show at Shea-fucking-Stadium?! During a pause in band and crew activity on the stage, I walked out to the very lip of it and stood for a moment, taking in the thousands of empty seats, picturing what had transpired there eighteen years before. I couldn't resist, I found a pay phone and called my mother. She teased me a little, but I knew she knew what a big deal this was for me.

The enormity of it all made the show go by so fast. Despite some rain and a shortened set due to the third act being added, R.E.M.'s performance was spectacular, and the crowd seemed to dig it too. Peter was especially athletic, leaping around like a madman. After the band finished and we packed up the equipment, I needed to catch my breath. I hid out in the relative calm of our trailer, so I didn't see Joan Jett. I did watch a fair bit of the Police set, though I think I paid as much attention to the insane crowd as I did to the band. After the final encore, Sting said something like, "Thank you to the Beatles for letting us use their stadium." This got me a little choked up; it was a very sweet way to close the show.

Two days later we were at JFK Stadium in Philadelphia for a daytime show. If I thought the crowd at Shea was big (70,000), JFK dwarfed it

(125,000). In addition to the Police, R.E.M., and Joan Jett, the English ska band Madness was also scheduled to perform. An unwelcome addition, however, was the heat. At the 1:00 PM showtime, the thermometer was pushing 100 degrees. R.E.M. soldiered through their set, although the adrenaline had definitely kicked in, and they played faster than usual and managed to squeeze seven songs into their allotted fifteen minutes. Madness played second, and the audience ate it up, as did I. By the time Joan Jett went on, a number of people in the audience were suffering from heat exhaustion and were being passed hand-over-hand to medics beyond the barricade in front of the stage. During the Police's set, Sting actually sprayed the audience with a hose. I'm not sure it was a very enjoyable afternoon for all attendees.

From Philadelphia, we headed to Landover, Maryland, and the Capital Centre for the final two shows of the tour. I'd gotten used to the gargantuan machine that it took to put on a Police show, but I never ceased to be awed watching all the preparation in action. This was definitely the Big Time.

After the last show, the crews exchanged friendly thank-yous and goodbyes. At some point, I was walking through the maze of hallways backstage and ran into Sting, who gave me a friendly smile and a thumbs-up. Other than nearly hitting him with the van door at Shea, this was the first and only interaction I had with him the whole trip, but it was a nice way to end it. With the close of the tour, band and crew alike had a feeling of "mission accomplished." R.E.M. had held their own and then some on the largest stages they'd played to date, while the crew and I delivered on our end too. We were treated well, we had fun, and the exposure and experience were invaluable.

The next morning, I flew back to Atlanta with the band. We had three days off in Athens before the final show of the summer, when R.E.M. was headlining at the Six Flags Over Georgia theme park outside of Atlanta on August 26. This was going to be interesting, as I had to be back in Minneapolis the next day for a recording session to begin the Replacements' next album. I had a red-eye flight booked after the show.

R.E.M.'s set time wasn't until 9:30 PM, but due to theme park proto-col, we had to load in early afternoon. There was a lot of hurry-up-and-wait that day. That evening's performance was a good one. The set featured a few as-yet-unreleased tracks, including "Harborcoat," "7 Chinese Brothers," and "Pretty Persuasion," as well as cool obscurities "That Beat" and "White Tornado."

Packing up at the end of the night was bittersweet. R.E.M.'s next scheduled dates weren't until October, so I wouldn't be back in Georgia for at least a month. Peter was meeting me in Minneapolis in a few days to sit in on the Replacements' sessions, and he asked me to take two of his guitars with me, which was stressful. Several scenarios ran through my head, all involving weapon-wielding villains running off with his precious Rickenbackers.

The recording sessions at Blackberry Way were fruitful; it was the start of the Replacements' masterpiece, *Let It Be*. After Peter Buck arrived, much carousing ensued. I have hazy memories of late-night record listening in my apartment, and of Paul Westerberg and Peter decked out in eyeliner at First Avenue or at one of our favorite after-hours fast-food haunts, the White Castle.

A week or two later, I was at home in my apartment and got a phone call I wasn't expecting. It was Jefferson, and he got right to the point. He and the band had decided they were ready to hire a professional, full-time road manager. They'd no longer be needing my services. I'd known that I was a stopgap for them, but I hadn't expected it to end so soon. Jefferson assured me there hadn't been any problems with my work; they just needed someone permanent. He then added that they wanted someone who was more forceful, more of a bulldog, on the business side of things. This was no surprise to me. I wasn't exactly a hard-ass who could intimidate troublesome venue managers. In a subsequent conversation, an old girlfriend of Peter's said there was a general feeling among the band members that I might have been "too nice" in some circumstances. Frankly, it wouldn't be the last time I heard something along those lines, and I was okay with that.

Over the years. I've thought a lot about my time working with R.E.M. It caused a rift between the Replacements and me that I wasn't fully aware of for a very long time. Maybe if I could have anticipated that, I wouldn't have taken the gig. But had I not, I would've missed out on an extraordinary experience. It goes without saying that R.E.M. is one of the greatest rock 'n' roll bands of all time. In my mind, their legacy is one of colossal originality and integrity. I respect the band and the people who work with them. It was an honor and a privilege to be in their employ, even briefly.

Seven

The Replacements, Part II:
On the Road, Crash Landing

When I agreed to take on the road-managing job with R.E.M. in the spring of 1983, I knew that it could lead to new opportunities for the Replacements, a band I remained deeply committed to. And sure enough, within six weeks of my accepting the role with R.E.M., the Replacements were heading out on the road to do several opening gigs on R.E.M.'s tour. Unfortunately, it wouldn't be smooth sailing for long.

The tour was kicking off in Indianapolis on Saturday, July 2. The Replacements van pulled out of Minneapolis on Friday with the same seven who had been on the April East Coast run. It was about a nine-hour drive to Indy. The plan was to travel most of the way, get a cheap motel room outside of town, and have a short drive into the city on the day of the first show.

As usual, after a few hours on the road, the band wanted a cocktail. I knew of a hotel bar just off the freeway in rural Wisconsin where we'd stopped before. It was a dark, lodge-like place, with few other patrons that night. The excitement of being back on the road was in the air, but as we talked, I began to sense a strange vibe from Paul. At one point I made a comment about his snarky attitude. He turned to me and said, "Don't you get it, Pete? You're not one of us anymore." *Huh?!* For a moment I thought he was joking, but it quickly became clear he was not. There was real bitterness in his eyes, and he made a derogatory crack about me taking the gig with R.E.M. Tommy seemed to be siding with Paul, while Bob and Chris appeared uncomfortable with the rebuke. There was an awkward silence. Though I was completely dumbfounded by what Paul had said, I did the only thing I felt I could under the circumstances: I kept my nose down and continued to do my job as best as I could.

When we got to Indianapolis, the R.E.M. guys were welcoming, and the partying started soon after. Paul and Peter seemed to egg each other on. The 'Mats had the next two days off while R.E.M. headed to Milwaukee for a Summerfest show. We hung around Indianapolis, and the band was invited to do an impromptu performance in a fan's used-clothing store on July 4, but otherwise, we were just killing time. On the fifth we headed to Cleveland and the Pirate's Cove. It was another okay night, performance-wise, but a pattern was developing. The Replacements got a lukewarm response, while R.E.M. was unanimously adored. This aggravated Paul, but he did little to quell the causes of the crowd's indifference: excessive volume and sloppy performances. The two bands were scheduled for seven more shows together, and I was hoping that would change.

Bogart's in Cincinnati was next. When we arrived, the drinking began again, and after sound check Tommy, who'd yet to fall under the spell of the bottle, announced he'd had it with the drunken, sloppy performances and was leaving the band. He called his mom from a pay phone and asked her to send him money for a plane ticket. It took some doing, but we finally talked him out of quitting. I thought this episode might have a constructive effect on the band's alcohol consumption, but that was not the case.

After one more show in Detroit, the two bands went their separate ways and would reconvene at the Paradise in Boston on July 13. The Replacements had four days off, so we drove straight from Detroit to Boston. This much downtime was difficult for our finances and morale. I'd been coordinating the tour dates with Frank Riley, but it wasn't easy for him to book what was still a fairly unknown band. Being on the road with very little money and having to rely on the kindness of friends or fans for even floor space to sleep on could be exasperating, and Paul in particular would get ornery. What frustrated me about this was that I had discussed it with him beforehand. I'd shown him the dates we had booked and explained that there were times we'd have more days off than was ideal, and he said he understood.

Holes in the calendar, on top of the knowledge that I was about to part ways with the band for the next little while, certainly caused problems, but the familiarity that came with being back in a city we had been in just a few months earlier helped offset the tension. Distraction wasn't hard to come by in Boston. The band had no trouble finding a party, that's for sure.

The downtime in Boston had an upside. Paul asked if I could find a place for the band to rehearse. This was a surprising and uncharacteristic request, but I contacted Lilli Dennison, manager of the Del Fuegos, and she generously offered up their practice space. I didn't know what Paul had up his sleeve until we got to the Paradise the next night.

For sound check, the 'Mats ran through snippets of their usual set, then they kicked off a song I didn't know. It had the feel of an original. I thought, *This must've been why he wanted to rehearse. He had a new song to teach the band.* I was trying to catch the lyrics when I heard:

Your age is the hardest age.
Everything drags and drags.
You're looking funny.
You ain't laughing, are you?
Sixteen blue
Sixteen blue

It hit me: *He's written a song about Tommy.* They played it live that night for the first time. Another killer song for the next album.

The end of the night was strange, indeed. Since first meeting them in 1980, I'd missed only a couple of Replacements shows. I would miss fourteen more over the next month, and that was a tough pill for me to swallow. The goodbyes seemed heartfelt, even though the bands' schedules would intersect a few times in the coming week. When we met back up, I'd get razzed a bit by the 'Mats guys for my new, cushy travel arrangements—two vans, multiple drivers, only two people to a hotel room—but it was always in good fun, and it seemed that whatever acrimony there'd been between us had dissipated.

After wrapping up that leg of the tour on July 23, I returned to Minneapolis, where I had plenty to do before the next set of R.E.M. dates. I was still doing a fair bit to assist Tom Carlson with advancing the Replacements' shows. They were doing dates in the South in July and August, so much of the driving would have to be done at night because our old van's engine and air-conditioning wouldn't cut it in the kind of daytime heat they'd be traveling through.

I reconvened with R.E.M. for the Police tour and then flew back on a red-eye from Atlanta to Minneapolis the night before the Replacements were to begin recording their album. I caught a few winks on the plane, and three or four more at home before picking up the band and heading over to Blackberry Way studio.

Recording for the 'Mats' fourth album began on Saturday, August 27, 1983. It felt good to be back at Blackberry Way with our old pal Feljy engineering. The sessions were the most focused the band had done so far. Over a five-day period, the 'Mats quickly laid down backing tracks for the songs they'd been doing live: "I Will Dare," "Sixteen Blue," "Favorite Thing," "Tommy Gets His Tonsils Out," "Adult" (which later morphed into "Seen Your Video"), "Gary's Got a Boner," and a cover of Kiss's "Black Diamond." They also cut one called "Who's Gonna Take Us Alive," but it was left unfinished. Peter Buck came to the rescue on "I Will Dare" after Bob had trouble finding a guitar part he and everyone else liked. Peter filled in Bob's section perfectly with a kind of rolling, poppy guitar solo.

When we were listening back to one of the "Dare" takes, Paul off-handedly commented that a mandolin might sound good during the breakdown in the middle of the song. I snuck upstairs and found a phone where I wouldn't be heard. I called Mark Briar, the mandolin player in my brother Alan's bluegrass band (the Middle Spunk Creek Boys), and asked if he would be willing to rent me his mandolin for a recording session. He said yes, and we made plans for me to stop by his house.

The next day when I picked up Paul to go to the studio, he spotted the strange little hardcase on the back seat and asked what it was. I said it was a surprise for him. He opened it, pulled the mandolin out, and started tinkering with it. It might've been the first time he'd ever played one. In the studio he added some perky licks to the "Dare" track. Listening to the playback, we all agreed it fit perfectly.

Paul and I were working well together, maybe better than ever. We spent a lot of time after the sessions listening to rough mixes and talking about what needed to be done next. It seemed as if he'd forgotten whatever grievance he'd had over my taking the R.E.M. gig—or at least he put it aside to focus on the recording. I believe *he* knew that *I* knew he was having a kind of artistic breakthrough in terms of the sophistication of the new songs he was writing, and the relationship we'd long had with me as his sounding board was restored (for the time being, anyway). And, though I had been surprised to receive a phone call from R.E.M.'s manager in early September telling me I would no longer be needed, as they were hiring a full-time tour manager, this too likely helped reinstate my standing with Paul.

September was light for band activity. Which was good because everybody needed a little downtime after the hectic summer. Paul also needed time to come up with, or finish, a few more songs. We worked at Blackberry a couple of days that month, had dates at the Entry and Duffy's, then hit the road for most of October and November. The next clusters of studio time came in December and January.

October held two important happenings for the Replacements. On the eighth, the band did its first show in Coffman Union's Great Hall at the University of Minnesota. Being invited to play there was indicative of their rising stature. It was a big room with a capacity of 1,000. The 'Mats didn't fill it that night, but they would in the not-too-distant future. Second, on the eighteenth, they opened for LA punk band X at Merlyn's in Madison, which led to additional tour dates down the road and launched a lasting friendship between the bands. Like the Suburbs, Hüsker Dü, and R.E.M., X was incredibly supportive of the 'Mats, giving them much-sought-after opening slots.

I was working with Frank Riley on setting up the band's first foray to the West Coast, which was to kick off on November 14 in San Francisco. I had to miss the first three Replacements shows, however, because I had agreed to tour manage Figures on a short run to the East Coast, and the dates overlapped.

Regrettably, things didn't go smoothly on the other side of the country. During the drive west, the Replacements' van broke down in Wyoming. I was out of reach, so they called Twin/Tone, and luckily Paul Stark was able to wire them money. Tom Carlson and the band paid a local man to take them to the nearest airport, which was 150 miles away in Salt Lake City. From there they flew to the Bay Area for the start of the tour. Both San Francisco shows were with the Neats, who generously allowed the 'Mats to use some of their gear, and the venue supplied the rest. Meanwhile, Bill Sullivan stayed with the van until it was repaired and then made the long drive to San Francisco. He met up with the band and got them to gig number three, a house concert in Davis, California. The next day they drove the 400 miles to LA. I'd flown in the night before and stayed with my friend and former Oar Folk coworker Dan Fults. The guys picked me up there, looking a little worse for wear. Everyone perked up, though, as we headed to Club Lingerie for sound check. The Replacements' first show in Los Angeles was in the thick of Hollywood on Sunset Boulevard.

The show at Club Lingerie was moderately well attended. Those who were there made a lot of noise and were treated to a classic Replacements performance—opening with "Hayday," segueing into "Color

Me Impressed," a cover of T. Rex's "Baby Strange," and an impassioned "Unsatisfied." The latter song, along with early airings of new material like "Can't Hardly Wait" and "I Will Dare," provided strong evidence that Paul's songwriting was rapidly maturing. It was still a year before their fourth album, *Let It Be*, would come out, and the band was already doing six tracks from it live. They also threw in a couple of numbers that always got a laugh from audiences: "The Marines' Hymn" and an improv they called "Music Is My Life," both of which ended in farcical cacophony.

While in LA, we stayed at the famed Tropicana Motel in West Hollywood. Former long-term residents included Jim McGuinn of the Byrds, Janis Joplin, and Tom Waits. A signed photo of Jimmy Page hung on the wall above the reception desk. Celebrity tenants or not, I loved the place. It was surprisingly affordable, and we were able to camp out there for several days while doing shows in the area.

The next gig was at Cathay de Grande, a basement alternative-music haunt off of Hollywood Boulevard and Vine Street. Top Jimmy & the Rhythm Pigs were doing a Monday-night residency, which meant there was a built-in crowd. The Replacements were special guests and did another rip-roaring set.

The 'Mats also picked up an unannounced show there on Thanksgiving night opening for Social Distortion. It was their last performance in LA on this trip, and they effectively flipped the bird to the punk rock crowd. Seeing a room full of kids decked out in leather and mohawks, Westerberg put on his bumpkin voice and the band proceeded to do covers of songs by Hank Williams and Billy Swan, along with slowed-down, countrified versions of their own stuff. At first, the crowd was incensed and heckled loudly. But as the set progressed, a fair number of them got into the spirit.

All in all, our first experience in LA was a mixed bag. Attendance was modest, but the band made a significant number of new fans and got some great press. As music journalist Chris Morris put it in the *LA Reader* the following week: "On their records (and I wouldn't part with any one of them), the Replacements are unbeatable. Onstage, even when approaching the boundary line of chaos, they're among the most special of live bands."

After the long trek home from the West Coast, the Replacements had a few days off. They had only four shows in December and so devoted most of their time to the recording studio. We rolled tape on a handful of new songs and covers. The originals included "Unsatisfied," "Perfectly Lethal," and "Street Girl." Paul recorded two solo songs: "Androgynous," on which he played piano, and "Answering Machine," featuring a loud, distorted electric guitar. They also recorded covers of "20th Century Boy" by T. Rex, "Temptation Eyes" by the Grassroots, and "Heartbeat, It's a Lovebeat" by the DeFranco Family.

We continued working on the album at Blackberry through much of the first half of January—tweaking, tinkering, overdubbing, and mixing. As the album was taking shape, the feeling around Blackberry and Twin/Tone was that these Replacements recordings were a cut above.

A tour of the Midwest and East Coast was on the calendar from mid-January to mid-February—sixteen dates in all. We'd learned from past experience that we had to schedule at least one day off every three or four days, to let Paul's voice rest. Booking agent Frank Riley did an exceptional job, and the routing for this trip was great, as were the venues and the money. We left for Oklahoma City the morning of January 22 and headed across the Midwest to the East Coast for shows in Boston and New York City, before finishing at City Gardens in Trenton, New Jersey, on February 11.

We returned home after the tour and went right back into the studio to finalize the track order. We picked eleven songs for the album. Next we needed to have pictures taken for the cover art. We arranged photo shoots with our old friend Greg Helgeson and with up-and-comer Dan Corrigan. Greg tried a few different things, including some shots of the 'Mats crossing Minneapolis's Bryant Avenue, *Abbey Road*–style.

Twin/Tone's Blake Gumprecht then suggested to Dan that he take photos of the band at the Stinson house because it was essentially where the band had formed and it held such an important place in their history. Dan and the band liked the idea. They started shooting in the basement where the band rehearsed before heading outside, and the roof beckoned. The result was one of the most iconic pictures ever taken of the Replacements. Bruce Allen's grainy, blue-tinted treatment of Corrigan's photo added a beautiful design element to the album cover. Various titles had been kicked around, but at the last minute Paul decided to call the album *Let It Be* (I think partly as a poke at my Beatles' obsession).

As with *Sorry Ma*, we wanted to put out a single ahead of the album. "I Will Dare" was the obvious choice. We decided to do a 12-inch format, which gave us more room, audio-wise. We picked two songs for the flipside, both covers: the studio recording of "20th Century Boy" and, in a last-minute curveball, a raw, live version of Hank Williams's "Hey, Good Lookin'," featuring one of Bob Stinson's most preposterous leads—it was like he was playing a completely different song. It had been recorded at Merlyn's in Madison, and driving home after that show, we tortured Bob by playing the solo over and over again, while he tried to fight his way to the tape deck to destroy the cassette.

As Feljy and I were transferring the track at the studio, a funny thing happened. The cassette we were pulling the live recording of "Hey, Good Lookin'" from had been a mix tape that we'd recorded over. When "Hey, Good Lookin'" ended, one of the songs that had been on the mix tape started up. It almost sounded deliberate: the Hank Williams song segued perfectly into the beginning of "Feel," the opening song from the first Big Star album. I thought, *What if we leave just a few seconds of the Big Star track and then fade it out?* It would be a tip of the hat to one of our favorite bands. I played our edit for the 'Mats that night, and they loved the idea. When I met Alex Chilton later that year, he told me that sneaky move was how he'd first heard of the Replacements. A friend played the 12-inch for him, and he heard the little Big

Star snippet that we left in. Alex was not one to throw compliments around, but I could tell he thought it was cool.

By the time the album's audio masters and package design were done, it was too late to get *Let It Be* into production for a spring release. It was a tough decision, but, again for college radio purposes, we reconciled ourselves to a late August release of the single and early October for the album. In the meantime, the 'Mats did short runs to Madison, Chicago, and Milwaukee and a handful of local shows. One of the local dates was at Coffman Union's Great Hall for a rescheduling of a show that had been canceled under unusual circumstances a couple of months earlier. The band had been asked to play a benefit for a young heart transplant recipient, but it was postponed, apparently because the heart the beneficiary was set to receive was the wrong size. The situation was rectified, and the show was on. The 1,000-capacity Great Hall was sold out or very nearly so. The 'Mats went onstage at the designated time, and as Westerberg was strapping on his guitar, he walked up to the mic and said, "Let's hope the fucker fits this time 'cause we ain't comin' back," and then they crashed into the opening song.

The *Let It Be* promo campaign began in early August when "I Will Dare" was sent to radio. The 12-inch was released to record stores the twenty-fourth. We felt the song had real potential and wanted a month to let it circulate before releasing the LP on October 2. Bruce Allen designed a cover for the 12-inch using an outtake from the roof photo session, perfectly complementing the album.

Late that summer, it was finally time to retire our touring vehicle—a former electric company Ford van that Westerberg had dubbed "Bert"— and look for a new used van. After a bit of shopping, we found a gray Ford Econoline. Paul named this one "Otis."

As we were finalizing dates for the next tour, Tom Carlson called to tell me he'd decided to quit. He'd been a roadie, and more, with the band for three years and said he needed to stabilize his life and keep close to home for a while. We'd gotten used to having two road crew people and were trying to decide who could fill Tom's shoes. We'd previously discussed bringing a soundman along with us on the road, and this seemed like the right time. The money was finally good enough that we could afford one. The band had recently played a show at Duffy's, and the gent who mixed them there, Bill Mack, did an excellent job. I tracked him down and popped the question. He enthusiastically said yes.

The twenty-eight-date tour began on September 10 in Columbus, Ohio, and included seven shows opening for X, which were in bigger rooms than the Replacements typically played. We wouldn't be back home until October 15. It was the longest run we'd done up to that point.

The *Village Voice*, an influential alternative weekly from New York, flew journalist R. J. Smith out to ride with us for a few days and do a story on the band. Smith had reviewed *Hootenanny* the year before, claiming that listening to it was "like taking a warm beer shit." We said we'd be honored to have him! He was meeting us at a club called Stache's in Columbus. Every time someone walked in, Paul and I tried to discern if that was R. J. After several "definitely nots," we saw a serious-looking, bespectacled, dark-haired man enter, and we instantly pegged him as the *Voice* writer. As he approached our table with hand extended, Paul stood up and said, "Excuse me, I've gotta go take a warm beer shit." It was a great icebreaker and set the tone nicely for our travels with R. J.

The venues in Boston, New York, Trenton, and Hoboken were all places we'd been before, and the band delivered mostly good sets. Having our own soundman made a difference, but it didn't stop the 'Mats from going off the rails on many nights. I believe this was also the tour where "the magic slacks" entered the picture. One of the band members found a hideous pair of blue and white wide-striped bell bottom pants in a thrift store. They became a sort of punishment when someone did something stupid. When you were told to put on the magic slacks, you had to comply and keep them on for the entire night or risk more serious retribution. They really were ridiculous, and the routine was one of the funnier rituals in the Replacements' storied existence.

A few nights later we were in Athens, Georgia, where the band had a dedicated following. The show was in the back of an old building called Stitchcraft. The stage was in the loading dock area, and a big garage door opened onto the Oconee River. It was a very cool setting. The place was packed that night, and it was one of the best shows I'd ever seen the Replacements do. Friends of mine from Athens still say that show is legendary. One of the openers was a killer band called the Primates, with vocalist/bass player Eric Sales. He and I would hook up nine years later when he was playing with Jack Logan, whom I signed to a record deal. Worth noting: Stitchcraft was across the street from the church where R.E.M. had played their first show. Unfortunately, those boys were out of town.

After two more shows in the South, we made the long drive to East Lansing, Michigan, for the first date with X. The next night was Ann Arbor. Right after the 'Mats set, we left for Columbus, Ohio, where we had free lodging, and where the 'Mats and X would perform at the Newport Music Hall. At around midnight, just after we'd crossed into Ohio, the van started making a horrible racket. We limped our way to a motel and rented a room for the night. The next morning I called Curt Schieber, the promoter who booked the Newport and had offered to put us up. He gave me the number for a repair shop in Columbus, and I arranged to have the van towed there. Curt then borrowed a Jeep from a friend, picked us and our trailer up, and drove to his house. The repair shop said the van wouldn't be ready for three or four days. We still had five dates with X, so I rented another van.

After the Newport Music Hall gig, both X and the Replacements had the next day off, so with Curt's help, we drummed up an unannounced show at Stache's. X had an alt-country side project going called the Knitters. So, with them and the Replacements playing together, it became the Re-Knitters. It was a fun if slightly inebriated evening of old country covers and a few originals. The lineup onstage was fluid, with band members coming and going. At one point, the Replacements did a few of their songs and X's Exene Cervenka walked around the club telling people to stand up: "You can't be sitting down when the Replacements are onstage!"

We closed out our X dates in Pittsburgh, Chicago, and Madison and headed home. Everyone was exhausted and looking forward to sleeping in their own beds. Me? After dropping off the gear, band, and crew, I had to get back on the road and drive to Columbus, return the rental van, and pick up ours from the repair shop. Fueled on bad truck stop coffee and Campbell's soup, I did the 1,450-mile round trip solo in two days.

Bill Mack gets high marks for his first tour as soundman with the Replacements. He was very professional and did a good job making the vocals audible over the band's always challenging stage volume. He was also an alert and long-winded driver, and he didn't drink, which came in very handy for Sullivan and me.

Back home for a short break, I worked with Frank on coordinating two upcoming tours: an October and November trip to the west and a December run out east. He called me late one night and I could hear excitement in his voice. Frank said, "You'll never guess who just called me and wants me to book him some dates." I asked, "Who, Frank?" He replied, "Alex Chilton!"

This was big news. Alex hadn't made a record since 1979's *Like Flies on Sherbert*. We'd heard he'd quit playing music and was washing dishes at a bar in New Orleans. Apparently, Alex wanted to come out of retirement. Frank looked into booking dates for Alex and the Replacements together. Some club talent buyers were very excited about the prospect, while others didn't know much about Alex. Keep in mind, in 1984 Big Star's renaissance hadn't happened yet; they were still largely unknown. And even the clubs who knew about Alex and Big Star couldn't agree to the fee Frank was asking on Alex's behalf. The 'Mats and I were not discouraged. We offered to discreetly move some of our money into Alex's payment, but Frank said that wasn't going to work. For the time being, we settled for one show with Alex, at CBGB on December 9. But first, we had eleven dates to do in the west.

The first show was October 26, back at LA's Club Lingerie, playing with Love Tractor and the Unforgiven. From there it was six hours up the I-5 to the Bay Area and another club we'd been to before, Berkeley

Square, for a two-night stand. The club manager, Michael Bailey, had
called me a month or so ahead of the show to ask if it was okay to put
a local band on the bill. He said they were begging to open for the
Replacements. This was nice to hear and I asked who they were. It was
a band called American Music Club, and Michael said he could vouch
for them personally. They didn't have a record out yet but he described
them as a rock band with introspective, often sad lyrics. I took him at
his word and okayed them opening.

I was standing with Paul when American Music Club went onstage.
The lead singer, Mark Eitzel, looked terrified but I found him strangely
compelling. Paul said he thought Eitzel was putting on an act. I said
no, I think this guy is genuinely having a nervous breakdown. I loved
the band, and Eitzel's pathos, and have been a fan ever since.

Since we were there for a couple of days, we stayed in a motel
directly across the street from Berkeley Square. We also discovered a
nearby barbecue joint called Flint's in Oakland and ate there many
times. It was funny, for all the times we traveled through the South,
we always said the best ribs we ever had were at Flint's.

The 'Mats did shows in San Francisco and Pomona before they were
to perform at a Halloween celebration in Valencia at California Institute
of the Arts, the so-called Disney College. You can imagine what those
students did in terms of decorating the event. It was sensory overload.
The stage had a massive castle backdrop flanked by giant Mickey Mouses
with devil horns at the top. There were robotic mannequins, elaborate
haunted tunnels around the room, and blood-curdling sound effects
coming from all directions. We shared a dressing room with headliners
the Minutemen, which only added to the festive atmosphere. I don't
know if I've ever laughed so hard in my life. Minutemen bassist Mike
Watt was like an Energizer Bunny–comedian who never let up. At one
point, both Paul and I left the room, just to catch our breath.

The 'Mats' set staples on this run were mostly songs from *Let It Be*
and *Hootenanny*, with a few from the first two albums like "Kids Don't
Follow," "God Damn Job," and "Customer." They had a loose, bluesy

jam they called "Hear You Been to College" that I always thought was not much more than a time filler. The selection of covers included "Left in the Dark" by the Vertabrats, "Yeah Yeah" by the Revillos (sung by Bob), "Do the Clam" by Elvis Presley, "Hitchin' a Ride" by Vanity Fare, and "If I Only Had a Brain" from *The Wizard of Oz*, often sung with theatrical gusto in a cameo by roadie Bill Sullivan.

The final show on the West Coast was at Al's Bar in downtown Los Angeles. Best known for punk rock, it was a 250-capacity room and one of the best gigs in southern California. The club was run by a good bunch of people. The booker, Debbie Drooz, cooked delicious home-made dinners and brought them to the club for the bands.

We had the next day off to get to Tucson, an almost 500-mile drive through mostly desert terrain. It felt like we were on the moon. The Tucson show was at the Backstage. Bob had recently been reprimanded by the other band members for leaving the stage during sets to go to the bathroom. So on this night, when he had to go, he just went behind the amps and relieved himself. I don't think anyone from the club saw it, but several people in the audience did, and not all of them were amused.

When we got to Edcels Attic in Phoenix the next day, we ran into our friend John Freeman, later the front man of Twin/Tone band the Magnolias. He had gone on a hitchhiking adventure, stopped in Phoenix, saw the Replacements listed in the local weekly, and decided to stick around for the show. John ended up riding with us for the rest of the tour. He earned his keep well, schlepping gear and tuning guitars.

We had three more shows on the itinerary after Phoenix: Fitzgerald's in Houston, the Continental Club in Austin, and the Bowery in Oklahoma City. The band was itchin' to get home, and there was talk of blowing off the Bowery gig, figuring it was a Sunday show and would likely be dead anyway. We couldn't afford not to do it, though, plus it was a good way to break up the long drive home from Austin. We'd been at the Bowery back in January, but it had since moved locations, into a former Episcopal church. The building was mighty impressive, though it looked deserted. I knocked on the large wooden doors, and when the proprietor saw me and the van in the parking lot, he exclaimed, "The Replacements, my favorite band! *Let It Be*, my favorite album! C'mon in, the drinks are on us!" To say he was generous to us would be an understatement. The liquor flowed freely all night long.

One thing about playing in Oklahoma City was that we could always count on one guy being there wearing the most outrageous clothes. Inevitably, as we'd be approaching the city, someone in the van would pipe up and say, "Hey, I wonder if the guy with the wild slacks is gonna show up tonight." We found out later his name was Wayne Coyne, and he had recently started his own band called the Flaming Lips.

The Bowery show could have been a disaster, but it turned out to be an unbelievably fun, drunken Replacements performance. The crowd was sparse but enthusiastic. When the band came on, Westerberg encouraged people to move closer to the stage, which they did, pulling up tables and chairs. Sullivan served a few of them drinks from our ample supply in the dressing room. The 'Mats kicked off the set with a rousing rendition of Larry Williams's "Lawdy Miss Clawdy." The audience was barraging the band with requests, so I thought I'd join in. I shouted, "Ye Sleeping Knights of Jesus." It was a song we all loved from the new Robyn Hitchcock album, and the band kicked right into it. The show continued on, bouncing between half-finished drunken attempts at classic rock and surprisingly coherent performances, including fine renditions of "Sixteen Blue," "Can't Hardly Wait," and the Vertabrats' "Left in the Dark." The camaraderie between band and audience made it a particularly special night. Most everyone in attendance seemed up for whatever the 'Mats did.

The Bowery was the last show of this run, and we left for home immediately afterward, a nearly 800-mile drive. Bill Mack was at the wheel, and at some point he put a tape in. It was a recording of that night's show. Mack said he'd spotted a tape recorder running in the balcony of the club and confiscated the tape. The more we listened, the more we laughed. Some of it was actually quite good, and overall it was a real hoot of a show. Paul floated the notion of releasing the recording in some limited form, which got unanimously positive responses.

After the sun came up, Paul asked Mack to pull over, and John Freeman took a photo of the bleary-eyed band and me at the "Welcome to Iowa" sign. In January 1985, Twin/Tone released a cassette of the Bowery show as a limited edition of 10,000, bearing the title *When the Shit Hits the Fans*. Chris Mars did the artwork, and the J-card included liner notes by Paul and John's state-line photo. I assumed I'd be cropped out, but Paul said, "Nah, you're part of the band."

Luckily, after wrapping up the tour out west, we had just over two weeks off before the next run out east. It's funny how it works: When you're home, you get restless and can't wait to get on the road. When you're on the road, you get tired of the long drives and cramped quarters and wish you were home.

For our final road trip of 1984, we worked our way to the East Coast and back—seventeen shows in twenty-one days. We were starting with a bang, as far as I was concerned. On December 1, the Replacements opened for the dB's at the University of Chicago. Founder Chris Stamey was no longer in the band, but the remaining members—Peter Holsapple, Will Rigby, and Gene Holder, augmented by new bassist Rick Wagner—had just made a terrific album called *Like This*, and I was jazzed to see them. I was thrilled when midway through their set, drummer Will Rigby pointed a stick at me and mouthed, "This one's for you." They went into the Replacements' song "Unsatisfied," with Will on lead vocal.

Our travel agent had found us a deal on a hotel on Lakeshore Drive in Chicago. We still did the trick of getting a room for four and sneaking the other three in. I was sharing a double bed with Tommy, and at one point after we'd all been asleep, he woke me up, shouting and shaking me. A woman was standing over me, unzipping my pants! I sat up and pushed her away while trying to get my bearings. The commotion woke up Chris, who was sleeping in the closet across from the bathroom. He had a clear view of a second woman, sitting on the toilet relieving herself, with the door wide open. It turned out Bob had gone down the hall to get something from the vending machine and ran into a couple of sex workers who were leaving another room, so he invited them to ours. I can still picture Bob, cackling in the corner.

We continued on to shows in Ann Arbor, Kent, Buffalo, Albany, and New Haven. Back in familiar territory, we hit the Rat in Boston, headed down to Maxwell's in Hoboken, and then into Manhattan for the Sunday-night show at CBGB with Alex Chilton.

One of the Del Fuegos had told me about a reasonably priced hotel on West 44th Street near Times Square called the Iroquois. It had been a luxurious place when it first opened in 1902, but in 1984 it was clearly between renovations, which I'm sure had something to do with its affordability. It still had plenty of its old glamour, though. It had suites with two bedrooms and a living room with a sofa bed. There were ample choices for food and alcohol nearby, twenty-four hours a day. It became our go-to place to stay for the next couple of years.

At this point, the Replacements' star was rising fast. *Let It Be* was all over college radio and indie retail. It had become somewhat of a sensation, in the alternative-music world at least. One hitch that developed from this growing buzz, however, was that the much-larger Irving Plaza wanted to book the band on December 14. Because Irving Plaza had a no-compete clause, which restricted any other area shows within two weeks, the CBGB date on the ninth would have to be unannounced. We were worried that without being able to advertise the Replacements, CB's owner Hilly Kristal wouldn't go for that, but he generously agreed. The Replacements chose a rather obvious pseudonym for the gig: Gary & the Boners. Even though Alex was making a comeback, he figured he should play under a fake name too and decided on the Deteriorating Situations.

Adding to the frenzy, we arrived in New York to discover that R. J. Smith's article on the band had come out, and the Replacements were on the cover of the *Village Voice*! I'm not sure we knew in advance that was going to happen. It was a very surreal experience to have the band's mugs looking out at us from every newsstand.

After sound check at CB's, the 'Mats had a photo shoot down the street at the studio of legendary artist Stephanie Chernikowski. In an effort to cram as much as possible into our short time in the city, the band was also doing an interview at Stephanie's place with Richard Grabel, the US correspondent for British music weekly the *NME*.

I left the band at the studio and went back to the club to sort out our guest list. As I was sitting in the van gathering the names, I heard Alex and his band start their sound check. My mouth went dry and my heart rate went up. I took a deep breath, pulled open CBGB's big wooden door, and stepped in. Alex was singing an old Goffin–King song called "Let Me Get Close to You," and it sounded magnificent.

The show that night was both good and bad. By that I mean Alex was good and the Replacements were bad. Alex's trio played a terrific set of mostly new originals, a couple of old standards, and just one Big Star song, "Watch the Sunrise." The Replacements were in rough shape by the time they took the stage. Paul and Tommy had been up front watching Alex's set, and perhaps the excitement of seeing him for the first time influenced how much they drank. Even though the Replacements weren't advertised, word got out. The *Voice* cover story had attracted nearly every A&R person in New York, many of whom wondered who was this band they'd never heard of gracing the front page of such an influential newspaper. The place was packed, and I stayed at the soundboard with Bill Mack and house soundman Robin Danar. Some of the Replacements' drunk shows could be at least fun and entertaining. This one was neither. One funny moment occurred when Robin nudged me and pointed at a very tall man standing a few feet to our right. I didn't recognize him and shrugged my shoulders. Robin whispered, "That's Gene Simmons." The soundboard had a talk-back button that allowed us to communicate through the stage monitors. I told Paul, "Gene Simmons just walked in, no shit," and the

Replacements crashed into a very loose approximation of Kiss's "Black Diamond." Gene quickly exited.

At the end of the night, I went to Hilly Kristal's office nook to get paid. He never liked the Replacements, but he and I always had a great rapport. The club had been extremely crowded, so the bar must've made a fortune. Hilly was going through ticket receipts and counting money when he looked up and said, "Peter, do you know Alex?" I hadn't realized Alex had walked up and was standing right beside me. I didn't have time to get nervous; I just said, "Hello, nice to meet you," or something on that order. After the three of us had some chit-chat, I managed to eke out an invitation: "Alex, I'm a big fan of your work. Could I buy you lunch in the next couple of days?" He said he'd like that, and we made plans to meet the next day at the corner of St. Marks Place and Second Avenue.

The next morning, I got up around 10-ish, had a light breakfast and a shower, and got ready to meet Alex. Paul had a couple of interviews later in the afternoon, so I stopped by his room to remind him of that before I left. I had to wake him up, and he was grumpy, but I told him I'd be back to take him where he needed to go. As I was closing the door, Paul asked where I was going. I said I was going to meet Alex, and he shot out of bed and asked if he could come along. I said of course. Ten minutes later we were in a cab heading downtown to the East Village.

We pulled up at our destination, and there was Alex, standing on the corner. I paid our fare and hopped out, greeting him and trying to keep my cool. Alex wanted Indian food and led us to one of those two-steps-down basement places in that neighborhood. He was so laid back and friendly, Paul and I quickly calmed down. The conversation flowed easily, and the food was sensational. At one point, Paul excused himself to run to the bathroom, and when he was out of earshot, Alex leaned over and said, "Man, I loved the Replacements' show last night. I'd love to work with them in the studio sometime." I about lost my lunch! The band had been so irredeemably terrible the night before at CB's,

I wondered if he was kidding. But I replied, "If you're serious, we'll fly you in, and I'll book the studio time right now!" He said he was. When Paul got back to the table, I told him what we'd just discussed, and no surprise, he was all for it. We settled on the week of January 7. I called Steve Fjelstad from the restaurant pay phone and booked time at Twin/Tone's new facility, Nicollet Studios. We offered to put Alex up in a hotel, but he asked if he could just crash at my place. I didn't mind that one bit.

We had the next two days off and mucked about in New York City. Everyone needed a little relaxation and recharging after CB's and the excitement of the upcoming studio session with Mr. Chilton. I spent some time at Frank's office and did my requisite record shopping.

On Wednesday, we took off for a show in Philadelphia that night. Thursday was Washington, DC, and the 9:30 Club, which was a bear to load into. You had to drive down an alley and make a sharp right turn to get to the back door of the club. Sullivan was the only one who could maneuver the van and trailer in that tight space.

On the morning of Friday the fourteenth, it was back to New York, the Iroquois, and Irving Plaza for the big show. Since the 'Mats' reputation among major label talent scouts was heating up, we retained the services of New York–based lawyer George Regis to represent the band and handle any interest that might arise. George alerted me to the fact that a lot of key people were coming to the gig that night, and I did my best to keep that from the band. Knowing there were important people in the audience often caused Westerberg's contrarian nature to pull an unproductive stunt of some kind (like getting liquored up and doing an all-covers set).

When the 'Mats were getting ready to go on, it was a full house, and it was hot in the room. Paul was wearing a flannel shirt, and I said he might want to rethink his wardrobe, but he shrugged it off. They started the set with a twist, launching into an impassioned "Go" from the *Stink* mini-album. I moved around the room to hear and see from different angles. The Replacements were performing at the top of their game. They knew they had something to prove after the shambles of a set they'd done at CB's. The audience was enthralled. I returned backstage to watch from the wings. Paul was sweating profusely. When they finished a song, he looked around, spotted me, and ran over while removing his flannel. Without asking, he yanked my T-shirt over my head, put it on, and ran back onstage. I wasn't exactly happy about putting on a thick, wet hunk of flannel, but I got a kick out of seeing Paul wearing my Neil Young T-shirt.

I'd seen zillions of Replacements shows, and this was one of their best. Toward the end of their set I noticed George talking to a rather rotund older man who was gesturing frantically. When the man walked away, George came over and said, "That was Seymour Stein from Sire Records, and he just said he's going to have you guys signed before you even get home from this tour."

It was hard to beat the Irving Plaza show, but the next two nights at City Gardens in Trenton were pretty great too. Saturday, the 'Mats opened for the dB's again, and Sunday they headlined their own all-ages show. We headed back west, stopping in Pittsburgh, Cleveland, and Columbus before ending the tour on December 21 at Chicago's Cabaret Metro, another favorite room of mine with a powerful PA system. Back home, we had one more show before the end of the year, at First Avenue on the twenty-sixth. And then, we rested.

The year 1985 was looking good. We were confident the Sire Records deal would go through, but to be honest, Alex Chilton coming to town might have been even more important to us at the time.

The only negative aspect to that first month of the year was that the band decided they wanted to bring in a new soundman. I always liked Bill Mack, thought he was a very good soundman, a hard worker, and a reliable driver. But I think the band felt he didn't fit in somehow.

We hired Mike Bosley, another Minneapolitan, as the new sound person. We'd frequently crossed paths with him around town, as he'd been doing sound locally as well as for some national and international bands like the Long Ryders, Jason & the Scorchers, and Lloyd Cole and the Commotions. Everyone he worked with gave him high marks. We had a gut feeling that he'd be compatible with the Replacements, and we put him to the test very soon.

Frank Riley had set up another substantial tour for us. It was three weeks long and would start January 18, so I had plenty to do in advancing the dates. We were going to a number of cities we hadn't been to before, including four in Florida. Before all that, though, we had some recording to do, with one of our heroes.

Alex Chilton flew in from New Orleans on Monday, January 7. Westerberg and I picked him up at the airport and brought him back to my humble abode. The recording wasn't scheduled to start until the next day, but Alex was hot to see the place, so we took him over to Nicollet Studios. It was fun to see people's faces when Alex walked into any of our regular haunts. He was so revered, it was like rock 'n' roll royalty was in the house. We introduced him to Paul Stark and Steve Fjelstad, and they gave Alex a tour of the studio and filled him in on what type of gear was available. I showed him the Twin/Tone offices upstairs. He seemed impressed with our operation.

After we left the studio, Alex wanted to chill out and reserve energy for the next day. Paul went home, and Alex and I had a quiet night at my place, listening to records and talking. I quickly made note of one subject that it was best not to dwell on around Alex: Big Star. He was certainly proud of the work that band had done, but in his mind, they were a failure. The records didn't sell and the band barely toured. What's more, he didn't think their three records were as big a deal as a select cult following (including me) thought they were. He could get quite prickly when someone raved too much about the band.

When we convened at the studio, there was no question Alex was there to work. We weren't sure how much of the Replacements' music he was familiar with, but Alex loved the three songs Paul brought to the sessions: "Can't Hardly Wait," which had been road-tested and was ready to go, and two new rockers with a melodic bent, "Nowhere Is My Home" and "Left of the Dial." The band ran them down for Alex, and the consensus was to start with "Can't Hardly Wait."

Paul's idea was to record an acoustic version of the song and then pipe it through the band's headphones for them to play along. Paul said he'd like the track to have the sound of a large room, so Fjelstad suggested an echo chamber that was located above the receptionist's desk. The space was where the film projector had been when the building was a movie theater in the 1920s. To get into this space, you had to climb a ladder in the lobby. Paul asked Chris to join him with a snare drum to keep time. The resulting acoustic take didn't work as a template because it wasn't audible in the headphones when the full band cranked it up, but it was a gorgeous, ghostly version. Even with an unfinished lyric, the track, with Paul singing lead and Chris doing backup, was quite stunning.

Without a backing track to play along with, the band went ahead and knocked out a very strong, electric performance of "Can't Hardly Wait" with a different, but still incomplete lyric. Like with "I Will Dare" (or "Color Me Impressed," for that matter), I thought the band had a hit song on its hands. As it turned out, Paul decided not to include the song on the first Sire album. My theory is that he wasn't happy yet with the lyrics. They'd rerecord the song for the next album, *Pleased to Meet Me*, but I always thought that version was a little too slick, with the horns and glossy production. It was good, but it lacked an edge.

The other two songs were a breeze to get basic tracks down for, as was Paul's vocal for "Nowhere Is My Home." This song has a special place in my heart for two reasons: it contains one of Bob Stinson's finest guitar solos, and it referenced touring. The opening lines were so sweetly optimistic:

Out to sea in a ship full of holes
Even so, with a heave and a ho
Gonna raise my sails

"Left of the Dial" took a little more time. I think everyone recognized it was another classic Westerberg song, and a certain amount of finesse was required to get it right. Alex added a perfect harmony vocal to Paul's "dial" on the closing refrain. And Chris's drumming on this recording was spectacular.

As we were wrapping up the sessions with Alex, Westerberg told Fjelstad to erase the acoustic "Can't Hardly Wait." He was of the mind that it hadn't worked as planned and was therefore dispensable. I panicked when I heard this but managed to quietly conspire with Steve and snuck a cassette dub of it before he erased the master tape. I hated to do this behind Paul's back, but I felt it was great art that needed to be preserved. To me, it's one of the best Replacements recordings ever. I kept it hidden for years, along with a compilation of all the solo songs Paul had given me. I wasn't aware until much later that someone who stayed in my apartment while I was away found my secret stash and made a duplicate for themselves. Then that person dubbed a copy for someone, and that person dubbed a copy for someone—and the next thing I knew, all those tracks were in circulation on the black market. I've felt wretched about it ever since.

While Alex was in town, my girlfriend, Maggie Macpherson—the booker at the Uptown Bar—asked if he'd like to do a solo show there. He said he would. The Replacements opened and various band members joined Alex onstage at different points throughout his set. It was a loose but fun night, and a good break from the long hours in the studio.

On the last night of Alex's stay, we hung out at my place. Linda Hultquist and PD Larson came over. A young, local fanzine writer had been pestering Alex all week about doing an interview, so we arranged for him to stop by my apartment. It was amusing to watch how Alex handled him—putting off the interview to repeatedly play the newly recorded Replacements' tracks he was so proud of. Once the interview was done and the writer left, I pointed to an acoustic guitar sitting in the corner and jokingly said, "Hey Alex, I haven't charged you room and board for your stay. Feel free to sing a few songs as compensation." He picked up the guitar and did just that. He started playing Big Star's "Thirteen," and P. D. casually pulled out his portable tape machine and hit record. Alex noticed but kept playing. He did fragments of other Big Star songs, "Give Me Another Chance" and "Nighttime"; a couple of his solo songs, "All of the Time" and "All We Ever Got from Them Was Pain"; and a handful of covers, like "Rubber Room" by Porter Wagoner, Memphis Minnie's "Won't You Be My Chauffer," and "In My Girlish Days." He also did one called "Scrambled Eggs," which I think he said was by Furry Lewis. The next day, Paul and I dropped Alex off at the airport. It had been an inspiring and productive few days, and we couldn't have been happier. It was also the start of a long tradition; Alex would become a regular guest at my place in the years to come.

The first gig on the January tour was in Oklahoma City on the eighteenth, back to the Bowery. Once again, the club manager was generous with the drinks, and the band was well oiled by the time they took the stage. Around this time, alcohol began affecting me in unpredictable ways. Late that evening my head started to spin, and I passed out in some dark corner upstairs. The manager couldn't find me when it came time to pay up, so he paid Paul instead. I was embarrassed, but the rest of the guys were pretty wasted too, so nobody made a big deal of it, at least not when I was within earshot.

We headed from Oklahoma City to Austin, then east to Lafayette, Louisiana, and into Florida. The dates went okay until we got to Orlando. The show there was being promoted by a fan who'd put up his own money and rented out a VFW hall. Everything was in order until after sound check, when the police walked in and said something to the effect of, "We don't want any punk rock in Orlando," and canceled the show on a technicality. Not being paid was hard on our finances, but we felt worse for the young promoter. We had one more date in the Sunshine State, at the University in Tallahassee, then we were outta there. The overall vibe in Florida did not feel welcoming to us.

The next two shows were in Tuscaloosa, Alabama, and Athens, where we could always count on wild crowds and gallons of mischief. From Athens, we drove to Nashville and found a decent-looking hotel. Later, when we were loading into Cantrell's for the gig, one of the stagehands asked where we were staying. I told him, and he casually replied, "Oh cool, that's where Bob Dylan stayed when he was recording *Blonde On Blonde*."

The next stop on the tour, in Charlotte, North Carolina, was a trip— the band played a fabled punk rock room called the Milestone. The next night, at the Cat's Cradle in Chapel Hill, the band earned a special honor. While I was getting paid at the end of the night, the promoter smiled and said, "You guys just beat the attendance record for the club." I asked who had it before us. He replied, "NRBQ." Now that meant something! Pretty much the only music you could put on in the Replacements' van and not get any complaints was NRBQ or Big Star.

We had two more shows up the East Coast before heading toward home. There were two notable incidents. For the show at the Decade in Pittsburgh on February 4, I'd picked a hotel specifically because it had a secure parking lot. I'd been in and out of the hotel running errands that day and had gotten to know the kindly old security guard. After the gig, we got back to the hotel shortly after midnight. As usual, we took all the guitars into the rooms with us, along with everyone's personal bags. Around 2:30 in the morning, the front desk called to say that someone tried to steal our van. I got dressed quickly and ran out to the parking lot. The van was parked near the exit, with the doors wide open and the motor running. The security guard told me he saw the van coming toward him with someone he didn't recognize driving. When he flagged them down, two guys jumped out, knocking him to the ground as they ran away. They'd hotwired the van and nearly got away with a trailer full of amps and drums.

The second notable incident on this final stretch of the tour was on February 6 in Champaign, Illinois, at a second-floor venue called Trito's

Uptown. The Replacements had done fairly well in this neck of the woods in the past, but on this night, the club was jammed. When the mass of people in front of the stage started jumping up and down with the music, the ceiling of the grocery store below started buckling. The promoter had to ask the crowd to spread out and stop the pogoing.

We finished the tour in Northfield, Minnesota, at Carleton College on the eighth. Lots of our Minneapolis pals made the forty-mile trek south for the show, an especially nice way for us to end the trip. Apart from a quick three-date Wisconsin visit the following week, we wouldn't be on the road again until April.

In late February, we got word that the deal with Sire Records was a go! We had a signing party at a house in Kenwood owned by Peter Kohlsaat, a friend of George Regis. Champagne was poured, and a toast was had. Then we all wandered off in our separate directions. It was a strange experience. This was what we'd always been hoping for, and yet everyone seemed a little melancholy. We knew things were bound to change; we just weren't sure how.

Seymour Stein, the cofounder of Sire Records, was a visionary music man and had instigated the Replacements signing, but our day-to-day liaison was A&R man Michael Hill, whom we'd met at Folk City two years prior. Michael was a real music person, very smart, and a genuinely nice guy. As we discussed producer ideas for the 'Mats first Sire album, Chilton's name naturally came up. Everyone loved the demos he'd done with the band in January, but Seymour and Michael were wary of Alex's eccentric and sometimes difficult history. Other producers were considered, but in the end Tommy Erdelyi, aka Tommy Ramone, was the consensus choice. We all loved how that first Ramones record sounded, and that was largely Erdelyi's doing.

Erdelyi flew to Minneapolis for a "test drive" to see how he and the 'Mats got along. The band recorded two songs with him at Nicollet Studios on March 30 and 31: "Little Mascara" and "Kiss Me on the Bus." We all liked Tommy right off the bat, the demos sounded good, and everyone agreed he was the man for the job. For comfort, we asked that Fjelstad be the engineer. We booked six weeks at Nicollet to record the album, starting June 3. The band hadn't had the luxury of that much consecutive recording time before.

Five days later, we were heading to Dekalb, Illinois, to start the next tour. The first date was at Northern Illinois University—for a daytime show—and they fed us like kings. It was on to Ames, Iowa, the next night, where the band did a show that did not meet the audience's satisfaction. Some of the more irate among them tried to tip over our trailer while it was still attached to the van. Now we had four days to drive to Los Angeles.

LA was pretty familiar to us by this point, and through a resourceful travel agent, we were booked into a hotel that wasn't typically frequented by the rock crowd. It was called the Hollywood Celebrity Hotel and was located just north of Hollywood Boulevard. It also wasn't far from the storied Hollywood Palace, where the band was playing the next night. With the band having just signed to Sire, a lot of the top brass from Sire's parent company, Warner Records, were in attendance, which was an iffy proposition for the Replacements. They didn't always rise to the occasion in these sorts of "showcase" situations. Matters were exacerbated by the fact that the Palace staff was very strict about what the band could and couldn't do on their premises. Unsurprisingly to me, the band gave the Palace staff and the WB crew a nose-thumbing performance.

Shows followed in San Diego, Santa Barbara, San Francisco, and Chico before we pulled into the UC Davis campus on April 18 for a gig at the Coffeehouse, the school's 300-capacity venue. We loaded in, and everything seemed to be going smoothly. I asked where the dressing room was, and a student volunteer led me to the Oak Room, a conference room–type place with a big oak table and cushy chairs. A deli tray was perfectly laid out, along with sodas, water, and the beer, whiskey, and vodka that was on our rider. I gulped and said, "Can you show me something in, say, concrete?" The volunteer thought I was kidding. I should have told him right then and there that this was a recipe for disaster. Set time was still several hours away, and I could only hope for the best. The band started cracking beers and pouring drinks. Tommy, Chris, and I went downstairs to a lounge area and shot a few games of pool. The drinks seemed to be going down awfully quickly. I was concerned.

The Replacements' performance was not one of their best. Afterward, when I went back to the Oak Room, it was trashed. It looked like a bomb had gone off. The paneled walls were covered with remnants of deli-tray food and dented from beer bottles that had been hurled at them; the phones were destroyed; the conference table was chipped all over; many of the chairs were broken and their padded seats ripped open; and the carpet was soaked with whiskey, Coca-Cola, and beer.

I suggested we pack up and leave, fast. When we got to our motel, the band was worn out and crashed pretty quickly. It wasn't too hard to get them going early the next morning when, again, I said we best leave ASAP. Once we got out of town a bit, we stopped to eat and gas up. While there, I called the Venture Booking office in New York and asked for Frank. He picked up the phone and immediately asked, "What the hell happened in Davis?!" He said the school's concert liaison called him about the damage to the Oak Room, and they estimated the repairs would cost roughly $2,000. Frank also told me to stay away from the band when we got to our next stop, Fresno, because my name was on the contract for the Davis gig and a warrant had been issued for my arrest. As it turned out, Frank assured the college we would cover the expenses, and if we didn't, Venture would. The warrant was withdrawn.

The shows continued to be up and down, but mostly up. We were scheduled to play the Palomino in North Hollywood on the twenty-fourth, and after sound check most of the band and crew stayed at the club, but Paul wanted to go back to the hotel. I was happy to hear this because it meant Paul wouldn't be sitting at the bar drinking for three or four hours before set time. Back at the hotel, Paul and I just took it easy. He had a couple of drinks and called home. Shortly before it was time to head back to the Palomino, Paul put on some eye makeup and some kind of scarf-headband. This was unusual. I'd seen people put makeup on him before, but never the headgear. I thought he looked seriously cool. We headed back to the club but had to park a few blocks away. We didn't know it yet, but the show had sold out, and a line of people extended all the way down the block. I got a big kick out of walking past them as we made our way to the entrance. The folks in line would glance at us and do a double-take when they recognized Paul. He really did look every inch the rock star.

At showtime, the place was full to the brim. The Replacements walked onstage, kicked into "Color Me Impressed," and played their asses off. They were stupendous. It was the best show of the tour.

The next night was our last show in California on this tour, at a joint called the Cornhusker in Azusa. It was basically a restaurant with a stage. The owner introduced himself to me and initially seemed nice enough, but something about the way he looked made me uncomfortable. He said he knew we had an underage band member, but I assured him Tommy didn't drink. I then told Tommy this guy would be on the lookout, and Tommy said he didn't feel like drinking that night anyway, so not to worry. A few minutes later, I saw a waitress walk up to Tommy, grab his glass, and smell it. He laughed it off the first time. Then, after sound check, another waitress pulled the same move, and Tommy didn't think it was funny anymore. I hoped that was the end of it. I went into the dressing room and all the beer was gone. I asked one of the waitstaff for more and was told no, they'd given us all we could have. I said I had advanced the date and gone over what was on our rider and was told it would all be honored. The owner apparently changed his mind. It was starting to feel very uptight in there. Finally, Paul told me that everyone who worked there was treating the band like lackeys, and he wanted to leave. I said, "Okay, but we're going to have to move fast, and you guys need to help pack up." He agreed, and we rallied the rest of the guys and went into action. When the boss man realized what was happening, he started yelling. But we kept our noses down and got out in record time. The last thing the owner said was, "I'll make sure this band never plays LA again!" As we drove off, a crowd of twenty or so people who had driven out from LA began applauding. They'd witnessed the harassment the band had gotten. The funniest thing about all this was, two or so hours later the band played a short set at the Club Lingerie, using the gear of our friends Thelonious Monster. Next on the agenda, a 1,300-mile drive to Oklahoma City.

It was April 26, so we weren't expecting weather issues, but as we got close to Flagstaff, we hit a full-on blizzard. I white-knuckled the drive as long as it felt safe, then took a random exit with a number of hotels where we could wait out the storm. Luckily, we had three days before the next show.

We got rooms and took our bags and guitars in. I said I needed a drink, and a couple of the guys joined me. It was a typical hotel bar, with an older man playing piano in the corner. Through the windows, we could see the snow was really coming down. It was a relief to be inside. We were enjoying the piano music and talking when I noticed two men on the other side of the room laughing and tossing ice cubes at the piano player's back. He was noticeably irritated but doing his best to ignore it. I was still a little wired from the drive, and this disrespectful behavior riled me up. I couldn't take it anymore and marched over to give the two creeps a piece of my mind. As I got closer, I recognized one of them. It was Gene Clark, formerly of the Byrds. I went from mad to fanboy in about two seconds. I said I hoped I wasn't intruding but I told Gene I was a big fan and mentioned a great show of his I'd seen in New York a few months back. He was very drunk and slurring his words, but he responded, "What'd you say your name was?" I said, "Peter." Gene said, "Thank you, Peter." Then gestured to his left and said, "This is my friend Rick. Rick Danko." I hadn't recognized Rick because I'd been so focused on Gene, but I was also a huge fan of the Band. Now I was doubly starstruck. We exchanged a few words, but they were so tipsy I just shook their hands and politely excused myself. I went back to our table, all abuzz, and filled the others in on who I'd been talking to. A few minutes later, we saw Gene and

Rick get up, look around furtively, and duck out of the bar without paying their tab. The waitress chased after them into the parking lot, shouting epithets as they slipped and slid around in the snow. I don't think the waitress ever got her money. It was sad to see these guys I admired so much behaving so badly. I also couldn't help but laugh at the absurdity of it all.

Oklahoma City was a blast once again, and the band played well. Wichita was next, where attendance was very light—maybe a dozen people when the Replacements went onstage. Fortunately, the room filled up more as the night went on, and the band played a fantastic set. We went on to Lincoln, Nebraska, and a club called the Drumstick that had been around for a while. The 'Mats played another good show, but everyone was getting antsy to get home.

The grumbling started the next morning. We had one more show in Moorhead, Minnesota, which meant we'd be driving past the signs that pointed east to the Twin Cities as we drove north another 200-plus miles. It was a good payday for us, and we needed the money. Another consolation was that a few of our friends were driving up for the show. When we got to town, we were pleased to find there'd been some decent press. One of the papers referred to the Replacements as "a punk rock band from New York," and we had a good laugh over that. Bosley got the magic slacks treatment that day, which was especially funny when his girlfriend, Sally, arrived.

After the gig, we loaded up the trailer and headed back to the hotel. Mike and Sally had left right after the show to drive back to Minneapolis. With some pals from Minneapolis in attendance, I probably partied a bit more than I should have, and I was relieved when Sullivan took the wheel. We were maybe four or five blocks from the club when we were pulled over by multiple police cars. I didn't know how much Bill had had to drink, but I was worried. He failed the Breathalyzer test, so they handcuffed him and put him in the back of a squad car. The police then asked who was sober enough to drive. I shrugged my shoulders and took the Breathalyzer. I was over the legal limit as well. None of the band members had driver's licenses, so they were off the hook. The police impounded the van, and we walked back to the hotel, feeling awful about Bill. As we were fretting and talking about what had just gone down, someone noticed the magic slacks lying on the floor of the hotel room. Apparently, Bosley had come back to the hotel and changed before he and Sally drove home. He hadn't been respectful to the slacks, and we credited that with being responsible for Sullivan's DUI.

I set an alarm for early the next morning to call George Regis for lawyerly advice. George hooked us up with a local Moorhead attorney who would take care of getting Bill out of jail and the van out of the impound lot. I taxied to his office. He told me he thought the police might still be watching us and so it might be best for me to eat a good meal and wait a couple of hours, just to be sure my blood alcohol level would be under the legal limit from the night before.

Around noon, the lawyer and I picked up the van, drove to the jail, and rescued Bill. Then we went to the motel to pick up the rest of the gang. The lawyer followed us to the city limit, just in case the cops wanted to mess with us again. Our big payday in Moorhead was gone and then some. Bill's legal fees were four or five times what we'd made for the gig.

Tommy Erdelyi flew into Minneapolis on June 2 for the recording of the Replacements' fifth album. Tommy, the band, and I got together at my place for a last-minute huddle before the sessions were to begin the next day. Out of the blue, Paul informed me that they didn't want me in the studio for this project. I didn't know what to say. I'd planned my next six weeks around these sessions. The only explanation I got was from Chris, who said something about feeling like he might be more open to doing new things if I wasn't there. None of it computed to me, but what could I say? Thirty-one years later, in Bob Mehr's Replacements biography, *Trouble Boys*, Paul and Tommy admitted that uninviting me to these sessions was payback for me taking the temp job road managing R.E.M. back in 1983. *You remember, the job that I had specifically talked to the Replacements about before accepting, saying I would decline if they had any issues, to which they all replied that they had no problem whatsoever?* That's some messed-up, long-ass grudge holding, if you ask me.

Despite not being in the studio, I still had lots of logistical stuff to do—bringing the band per diems, running the odd errand for guitar strings or drum sticks. And we had another tour coming up in August, so I was doing a lot of coordination and advancing the dates with the various venues. The time went by fairly fast.

Unbeknownst to the band, Erdelyi called me almost every night to fill me in on what had gone down that day. I was especially pleased when he called one night to say the band had cut a brand-new song, and he'd run a cassette copy of the rough track for me. I went to his hotel to pick it up. The song was called "Waitress in the Sky."

After basic tracks for the album were done and it was just Paul, Feljy, and Erdelyi working in the studio, things loosened up. Paul seemed to want my opinion on a few things, so I was around a bit more.

I'd also been talking to our Sire A&R man, Michael Hill, who asked if Paul had recorded a solo song yet. I said no, and that as far as I knew, he didn't have one for this album. Michael said Paul told him he did. When I got to the studio, I mentioned this to Paul. He immediately looked uncomfortable. Then his expression shifted and he went into action mode. He told Steve he had an acoustic song to record. Steve cued up a fresh tape and set up the mics. Then Paul pulled me into the studio with him. We moved two large choir baffles in front of the control room window so he wouldn't be seen. It seemed that Paul was nervous about the song and wanted privacy. He grabbed his guitar, sat down, and asked me to turn the lights way down. I shut the door and headed into the control room. Steve punched the record button and said, "Tapes rolling," and we heard "Here Comes a Regular" for the first time—as intimate a confessional as Paul had ever penned.

By mid-July, despite some disagreements between Erdelyi and the band, the album was mixed to everyone's relative satisfaction. I had not been the only one missing for much of the recording. Bob had been a ghostlike presence, coming in sporadically, missing some sessions altogether, and not always playing up to par. It was obvious he didn't have his heart in these songs. Or maybe he no longer had his heart in the group, period.

We left for the next run of tour dates on August 7, beginning in Milwaukee. We worked our way east, did two shows in Boston, followed by a sold-out gig at Irving Plaza that devolved into one of the Replacements' cover sets. Nonetheless, the promoter was over the moon about the box office receipts and ended up coming back to hang out in my room at the Gramercy Park Hotel after the show. We were up very late, and I made a poor showing the next day. When we got to City Gardens in Trenton, I excused myself from load in, went in the back, and took a nap. That didn't go over well.

On Sunday, August 18, we went to DC for a show at the 9:30 Club. As the band was setting up for sound check, I noticed a club staffer shinnying up a pole in the middle of the room with a video camera. I told him there was to be no filming of the band. He said I'd have to talk to management about that. Frank Riley had come down for the show, so he and I went to the office to speak with the manager. She said it was standard procedure at the club. I replied that there was nothing in the contract stating that, and the band wouldn't play if there were cameras going. She agreed not to record them, but they needed the camera there to show the performance on a TV monitor in the back bar. Frank and I maintained that if the people in the back bar wanted to see the band, they should come into the music room. It was an uncomfortable argument, but we stood our ground and the manager relented.

We finished the tour with dates in Ann Arbor, Chicago, and Madison. Soul Asylum was scheduled to open the first two. Ann Arbor went as planned, but Soul Asylum's van broke down on the way to Chicago, and they rolled in too late to do their set. When the Replacements finished theirs and got an encore, Paul told the Soul Asylum guys to take the stage instead. Guitarist Danny Murphy and I were reminiscing about this recently, and as he put it, "We played our single 'Tied to the Tracks' and 'Long Way Home.' The crowd went mild."

As things ramped up with Sire, I was getting less comfortable in my role as the Replacements' manager. Interfacing with a major label was just not my world. I wasn't thinking about leaving the band; I just thought we needed to bring in proper business management. I talked about it with the band, Frank Riley, and Michael Hill. We got advice from our lawyer, George Regis, and other industry people we trusted. In late August, we decided to put the word out: The Replacements were looking for a professional manager.

After a month or so, only three parties had raised their hands. Gary Kurfirst, a New Yorker who had worked with big names like Blondie and Talking Heads, bailed before we even had a meeting with him. The Arizona-based Mike Lembo had worked in both publishing and management and had an impressive track record, working with the likes of the Church, songwriter Jules Shear, and NRBQ. Mike withdrew his hat from the ring after he met with the band. The fact was, most professional managers wouldn't touch the Replacements with a ten-foot pole. High Noon Management's Gary Hobbib and Russ Reiger were the young bucks. They had a small roster but had complementary personalities and were motivated to establish themselves. They came to Minneapolis and were subjected to the Replacements' unique screening process, which always involved an abundance of alcohol, and yet miraculously they remained interested in working with the band.

For some time the title of the new Replacements album was going to be *Let It Bleed*, which I thought was the perfect way to follow up *Let It Be*. But at the last minute Paul decided to call it *Tim*. I was never clear on exactly why. When I asked him, he just said, "Because it's such a nice name." The album was released in September and the response was overwhelmingly positive. Reviewers were unanimous in calling out several tracks. "Bastards of Young," "Left of the Dial," "Swinging Party," and "Here Comes a Regular" were hailed as band classics.

For the Twin Cities record release, instead of doing one big show at First Avenue, the band opted for something novel: a five-night stand in the 7th Street Entry, including an all-ages show. Openers in order of appearance were Soul Asylum, A Few, Good Joe, Bad Trip and Lou Santacroce, and the Form. Seymour Stein flew in and was delighted by the reception the band received.

Shortly after the Entry shows, I was disappointed to get a "Dear John letter" from Mike Bosley. When the Replacements weren't on the road, he was working with Lloyd Cole & the Commotions and had been spending a lot of time in London. He wrote that he'd been offered an apprenticeship in a recording studio there, and he couldn't say no. He apologized for the last-minute notice, but I certainly couldn't argue with his decision.

There was no way we could go on without someone to run sound, so I scrambled to find a soundman fast. I started asking around, and two or three good prospects came up. When someone told me about a young gent from Duluth who was a bit of a sound prodigy, I had a gut feeling this could be the right person for the task. His name was Monty Lee Wilkes. I called him at his home in Duluth, and when I told him why I was calling, he was practically in Minneapolis before we hung up. Within just a few hours, we were sitting across from each other at the CC Club. I liked him immediately. Monty was an audio geek, as well as eager and smart. After talking for thirty or so minutes, I told Monty I'd have to run it by the band but I thought the job was his. When I gave the 'Mats the lowdown on Monty and his experience with bands in Duluth, and a stint running sound for former Flamingo guitarist Johnny Rey's solo band, they were willing to give him a try.

Another issue that needed to be addressed was that in many of the clubs the band was playing in, the stage monitors for them to hear themselves were subpar. We'd been talking for some time about bringing a monitor guy and our own monitors, when the money was right. I talked to Monty, we looked at our budget and projected income, and we determined it could be done. Our friend Casey Macpherson had just left a long spell road managing the Suburbs. He was no audio expert, but with Monty's guidance, he could handle monitor mixing, and we knew he'd be a super easygoing guy to travel with.

I thought these incremental improvements would make everyone feel better, but Paul had gotten into a different mindset. There was just no pleasing him anymore. He was impatient to be further ahead in his career. The way I saw it, the reason he wasn't was largely of his own making.

The next set of tour dates started on November 5 in Iowa City, then on to Norman, Oklahoma. The promoter of the show was the girlfriend of Wayne Coyne (of the Flaming Lips), Michelle. She had rented a small hall and brought in a sound system. It wasn't a formal establishment, which meant there was no liquor license. Michelle told me she would honor our rider, but we'd have to be discreet and keep all alcoholic beverages in plastic cups. Unfortunately, shortly before showtime, Tommy had gotten a little tipsy and was goofing off, swinging on the back door of the dressing room, which opened into the alley. A police car happened to be driving by and stopped to see what was going on. Tommy later told me he had a fresh tumbler of vodka and OJ, so they arrested him for public intoxication. Tommy was nineteen at the time, and the drinking age in Oklahoma was twenty-one. The arrest happened at about 9:00 PM, and I was told they'd need to keep him in custody for a minimum of six hours. The band started the show as a trio but soon dragged Monty up to play bass. That left me at the soundboard, doing my best with my limited technical abilities. The performance had its moments, and the novelty of it seemed to satisfy the crowd. Wayne gave me a ride to the police station at 3:00 AM to spring Tommy. While we were waiting, I made a flippant crack to one of the cops. He got in my face and said, "Look buddy, I can smell liquor on your breath from here. How would you like to join your little friend?" I kept my mouth shut, paid the fifty-dollar fine, and we were outta there.

The next day, after loading into Dallas's Theater Gallery, Paul and I were sitting at the bar. I hadn't been minding my alcohol consumption very well, and Paul brought it up. We had a surprisingly adult conversation about it. He admitted that most of us had a drinking problem, but since I was older and had been at it longer, it was affecting me more. He said if I didn't do something about it, it could affect my job. I took him seriously and swore to myself I was going to slow down. Ironically, the next night was one of the band's most legendary drunk shows.

We were excited about the next two nights because Alex Chilton (solo) was the opening act. Up first was the University of Houston's Lawndale Art Annex on November 9. We got there a little early, and I had done my typical instruction, telling the promoter not to put all the alcohol from our rider in the dressing room at once: just a couple of six-packs.

When Alex got to the club and finished his sound check, he asked if I could drive him to our hotel so he could get a room there. I agreed but said he needed to be quick. I didn't want to leave the band unattended for too long.

At the hotel, Alex got a room, no problem, but proceeded to take his sweet time. I had some kind of premonition and was antsier than usual. When we finally got back to the Annex, I walked back to the dressing room. The door was closed, there was liquid streaming out, and an extension cord was going in under it. I opened the door to find a temporary work light hanging from the ceiling, full bottles of Heineken embedded in the drywall like darts, and near-empty bottles of whiskey and vodka. No sign of any band members. They were hiding.

Alex went onstage to do his set, and I was determined to forget the issues at hand for a moment and enjoy it. Tommy and Paul had found a plastic children's swimming pool in a storage room, dragged it in front of the stage, and sat in it while watching Alex, full cups of booze in their hands. No one had bothered to check Tommy's ID. By the time the 'Mats went on, they could barely stand up. No one in the audience was the slightest bit amused. I was with Monty at the sound-board, and after a few bad covers, the promoter came over and said people wanted their money back. I said I was sorry and that he should give a refund to anyone who asked. He said, "No, I mean everyone wants their money back." As the room emptied out, he came back and told us we had to stop the band. So Monty shut off the PA. The band still didn't stop. Finally, the police came in, walked onstage, and took the Replacements' instruments away from them—something I've never seen before or since. The promoter would barely speak to me, but I assured him we'd cover his losses.

The rest of the tour was fairly uneventful. I had always thought that once the Replacements got their road chops down, they'd be unbeat-able live. But the shows were as inconsistent as ever.

We had a week and a half off in Minneapolis before a short pre-Christmas West Coast tour. During this break, I was at Paul's apart-ment and we talked about the potential managers we'd met with. The other three 'Mats had voiced support for High Noon, and Paul and I agreed, so we decided to do something about it right then. I called High Noon to tell them they were hired. Russ Reiger answered the call and screamed when he heard the news.

The West Coast dates kicked off in Vancouver, British Columbia. Bill, Monty, and Casey left on December 2 with the van and the equip-ment truck and drove to Seattle. The band and I flew there two days later, and we all drove together into Canada for the first show, at the Commodore Ballroom. Replacements shows may have been up and down, but when they were up, it was amazing. Their roughly thirty-song set lists, with five albums' worth of originals and some choice new covers, could be stunners. At the Commodore they did fabulous rendi-tions of T. Rex's "20th Century Boy" and the Beatles' "Nowhere Man."

Moving down the coast, the band played Seattle, Portland, Eugene, San Francisco, and two nights at Berkeley Square. On the fourteenth, they had a show at San Diego State's concert space, the Backdoor. The first time we'd been there, a couple of years back, Bob played buck naked, with his guitar strategically placed, and people in the audience were encouraging him to do it again. Bob complied. Bill Sullivan was doing another cameo appearance with the band on Alice Cooper's "Be My Lover" when Bob set down his guitar and jumped him from behind. I'll never forget Bill's face when he realized he had a naked Bob on his back!

We had the next day off, but Paul and I had a meeting at Warner Records in Burbank. It was terribly exciting to tell the taxi driver we were going to 3300 Warner Boulevard; I had hundreds of records with that address on the back. The rustic office building, known as the "Ski Lodge," didn't look like any record company I'd seen, all dark wood and windows. We were ushered into the office of creative director Jeff Ayeroff. After exchanging pleasantries, Ayeroff got right to the point: "I don't want to talk about the fact that you guys don't want to make a video. I want to talk about the video you will eventually make." I thought to myself, *This is no way to motivate Westerberg. This guy clearly hasn't done his homework.* Westerberg quickly fired back: "Get us on *Hee Haw* and I'll lip-synch 'Waitress in the Sky.'" I laughed out loud, but Ayeroff wasn't smiling. The meeting devolved from there, and we left with Paul saying the band would do live TV, if the label could ever arrange such a thing.

The last two shows of the tour were at the Roxy on the Sunset Strip—yet another fabled LA venue. Seymour again flew in for the festivities, which made the band feel like they were getting proper label attention, although it didn't curb the aberrant behavior. Bob had gone shopping in a novelty store somewhere along the way and showed me a bottle he'd bought with a label that said "Morning Breeze." It smelled horrible, like rotten eggs (though it was supposed to smell like someone had passed gas). The Roxy has a small VIP balcony above the right side of the stage, which is where Seymour, John Doe and Exene Cervenka, and some other movers and shakers were watching the show. At one point, I saw Bob reach into his pocket and pull out the Morning Breeze.

He walked behind Paul and smashed the bottle on the stage. I wasn't close enough to get a whiff, but Paul sure was! So were the people in front of the stage and, if I'm not mistaken, some of the VIPs too. One of Bob's best stunts!

The shows were done for the year, and everybody was wiped out. The band was going to fly home. Monty and Casey would drive the rental, and I'd drive our van, Odie. I'd made an offer to the band that, if anyone wanted to keep me company, they could have the equivalent of the plane fare in cash (around $300, I think). Tommy jumped on it. We dropped off Paul, Bob, and Chris at LAX, hooked up with Monty and Casey, and the two vehicles caravanned out of town. I have a distinct memory of driving through Colorado late at night with a very bright full moon. Casey and Monty were in front of us, and Casey turned off their headlights. I followed suit. We did it for just a minute or so, and it was spooky but cool, driving with only the moonlight to light the way. I loved traveling with Casey. Sadly, this would be our last trip with him. We decided that hauling our own monitors wasn't worth it. Casey would keep busy though; he was soon road managing Hüsker Dü.

We were preparing for an upcoming series of dates on the East Coast starting at the end of January, including a live twenty-four-track recording that Sire was setting up in Hoboken. Before that, we had a one-off, good-money gig in Chicago on Saturday, the eleventh. On Monday, back home in Minneapolis, I got a call from George Regis. He said, "You guys gotta get on a plane to New York on Wednesday." I asked him what for. He said the band was booked to play on *Saturday Night Live*. I was flabbergasted. I called the band members—*shocked* is the only word to describe their reactions. The predominant thought rolling around in my head was: *I cannot believe somebody at NBC wants to put the Replacements on live TV.*

The seven of us—me, Monty, Bill, and the band—flew out Wednesday the fifteenth. Sire had graciously agreed to fly the girlfriends out by showtime. Paul Stark came on his own dime; he wouldn't have missed it for the world. The label put us up at the Omni-Berkshire, conveniently walking distance from Rockefeller Plaza, the HQ of NBC Television. Once we got settled, I wanted to go downtown to see Frank Riley at the Venture Booking office. Monty had never been to New York, so I asked him to come along to see some sights and meet Frank. As we were walking out of the lobby he pointed to a line of cabs. I said, "Too expensive; we're taking the train." He looked at me all bug-eyed and said, "I'm going to take the *subway*?!"

Rehearsals started at 10:00 AM Thursday, and we were basically locked in at NBC for the day. Our dressing room was well stocked with coffee, juices, and a deli tray. Bob wanted beer. I asked one of the assistants if they could accommodate and got a horrified look, as if to say, *You want beer at ten o'clock in the morning?!* I was told NBC was not allowed to purchase alcohol for its guests. So, I snuck out and found a convenience store where I bought a six-pack of Heineken for three times as much as I'd ever paid. When I brought it into the dressing room, Sullivan looked at me incredulously and said, "You only bought a six-pack?"

The rehearsals went alright, though we were treated like the last-minute replacements we knew we were. Monty was his diplomatic self and coached the NBC staff engineer who was mixing the sound. This was the first band function with Gary and Russ from High Noon Management officially on duty, and I was interested to see how that went. When Russ walked onto the SNL stage, he started explaining to the band what camera blocking was. "That's when they tell you where you have to stand." I thought, *Wow, does he really think the Replacements are going to take those sorts of orders?* It made me wonder.

We had Friday off, and on Saturday the eighteenth we were back at NBC at 10:00 AM. The two songs selected for the show were "Bastards of Young" and "Kiss Me on the Bus." There were two complete performances of the program in front of an audience: a warm-up and the live-on-TV segment. It was hectic on the set, and we pretty much stayed sequestered in our dressing room. A couple of different kinds of liquor were smuggled in. At some point, the guest host, Harry Dean Stanton, popped in and introduced himself. We'd heard he was on the wagon, but he sure seemed excited to have a taste from our stash.

The band's two performances were looser than what you'd normally see on network television, but I was surprised at how well they pulled it off. On the live portion, however, during "Bastards of Young," just before Bob's solo, Paul said off-mic, "C'mon fucker!" I didn't think it was audible, but if you were watching closely, you could read Paul's lips.

Afterward, I ran into SNL producer Lorne Michaels in the hallway, and he was livid. Russ got the brunt of Michaels's ire. I wasn't sure they were going to let the 'Mats do the second song. But the band did a spunky take of "Kiss Me on the Bus," and in a perfectly Replacements-esque move, they had traded clothes between songs. Once again it was a solid performance. After-show festivities were at the Café Luxembourg, an uber-fancy place where none of us felt comfortable and where, once again, we were treated like interlopers. We didn't stay long.

The night of the SNL airing, the program was preempted in the Twin Cities by a Jerry Lewis telethon. In an ingenious move, First Avenue made arrangements for one of its employees to go to the local NBC affiliate, record SNL in real time from the live feed, and rush the tape back to the club. They then showed the Replacements' two performances on the mainroom screen to a full house of fans. I heard from many people who were present that it was the loudest audience reaction they'd ever heard the band receive.

The East Coast dates were set to start in Providence, Rhode Island, on January 29. Odie seemed like it was on its last legs, so we decided to rent a van in Providence. Bill and Monty drove the equipment truck; the band and I flew in. When I got to the car rental desk, they apologized and said they didn't have a van, and the biggest thing they had was a station wagon. This was a huge drag. We'd flown in with all our personal bags plus guitars, so the station wagon was packed tight, but we made it work.

After Providence, we hit Boston, New York, and Trenton. The next gig was Maxwell's on the fourth, and Michael Hill had arranged for a twenty-four-track mobile truck to capture the performance for a possible live album. Monty was totally in his element, rushing back and forth from the truck to the stage and interfacing with the technical crew. The live album wouldn't surface until 2017, but it's a wonderful document of the original lineup of the band. The remainder of the February dates were down south—DC; Charlottesville and Richmond, Virginia; and Raleigh, North Carolina.

After a show in Duluth on February 21, we had a month off. I'd been researching a bigger vehicle to rent, something with a toilet. The band's drinking while we traveled was a pain because we had to stop so often for someone to go to the bathroom. We couldn't afford a tour bus, but I was looking to find something in between, expense-wise. Calling RV rental places around the Twin Cities, I couldn't find a single one that would rent to a rock band. I finally found a custom RV company that would, about thirty miles north in Elk River, Minnesota. The man I spoke to, Rollie Stevenson, said, "I'm tired of rock musicians being treated like second-class citizens. I will rent to you, Peter!"

When the time came, Monty and I drove to Elk River in his van. Rollie was very friendly and proud to show us the beautiful custom RV. He also assured us it was fine to leave Monty's van there for the two weeks we were away.

After driving south to Lincoln, Nebraska, and Lawrence, Kansas, for the first shows on April 1 and 2, we headed east to Indianapolis and Ann Arbor. Upon arriving in each city and checking into our hotel (we upgraded to two rooms now for the seven of us), I'd sweep out the RV and do some general cleanup. I was sure a vehicle like this was the solution and was going to make touring so much better. The band seemed to like the RV, but nobody was overly complimentary.

From Ann Arbor, we drove east past Detroit and crossed into Canada for a show in Toronto on the sixth. I had all the papers in order to bring in the gear, and customs went smoothly. The next show was in Columbus on the eighth, and since the drive was over 400 miles, I opted to break it up and stop in Cleveland for the night. I talked to Bill and said

I was a little worn out from driving with the band. I asked if we could trade, to let me have a little peace and quiet for one day. He was cool with that. Since the equipment manifesto was all in my name, the two vehicles went to the border together. I'm not sure how this happened, but Monty and I were waved through while Bill and the band were still talking with the customs agent. It looked like everything was okay, so we took off. What I didn't find out until later was that I had forgotten to give Bill and the band their passports. Their border crossing was touch and go, but they were finally allowed through.

It was so civilized riding with Monty, listening to music and talking. Monty had a Fuzzbuster, a unit that monitored police radar. When none was detected, we could push the speed limit, and we made great time. We got to Cleveland well ahead of Bill and the band. Our travel agent got us a cheap rate at the Bond Court Hotel downtown. Monty and I checked into the hotel, showered, and had a nice dinner. We asked at the front desk if the rest of our party had checked in but were told no. After a while, I got concerned and went back downstairs to ask again. While I was talking to the clerk, something came flying over my shoulder and landed on the desk. It was the RV keys. I turned around and saw Bill Sullivan, hair askew, covered in white paint from head to toe. He said, "You park that thing. I'm never getting in it again." I looked beyond Bill and saw the band, also paint-splattered but not making eye contact with me. I tossed the keys back to Bill and said, "I'll look at it tomorrow. You park it," and went back up to my room.

The next morning, Bill and I walked out to the parking lot together. He filled me in as we went. Apparently the band had found some cans of paint backstage at the Concert Hall in Toronto and stashed them in the RV. On the way to Cleveland, they got liquored up, and all hell broke loose.

I stepped into the RV and took inventory. They'd torn the storage cabinets off the walls, shredded the bench cushions, yanked the toilet out of the bathroom, and apparently threw it out the back door while driving down the freeway. They'd broken out every window in the RV except the windshield. Bill said at one point Bob was in the front passenger seat with his feet pressed against the windshield, about to give that the ol' heave-ho too. Bill stopped him. The front passenger seat was bent all the way back, like a chaise longue. And with the toilet gone, they'd just peed into the pile of broken lumber in the back. We had five shows left to do before getting home, which meant driving through cold, rainy April weather with nothing but the windshield to block the elements.

The last date on the tour was April 12 at Headliners in Madison, Wisconsin. There was little of the usual end-of-tour joy going home.

On our way back to Minnesota, I began concocting my story for Rollie at the RV rental company. I didn't want to admit to him the band had done all the damage. I thought back to the Lincoln gig. It was at a college, and they wouldn't let us bring in any alcohol, so we used the RV as a dressing room. After the show, it took a little longer than I expected to get paid. I was anxious to get back to the RV and make sure it hadn't turned into party central. When I got there, the band had invited in a handful of fans, but everything was fine. I thought, *Okay, here's what I'll do: I'll tell Rollie that I'd gone to get paid, and when I got back to the RV, it had been trashed.* I'd tell him that I wasn't sure, but I suspected some of our guys had something to do with it, but either way I understood it was our responsibility and we would cover all repair costs. Once I'd rehearsed the explanation in my mind a few times, I called Rollie and laid it on him. He said he appreciated my honesty (ouch!) and willingness to pay for the damages, and he would assess things when we got back and he could see for himself.

As we were pulling into Minneapolis, I asked who wanted to help me clean out the RV before returning it. Monty had to ride along because his van was at the rental place, so I knew I'd have at least one person to assist. Chris said he'd come along. The rest of the guys declined, and I dropped them off at their respective homes. On the way to Elk River, Chris, Monty, and I stopped at a K-Mart and bought rubber gloves, spray cleaner, disinfectant wipes, air freshener, and a cheap shovel. We got directions to the nearest dump and made our way there. I backed the RV up to a garbage pit, and we threw out all the broken furniture, cabinets, and fixtures. Then we swept it out as best we could, sprayed it down with air freshener, and drove the rest of the way to the RV company. I went straight into Rollie's office and handed him the keys. He went out to inspect the vehicle. Other employees began to gather around. It was like they were looking at a horror film. These were people who took their jobs seriously, and they were very proud of their custom RVs. This was disgraceful to them.

When Rollie came back in, I was sitting there with checkbook in hand. He said quietly, "I want a check for ten thousand dollars, and if repair costs are less than that, I give you my word you'll get a refund." I wrote the check, apologized again, shook his hand, and we left. Rollie called me back about ten days later, saying he needed a check for another $6,000.

We had some West Coast dates coming together for May, and we were making plans to go overseas for the first time in June. For me, the excitement was mixed with a feeling of dread, like, *Uh-oh, here we go again.* During the break, I kept up with the band work that needed to be done, but I had a lot of conflicting thoughts running around in my head. Nobody seemed happy. Everybody except Chris was drinking too much. How long could we keep all this up?

Recently I was involved in a podcast, and a Replacements' fan asked me, in retrospect, was there any one thing I'd do differently? I was a little stumped by the question and threw out a couple of comments off the top of my head that I can't even remember now. Reflecting on that question later, I thought, *D'oh! Yeah, I wish I'd had the foresight to curb my damn drinking.*

At first, the drinking had been social and fun for both the band members and me. As time went on, it was something we did too much of during the downtimes on tour. Then I think it became, at least partly, a way to dull the pain of things not going the way we had planned/ hoped/thought/wished they would. There was so much promise in the beginning, and I think we were all a bit afraid it was slowly unraveling. Being signed to a major label had done very little to change the band's fortunes. For Paul specifically, as his songwriting developed, the material called for more finesse, and it was my impression he began to think maybe he could do it better on his own; he began to think he *was* the Replacements. To me, that was a big part of what was wrong.

None of this is to say that I thought the band was completely unsuccessful. They'd made five records of extraordinary quality, played many brilliant shows, and had a substantial influence on other bands. But they hadn't truly "made it big." When you're writing songs like "I Will Dare," "Can't Hardly Wait," or "Left of the Dial," it had to be crushing that they weren't connecting with a wider audience.

It's also undeniable that the Replacements' refusal to play the music biz game, and their flagrant disrespect for many music industry people who were trying to help them, had a lot to do with limiting their success. As did their penchant for doing drunken shit shows way too often. I still hear from people who love the Replacements' songs and saw the band live many times but claim they never witnessed a decent performance. I saw them hundreds of times and can testify that they did more good shows than bad, but for the average concertgoer, it was always a crapshoot.

Such was the state of things when, in late April 1986, Paul called to let me know there was a band meeting at the Uptown Bar. I said I had other plans and was just running out the door. He could fill me in later on what went down. He said no, I needed to be there. So, off I went to meet with the band. Only Paul and Tommy were there when I arrived. Apparently, Chris and Bob had declined to attend.

Paul got right down to business. He said he wasn't happy with how things were going with the band, that he wanted to start swinging when he was mad, and he didn't want me in the way catching any punches. I thought those were strangely benevolent words for Paul.

But he was dead serious. My time with the Replacements was over. It was clear there was no room for discussion. I didn't argue. I swallowed the bitter pill and left.

I was full of regret and felt cut to the quick. I walked home and had several cocktails. The next night I went out to dinner with Steve McClellan. He and I had been close friends for a number of years, and I knew just being with him would make me feel better. We had a real heart-to-heart. I spoke my mind, and it was cathartic.

I'm not sure I was 100 percent rational, but over the next few days, as I tried to come to terms with the severing of ties, I was of two minds. Part of me hadn't thought this would ever happen, so I felt blindsided. When we'd hired High Noon Management six months earlier, I assumed they'd handle the business and I'd stay on board as personal manager. The five of us had gone through a lot together, and I thought that kind of bond was indestructible.

The other part of me had seen it coming, if subconsciously. Looking back, it occurred to me that Paul may have been trying to make me quit with his ever-increasing cold and churlish behavior. If he was, I obliviously put up with it out of loyalty.

What hurt the most, though, was suddenly being cut off from the four guys I had practically lived with for the past six years. Then, as word got out that I was no longer working with the band, I was devastated to hear from people that Paul had told them I'd been fired. So much for his seemingly compassionate words to me in person.

I think it's fair to say a big part of my dismissal from the Replacements was because I had made myself dismissible with my excessive alcohol consumption. But my drinking wasn't the only factor. Maybe Paul felt I was holding them back. Maybe in his mind I represented the band's failure to be more successful and my presence was an ongoing reminder of that. But I think the band also simply wanted to move into the next phase of their career without me—a bit like moving out of your parents' house. I didn't understand all that at first, and it would take some time before I did. It was hard for me to care about anything for a long time.

Eight

Euphoric Recall

For the first fourteen years of my life, I had no interest in alcohol or drugs. The prevailing altered state I witnessed as a little boy in the late '50s and early '60s was alcohol-induced. My first exposure to intoxication was on television through comedians like Dean Martin and Red Skelton. They made me laugh, and it seemed benign. I first became aware of intoxication being a problem through my mother, Carolyn.

Carolyn and my father, Chet, were dedicated bridge players, and their social life largely centered around cards and cocktails. It began as harmless, social drinking, but as time went on, the alcohol consumption gradually grew. Seeing my mother's drinking increase, my father took the initiative to quit and became the designated driver. While it was of course good that there was always a sober person behind the wheel, my dad all too frequently was on the receiving end of Mom's inebriated ire, which my big brother Alan and I witnessed on a number of occasions. My mom eventually was able to curb her drinking, but for me, the seed had been sown. I thought alcohol was something for old people and sometimes it made them unpleasant, even angry. I wanted nothing to do with it.

I was a good and moderately well-behaved student in elementary school, but by the time I hit junior high I became enamored with a bit more of a rebellious crowd. Clandestine drinking on the weekends was fairly common for this clique. Although I was pretty anti-alcohol, I eventually succumbed to peer pressure. A time or two some friends and I pinched liquor from various parents and combined different kinds that should never be mixed, and it made me really sick. I grew weary of the drinking set very quickly.

In the summer of 1968, between eighth and ninth grade, my best friend, Paul Sylvestre, and his family went on vacation to Arizona. Paul and I had met the year before and had become inseparable. How was I going to survive for two whole weeks without Paul?! I made it through, of course, and as it turned out there was a substantial upside to that vacation. Paul returned with two things that were going to be important to me for a very long time: records by the Mothers of Invention, and marijuana.

Marijuana had been talked about ad nauseam on the television news, on the radio, and in the newspapers, always in warning tones. The reporters sounded hyperbolic even to me. The burgeoning alternative press regularly debunked those straight news people's notions, and I don't need to tell you which of the sources we trusted more.

For maximum privacy and secrecy on our first cannabis outing, we made a plan to sleep out in a fort Paul and some friends had built on a hillside in the woods behind his house. It was no slapdash kids' construction; it was a solid, properly roofed wooden structure, complete with a wood-burning stove.

We came prepared with sleeping bags, candles, flashlights, snacks, sodas, and the all-important transistor radio. I believe there were three or four of us in the little one-room structure that night, and we had an absolute blast, jabbering nonstop and laughing uncontrollably. But the biggest revelation from my first experience getting high was that the music coming out of the radio sounded better than it ever had. From that night on, for a small group of friends and me, marijuana became a staple of our existence. We weren't all-day, every-day consumers. For us, it was a ritual that we planned ahead of time and looked forward to. Smoking pot opened up my mind. I found it to be stimulating, pleasurable, and freeing, especially when listening to music. I felt I could truly get inside songs and crawl around to examine the different parts.

The basement of my house became a regular hangout because I had lots of records and my parents were welcoming, tolerant, and frequently away at night playing bridge. As soon as my parents pulled out of the driveway and were out of sight, my mates would leap out of the bushes and come running into the house. The lights were dimmed, joints were lit, and the turntable was set in motion. Albums du jour in those early pot-smoking days included Procol Harum's *Shine On Brightly*, *Sailor* by the Steve Miller Band, *Bless Its Pointed Little Head* by Jefferson Airplane, and Neil Young's self-titled solo debut. We memorized all the early albums of the Mothers of Invention too: *Freak Out*, *Absolutely Free*, *Lumpy Gravy*, *We're Only In It For the Money*, *Cruisin' With Ruben & The Jets*, and *Uncle Meat*. And we mustn't forget the latest from the reigning kings: the Beatles' *White Album* and the Rolling Stones' *Beggar's Banquet*. That basement was like a secret club for me and my closest friends, including David Aiken, Bill Gamec, Bob Ivers, Robb Henry, Mike Owens, Paul Sylvestre, Tom Mohr, Roger Harvey, and Steve Carlson.

By the summers of '69 and '70, psychedelics had entered the picture. We tried LSD first, then mescaline, and psilocybin (all in pill form) and actual mushrooms. The first time I ever got high for a concert was when Paul Sylvestre and I took mescaline for the Mothers of Invention at the Guthrie on July 13, 1969. We were higher than kites by the time the opening act came on, and their theatrics and the sheer volume had us cowering in our seats. The band was called Alice Cooper. As striking as they were, we forgot all about them when the Mothers took the stage. A ten-piece band with two drummers, led by genius composer/guitarist/satirist Frank Zappa—it was one of the greatest live shows I've ever seen, and, dare I say, the mescaline enhanced the experience.

Another hair-raising drug-and-concert experience came a few months later when Jefferson Airplane played the Minneapolis Auditorium to support their album *Volunteers*, on May 15, 1970. We got tickets, and five of us decided that dropping LSD was in order for this landmark event. Our seats were about fifteen rows off the main floor and maybe twenty rows from the stage. Great sightlines. We were absolutely giddy. There was fantastic preshow recorded music blasting from the PA. When the song "I Feel Like I'm Fixin' to Die Rag" by Country Joe and the Fish came on and it got to the Fish Cheer part ("Gimme an F! Gimme a U! Gimme a C! Gimme a K!"), everyone in the audience shouted along at the top of their lungs. I was on cloud nine. I remember thinking, *I'd have paid just to sit in a big room like this, with all these beautiful people, and listen to records!*

After the local band Crow opened the concert, fabulous recorded music was again played during the break. Suddenly, the recorded music stopped, the auditorium went dark, and a film of the Airplane performing *Volunteers* album-opener "We Can Be Together" hit the giant screen covering the stage. My head went numb and my heart started pounding. The moment that song was over, a second film began of the Airplane doing the title song, "Volunteers."

As that song ended, the music started again, much louder—and this time it was live. The screen was slowly raised, and there was Jefferson Airplane, onstage, performing "Volunteers." I'd seen them before, back in 1967, and they were brilliant then, but this was something altogether different. Three years and hundreds of shows later, they were at the peak of their power. The band's live improvisational skills were astounding. And, once again, I can't lie: the mind-altering enhancement of the LSD made the concert even more spectacular.

In May 1970, I finished tenth grade with the sketchiest report card of my life. Our drug intake was peaking—pot most every night and LSD or some other psychedelic every three or so days. We mostly took LSD in pill form, but sometimes we'd get it as a liquid, a micro-dot on a piece of blotter paper. We'd be told it was "Orange Sunshine" or

"Purple Haze" or some other name, but whatever we got was always surreptitiously purchased from a friend of a friend, so who knows what we were really getting.

In July, I attended the Crosby, Stills, Nash & Young concert at the Met Sports Center with my friends Paul and David. We opted to stick to pot for the night. It was an incredible performance, the harmonies were so perfectly done, and we all thought Neil Young stole the show.

I look back at that summer with much fondness. I had such a great group of friends, and we went on many wild, sometimes stupidly dangerous, escapades. For me, though, this phase was about to come to an end.

When I got the job at the Guthrie Theater, I began to rethink my life. Tenth grade had been a blur of screwing off, daily pot smoking, frequent tripping, and barely squeaking by in my studies. Beginning in eleventh grade, I seriously backed off on my substance intake. I still smoked pot but rarely imbibed in psychedelics. My grades improved. Between school, working at the Guthrie, and later distributing the NME around the Twin Cities, I kept very busy, and there wasn't a lot of playtime. Of course, I did a lot of record shopping. On the average, I was buying five or six albums a week.

As 1974 rolled along, I developed a relationship with Pam Williams, whom I'd met while we both worked at the Guthrie. I credit her, but don't blame her, for my introduction to alcohol, in particular Johnnie Walker Red Scotch Whisky. Helluva place to start. It was a crazy romance that lasted into 1977. We had tons of fun together, but my substance consumption hit new peaks. And it didn't stop with alcohol. We got acquainted with a motorcycle-riding drug dealer who became a friend, which made it all too convenient to purchase high-quality cocaine. We did it occasionally at first, but it became more and more frequent, and for a while there, it got just plain stupid. I will say, one thing I liked about coke was that it helped me stay awake longer, which in turn allowed for longer music-listening marathons. Luckily, though, we didn't have enough money to get in too deep. Being short on funds didn't stop coke from getting a grip on my peer group; too many spent too much on it. It got out of hand for lots of us, was a horrible waste of money, and led to plenty of bad behavior and questionable late-night revelations about life and love that never held up the next day.

An unexpected thing happened one night when we went to the dealer's house. He was out of cocaine, but he had heroin. At first we were spooked at the mere thought of it, but when he said it didn't involve needles and we could just snort it, we said, "Okay, we'll try it." He sold us one fifth of a gram of the brown powder to split and advised us to wait to ingest the drugs until we were back at home, because it usually made you throw up for a while before you settled into the high. I know this sounds absurd, but we had gotten to be good friends with our dealer and we trusted the guy. He was not a junkie; he was a smart fine-art painter who owned a house and was, generally speaking, a responsible adult. He dabbled but steered clear of addiction. As did we, off and on for the next few months, until our dealer friend was busted and went to jail. We never did find out what happened to him. And we never looked for anywhere else to buy heroin. I crossed paths with the drug another few times, but always kept it at bay.

My last LSD trip was with Steve Almaas, sometime in 1977. Steve was renting a room from a schoolteacher. His quarters were in a fairly private second-floor area, where we thought we could enjoy the experience without interruption. The dose we took was a strong one but not too much. I have vivid memories of listening to Eno's second album, *Taking Tiger Mountain (By Strategy)*, and laughing uncontrollably when we realized one of the "percussion breaks" on the album was actually a typewriter.

The next several years were a whirlwind of activity: working at Oar Folkjokeopus and the Longhorn, starting Twin/Tone Records, and then becoming manager and coproducer of the Replacements. I was working around the clock. I was so swept up in it, I didn't see that my substance consumption was on the rise again. There was definitely cocaine involved, but the real culprit was that old demon: alcohol. DJ-ing at the Longhorn gave me unlimited bar privileges, which was dangerous. Pam may have introduced me to scotch, but that club was where I really mastered it.

Working with the Replacements certainly didn't help keep my drinking under control, either. They were a highly talented bunch, but as their star rose, alcohol and other recreational substance use became more rampant. I was as guilty of overindulging as any of them, and that was irresponsible of me as their manager.

When my job with the Replacements was terminated in the spring of 1986, it hit me hard. Drinking was certainly part of the reason, but the band also wanted to move on and have someone they didn't know, someone with industry clout represent them. At the time I didn't understand that, and in my highly medicated state I just felt sorry for myself. This is where my serious descent began.

Even after I stopped working with the Replacements, I still received royalty checks for the records I had coproduced, but those checks were not enough to cover even my meager expenses. I needed to get a job, and I wasn't too interested in going back to Twin/Tone or anything involving music, for the time being, anyway.

My buddy Dave Postlethwaite was working in a warehouse for Gene Smiley Inc., an interior decorating supply company run by our friend Jay Smiley's father. Dave said he could use some help and I could probably pick up a few bucks there. I talked to Jay, who was the warehouse manager. He was all for it, and I started right away. I was thirty-two and it was the first "straight" job I'd had since high school, when I worked briefly in a restaurant. I was still going out to see live music several nights a week and got involved with two young bands in an advisory capacity (A Single Love and Bad Thing), but otherwise I was quite unmoored.

In the fall of 1986, being short on money, I moved out of my apartment in the Modesto on 26th and Garfield and rented a room in a house at 34th and Lyndale with Dave and another friend. It was short-lived. A fire broke out a few months later, and we had to vacate. Luckily, Dave's guitars and my records weren't touched by the fire—a little sooty, but okay. I couch-surfed for a bit before moving back to the 26th and Lyndale neighborhood into a two-bedroom apartment with Peter Bystol, an acquaintance who worked at a record distributor in St. Paul.

My father passed away December 5, 1988, at the age of seventy-six. It was difficult for me to process in my intemperate frame of mind, and I wasn't very good at consoling my mother. I will always regret that my life was such a mess when he died. My brother Alan had to take care of all the burial arrangements.

During this period, a band from Toronto called 13 Engines caught my ear. They were a hard-touring bunch who found a substantial audience at the Uptown Bar. Locals compared their ferocious live show to our own Soul Asylum, which was no small compliment. I went to see them every time they came to town, and we got to be friends. One thing led to another, and they asked if I'd manage them. I was wary of going down that road again, but I thought working with the band would give me focus and might help pull me out of my doldrums. I might also slow down on the alcohol intake if I took on the responsibility. We came to terms, and I jumped on board.

I got involved with another Minneapolis group in early 1990 called the Leatherwoods. They were like a dream band for me, mixing key elements of the Beatles and the Everly Brothers. They wrote catchy pop-rock songs and had beautiful voices, which made for tight harmony singing. The nucleus was two guys from Kansas. Todd Newman was a pop music aficionado and a terrific guitarist and songwriter. The drummer, Tim O'Reagan, had a voice that stopped people in their tracks. He became a bit of a sensation in town. The Leatherwoods also caught Paul Westerberg's ear, so when I arranged for the band to do some recording at Blackberry Way, Paul joined in. He even co-wrote one song, called "Wastin' All My Time." Paul's solo career was just beginning at this point, and he was reluctant to put his real name in the credits for some reason, so we came up with a pseudonym: Pablo Louseorama. Paul had frequently referred to himself as "The Louse." It was fun to be in the studio with Paul again, but he was on the wagon and I most definitely was not, which made things uncomfortable at times. Nonetheless, we got some good tracks down over four days, and the Leatherwoods did more recordings at a couple of other studios, catch as catch can. I had been in touch with Paul Stark about the band, and there had been some preliminary talk about me bringing the band to Twin/Tone.

One of the things 13 Engines was looking for was a deal with a bigger label. They'd made two albums for sturdy Detroit indie Nocturnal Records but felt they were ready for the majors. We traveled to LA and New York for meetings, and the band eventually signed with Capitol in Canada and SBK Records in the states. We hired David Briggs to produce their next album. David had worked on many of Neil Young's best albums, and we did preproduction at Neil's Broken Arrow Ranch south of San Francisco. It was such a privilege to work there. The Engines and I dubbed it "Neil World." We tracked the album at Sound City in LA and mixed at Indigo Ranch in the Malibu Mountains.

Over the years, I'd experienced producers who were hostile toward band managers, and Briggs definitely fell into that category. But he and I had several dealings on the phone ahead of time, and he was always friendly. Although he and I had one run-in early in the recording sessions, I was under the impression that David recognized me as a real music person, and not a meddling manager. I didn't learn until much later that that wasn't the case. Apparently, his resentment of my presence made it unpleasant for band leader John Critchley. Had I known, I would've left.

Though some partying did go on, I managed to keep my drinking somewhat in check throughout the album-making process, and I felt good about that. But back in Minneapolis, it wasn't long before things went from okay to bad to worse. Feeling rudderless following six weeks of concentrated activity, I plunged back into the bottle and was soon drinking regularly during the day. We were still going over final details on the Engines' recording contracts with Capitol and SBK. I'd be on conference calls with John and the band's lawyer, Rosemary Carroll, and I just couldn't follow along very well. I'd never been savvy with large legal documents, and in my state I was pretty worthless. I was sick, I was an alcoholic, and I had to admit it.

I finally called John and told him I couldn't handle the band's management any longer. He didn't see it coming and was not happy about it, but I know he perceived I was in real trouble. I'm glad I had the wherewithal to leave when I did, but I felt terrible that I'd let the band down. Which gave me all the more reason to drown my sorrows.

The Engines' album, titled *A Blur to Me Now*, was released in April. It received glowing reviews, sold modestly, and still sounds brilliant to me. Under the guidance of Rosemary and her husband, Danny Goldberg, the band released two more albums before breaking up in 1997.

In January 1991, my girlfriend Maggie and I flew to Georgia to visit Peter Buck. We spent the better part of a week with Peter and his wife, Barrie.

One night, Peter asked me to go see a band with him. We went to the Caledonia club and saw a group called the Dashboard Saviors. It was love at first sight; I was blown away. They were a rockin' alt-country quartet with two vocalists and a passel of well-written songs. Front man Todd McBride and bassist Rob Veal both wrote and sang; Mike Gibson was a devastatingly great lead guitarist; and John Crist was one of the loudest and most precise drummers I'd heard in years. Down-home southern boys all, they had an intelligence that really drew me in. After the show, Peter fessed up that he was going to produce their first album and was hoping I liked them enough to put them on Twin/Tone. I told him I was interested. We talked to the band. They were excited, and the seed was planted.

Unfortunately, I was in rough shape the whole time we were in Athens. I was sneaking drinks, and there were times I had the shakes so bad at dinner that I had trouble getting a spoonful of soup to my mouth without spilling. R.E.M. was working on some recordings at John Keane's studio near Peter's house, and Maggie and I were invited to stop by and listen one evening. At some point, I passed out on the couch in the control room, and Maggie had to prop me up and walk me back to Peter's house. So embarrassing. But I'm not sure anyone really knew how bad off I was.

Back in Minneapolis, I was drinking like a fish, and I couldn't stop. If I woke up and didn't have any liquor left, I'd walk the four blocks to Hum's Liquors, buy a pint, and have several slugs on the way home. Sometimes I'd be awake before Hum's was open, and I'd sit and watch the clock until 7:55 AM, then walk down and get there just as they were unlocking the door.

Over the course of my teens, twenties, and thirties, between, say, 1968 and 1991, I had tried most every drug in the book, and I'm still surprised that it wasn't one of them that took me down. It was the booze that eventually sunk its claws in.

March 2, 1991, was an evening like so many others. I was hanging out with Dave Postlethwaite. Dave had a drinking problem as well, but it was another couple of years before his caught up with him. That night we had a bottle of Jim Beam, a few beers, and a couple snorts of cocaine, listening to records all the while.

The next day, I knew I was in serious trouble. I'd been drinking way too much for months, but this was different. My internal chemistry was rebelling. I felt horrible, disoriented, and shaky; my equilibrium was off. I told myself I had to stop. But it was as if all the addicted cells in my body heard me and said, "Oh no, you don't!" I talked about it with my roommate, Peter Bystol. He'd had personal experience with alcohol as well. A couple of years earlier, he'd gotten a DUI and swore off the stuff for a while, and he knew enough to understand what I was going through. He levelled with me and said that in the fall of 1990, when I'd come back from California after working with 13 Engines, he started to see a change in me. And other people were noticing too. The alcohol was affecting me in increasingly extreme ways. Memory lapses and complete blackouts were not uncommon. Maggie didn't know what to do. A mutual friend, Mark Trehus (then managing Oar Folk), brought it up to Peter, saying, "Seems like your roommate's been on quite a jag lately."

On Monday, Peter went off to work as normal. Around midafternoon, apparently I called him at work and asked if he'd pick me up a pint of Jim Beam on his way home. I told him I'd had "an awesome nap" but I seemed to have bitten my tongue. My doctor later speculated that I'd probably had a seizure and done a freefall on my face, which was all splotchy purple and red. From our phone conversation, Peter could tell something was seriously wrong. After hanging up, he called Dave Postlethwaite and told him he thought I needed immediate medical attention—an intervention of sorts. He asked Dave to meet him at our apartment right away. When they arrived around 3:00 PM, they told me they were taking me to the ER. Peter said, "Maybe a doctor will give you something that will make you feel better." I didn't resist. On March 4, I marched forth.

They took me to the Hennepin County Medical Center emergency room, where we waited for an hour or so while the staff attended to people in worse shape than I. When I was finally being admitted, I had a second seizure and they had to cut off my clothes. A third seizure soon followed.

Peter called my brother Alan. He said Alan sounded angry at first, saying, "It was bound to happen." But when Alan got to the hospital and saw me unconscious, his mood changed, and he sat there quietly and held my hand. Peter said he'll always remember that as a "cool moment," despite the circumstances.

I was in the intensive care unit for eight days, in and out of consciousness. First I had to go through the DT's (delirium tremens) from alcohol withdrawal, and the hospital gave me Valium intravenously to counteract the effects. Then, I had to be detoxed from the Valium. Dave remembers visiting me in the ICU. I was strapped onto the bed and said to him, "Let's go to First Avenue."

I finally came to in a hospital room on Monday, March 11. As the fog in my head subsided and I got my bearings, I had a moment of clarity. I wiped my brow (figuratively) and thought, *Phew, I made it.* Two more thoughts followed in quick succession: *I'm never going to have another drink as long as I live.* Then, *I can't die yet; I still have a lot of records to make.* My doctor told me I'd had acute pancreatitis. Then he said, quite sternly, "I need to tell you something, and I'm not just trying to scare you: It's a complete miracle that you're alive. The toxic level in your body when you were admitted was off the chart." I didn't need to hear that to commit to staying sober, but it sure didn't hurt.

The next step was figuring out what the next step was. I was free to leave the hospital and resume my normal life, but my doctor recommended I get addiction treatment. Putting an extra buffer between my hospitalization and going back to the real world seemed like a good idea to me. I opted for a twenty-one-day program in a Hennepin County facility in downtown Minneapolis. I entered treatment broke, unemployed, and uninsured, but I'd gotten a second chance, and I was determined to get well. For the first time in ages, I felt energized and optimistic about the future.

My experience in treatment was half paying attention to the curriculum and half impatience to be done with it. One aspect that especially stands out, though, was the counselor who was assigned to me. She was nice enough, but we didn't have much of a connection. I thought she was mechanical, always on autopilot and throwing around rehab jargon. She never made an effort to understand anyone on a personal level. During one group discussion, we recounted our experiences with substance abuse. Everyone had distressing war stories. When the meeting was over, my counselor grabbed me firmly by the arm, brought me into her office, and closed the door. She proceeded to dress me down for the way I had talked about my drug and alcohol experiences. She exclaimed, "You exhibited euphoric recall!" In addiction recovery, "euphoric recall" refers to remembering past negative experiences in a positive light, which may increase the risk of relapse. The stern look on her face seemed so overly dramatic, and the term she used just struck me as funny—I couldn't help but burst out in laughter. I knew it was inappropriate, and I meant no disrespect, but the fact was, yes, alcohol and drugs had wreaked havoc on my life in a number of ways—hell, I nearly died—but I also couldn't deny that I had many positive experiences while under the influence. The notion that I was supposed to feel otherwise seemed untruthful to me.

On March 3, 2023, I passed the thirty-second anniversary of my last drink of alcohol. I don't celebrate that day every year, but I certainly acknowledge it to myself and may mention it to a family member or a friend. Having beaten full-blown addiction is one of the things I'm most proud of in my life, and it still buoys me every day.

Nine

Twin/Tone and Medium Cool:
Go West, Young Man

I completed the treatment program for alcohol addiction on Tuesday, April 2, 1991. The early part of the day is fuzzy, but I remember the evening quite well. I went to a bar with my pal Steve McClellan, just like I had after my job with the Replacements abruptly ended in April 1986. It speaks volumes about my friendship with Steve that at the times I was feeling most fragile, he made me feel safe. The bar was the Fine Line in downtown Minneapolis, and we went there to see a folksinger I love named Steve Forbert. There I was in an establishment that served alcohol and I wasn't tempted for a nanosecond. So far, so good!

I had many well-wishers over the next few weeks, and the support was overwhelming. I vividly remember a phone call with Steve Almaas. He said, "I think everyone's allowed a certain number of drink tickets in their lifetime, and some people just use them up quicker than others." Ha! But seriously, I was so grateful to have survived. I felt like the clichéd newly sober guy: "Look at this blade of grass—isn't it beautiful?!" And seeing the mornings without a hangover for the first time in years was a glorious thing.

Kicking off this new phase in my life, I moved in with Maggie and I went back to work at Twin/Tone. Maggie was living above Oar Folk. Just the idea of living above that store made me feel good. It was a large, airy, three-bedroom apartment with windows on all four sides. I moved all my records and assorted music stuff into the corner room, which overlooked my beloved intersection of 26th and Lyndale.

One fear I had when I quit drinking and drugging was that music might not have the same electrifying effect on me that it had for so many years. Music and altered states had gone hand in hand with me for so long, I needed to remind myself that my earliest inspirational musical moments happened long before I drank or got high, but I couldn't shake the apprehension.

My salvation arrived in April or May when a new Terry Reid album called *The Driver* came out. I've often joked that I practically remember what I was wearing the first time I heard Terry Reid's voice back in 1968. It was that startling. He falls into the great raspy-voiced, British, blues-rock singer category, along with Steve Marriott, Paul Rodgers, Rod Stewart, Frankie Miller, and the like. Some would say Terry's the best of the bunch, and I wouldn't argue. *The Driver* is overproduced, but regardless, that voice shines through on several tracks, and none more so than on Terry's cover of the Waterboys' "The Whole of the Moon." I loved the Waterboys' version, but something in Terry's delivery made me think about the lyric in a way I hadn't before. The song is written from the point of view of someone who admires another person and their accomplishments. But what I heard was Terry singing directly to me. I was someone who'd gotten "too high too far too soon." The composer only "saw the crescent," but the person he's singing to "saw the whole of the moon." In my own way, I believe I saw the whole of the moon too. I had looked death square in the face, yet lived to tell the tale. I was so moved by the connection I felt to Terry's recording that I cried tears of joy the first time I listened to it.

As for Twin/Tone, Paul Stark and I talked, and he encouraged me to come back into the fold. It was so easy and felt so right. I'd been kicking something around in my head. Invigorated by the idea of my new beginning, I thought, *What if I developed a new label imprint under the Twin/Tone umbrella to signify a new chapter?* Paul supported me on this, and off I went.

I called the new label Medium Cool Records. The name was inspired by a compilation album called *Medium Cool*, which featured older, jazz-flavored songs with a modern twist by Alex Chilton, Adele Bertei, and James Chance. For a label logo, Maggie suggested using a simple, noir-ish line drawing of a man walking that had caught her eye on the spine of a mystery novel. I had it slightly redrawn—and voilà, we had a logo and a name! Two groups I'd started working with earlier in the decade, the Dashboard Saviors and the Leatherwoods, were the first bands signed to the Medium Cool label.

Naturally, while I'd been away, the Twin/Tone office had gone through some changes. Chris Osgood left in 1990 to work for Resources and Counseling for the Arts in St. Paul. Dave Ayers moved to New York City to take a job with Savoy Music Publishing in the spring of 1991. During his time at Twin/Tone, Ayers brought in substantial groups like the Jayhawks, Run Westy Run, the Wallets, and Babes in Toyland. Jill McLean was handling production and manufacturing. I'd always liked her, and she was a fastidious coworker. She'd started her own imprint under the Twin/Tone umbrella, Clean Records. Jill also went to work for Soul Asylum part-time, helping with their mailing list and fan club, organizing their business, and keeping their books for years to come. Sarah Brace was doing publicity. Our longstanding office manager/receptionist, Roz Ferguson, was still there, as delightfully cool and efficient as ever. Tom Hazelmyer and his noise-rock label, Amphetamine Reptile, rented office space in the building as well. Unfortunately, Charley Hallman was no longer involved with Twin/Tone. He got too busy with the newspaper and gradually just drifted away.

One of the best things about being back at Twin/Tone was the people. It was fun to be in Paul Stark's orbit again. I have a deep affection for the man. He was an unorthodox character, exceptionally smart, full of ideas, and always on the cutting edge of audio technology. He was stimulating to be around.

The day I officially came back into the office, Sarah Brace, whom I'm not sure I'd met before, had set up a desk for me in the front lounge area. It was really just a small table and chair, but she'd equipped it with a phone, a tape dispenser, a stapler, a notepad, and a cup with pens and pencils in it. A small, practical gesture perhaps, but it really touched me. Sarah came to us from Hampshire College in Amherst, Massachusetts, and had moved to Minneapolis in June 1989 specifically hoping to get a job at Twin/Tone. This of course endeared her to me even more.

By the summer of 1991, Bob "Slim" Dunlap had been the Replacements' lead guitarist for four years, having stepped in after Bob Stinson left the band. Westerberg, who had a rough time replacing one Bob with another, dubbed Dunlap "Slim," a nickname that suited his lean, tall frame. I knew Slim well from his days as Curtiss A's guitarist in Spooks and Thumbs Up. Sometime in June, Slim popped over to our apartment. We were chatting and listening to records, but I could tell he had something on his mind; he seemed a little down. He finally made a rather cryptic comment. He'd just gotten the latest Replacements' tour itinerary, and it ended on the Fourth of July with a show at the Taste of Chicago festival in Grant Park. Slim said, "There are no more dates booked after this. You might want to be at this show." I got the message.

The morning of July 4, I flew to Chicago with Maggie and Slim's wife, Chrissie. We met Slim at his hotel. The band members all had separate limos take them to Grant Park. The three of us went with Slim. Material Issue and NRBQ were the opening acts. We were backstage for a while, but it felt awkward, and I wandered out front on my own. Even watching one of my favorites, NRBQ, wasn't appealing. I was quite blown away by the Replacements, though. They opened with "I Will Dare," and I just lost myself in their performance. I was doing fine until they went into "Talent Show." At the breakdown midway through the song, Paul stepped to the front of the stage and played the melody to "Send in the Clowns." I knew then they really were breaking up.

In 1992, LA–based record label Restless Records came knocking. They were looking to expand their company by purchasing catalogs from other indie labels they admired and were interested in Twin/Tone. Restless was the offspring of Greenworld Distribution's label, Enigma. Restless had been taken over the year before and relaunched by Enigma cofounder Bill Hein and a new partner, Joe Regis. The timing was fortuitous, as Twin/Tone had gone through a rough patch financially. Paul Stark was reluctant to sell Twin/Tone outright and proposed a long-term licensing deal, wherein the rights to any titles Restless did not keep in print would revert back to Twin/Tone. Initially, the complete Twin/Tone catalog was licensed exclusively to Restless. However, in September 1995, the deal was amended to projects from just six groups: the Replacements, Soul Asylum, the Jayhawks, Babes in Toyland, Zuzu's Petals, and Ween. Joe also became interested in what I was doing with Medium Cool and offered assistance there as well. He invited me to Los Angeles to meet the Restless staff and bring them up to speed on the artists I was working with. It wasn't long before Joe began trying to persuade me to move west and work with Medium Cool out of their office. That same year, Restless cofounded the Alternative Distribution Alliance (ADA) with the Warner Music Group. Paul was named to the board of directors. ADA was instrumental in providing global distribution for indie labels. In late '95, Paul started another imprint himself, TRG Records (Twin/Tone Records Group), which acted as a manufacturing and distribution entity for other incoming artists and labels.

Just as the audio work on the Leatherwoods' album was wrapping up and the album artwork was in progress, things started to head south on the project. Tensions between Todd Newman and Tim O'Reagan had been brewing for some time, and after a fiasco at a New Music Seminar showcase in New York in June, the strains escalated and the group disbanded. Their album, *Topeka Oratorio*, wasn't due to be released for another month. I was so brokenhearted, I couldn't bring myself to cancel it. The album came out in July and sold very little.

My next order of business was to reach out to Slim Dunlap. I had first talked to Slim about the possibility of making a solo album back in 1978, but he was so self-effacing I couldn't convince him to take me up on my offer. He largely had been viewed as Curtiss A's right-hand man, but he wrote songs of his own that I thought were outstanding. Now that the Replacements had broken up, I approached Slim again with a firm offer. It only took a year to get him to say yes.

Slim and I ironed out the details on how we wanted to go about making his first solo album. Brian Paulson and I would produce. We'd record it in the Rykodisc/East Side Digital offices in downtown Minneapolis. Brian worked for Ryko at the time and had amassed a considerable collection of recording gear, which he stored in an unused space there. Ryko, being the artist-friendly outfit it was, didn't object to Brian pulling the equipment out and doing a little after-hours recording in the offices. Still, it took some time to make the album. Slim is meticulous in some ways but requires spontaneity in others. He played the main guitar parts and most of the bass on the album but also used his regular band for some of it—Jim Thompson on second guitar, Johnny Hazlett on bass, and his brother Buck Hazlett on drums. Tim O'Reagan, Chan Poling, and Paul Westerberg all made guest appearances.

The album, *The Old New Me*, came out in July 1993. It was a rock 'n' roll record, and it was brimming with character. The album attracted lots of positive press attention. As the *Los Angeles Times* put it: "Dunlap . . . may have been overshadowed in the Replacements, but his album, *The Old New Me*, is a more endearing work than Westerberg's solo debut, *14 Songs*."

I wanted to broaden the scope of new artists at Medium Cool. Tom Hicks, a songwriter from Decatur, Illinois, had sent some demos to Twin/Tone, and I was so taken with the songs I rang him up and offered him a record deal. It was an impulsive move, but I don't regret it. Tom and his band, Ticks, also recorded their album in the Ryko building. It was titled *sun shinin on your rain* and was released in the fall of 1992. We did everything we could to help them make a go of it on the road, but they were never able to pull it together.

The Dashboard Saviors' debut, *Kitty*, was released on the same day as the Leatherwoods' *Topeka Oratorio* in July 1992. The album, recorded in John Keane's Athens studio, was produced by Peter Buck, and various tracks featured guest appearances by Peter on guitar, Mike Mills on organ, and Vic Chesnutt on vocals.

Besides the incredible music they made for Medium Cool, the Dashboard Saviors brought other dividends to the label. They were doing shows backing a young female country-rock singer named Marlee MacLeod, who'd moved to Athens from Alabama. When I first heard her powerful singing voice, I was won over, and we talked about making a record together. Like the Saviors, Marlee toured like crazy, which made the idea of adding her to the MC roster even more appealing. We recorded her album with John Keane in his Athens studio too. Additional overdubs and mixing were done in Minneapolis with John Fields (who also engineered and mixed parts of *Topeka Oratorio*).

Another dividend from working with the Saviors arrived via a tune the band had been working on for their second album, a simple rocker called "Pawnbroker." I liked the lyrics and asked Saviors' front man Todd what had inspired them. He said they weren't his, that the words were written by Jack Logan. "Who's he?" I asked. Todd shot me an incredulous look. "You don't know about Jack Logan?!" He proceeded to fill me in, and as he raved, it dawned on me I'd heard the name before. The Saviors' manager, Len Hoffman, had gushed to me about Logan a while back. As had Peter Buck, who told me about an amazing song called "Female Jesus," which R.E.M. had liked so much they considered covering it for one of their fan club Christmas singles.

Over the next few days, I got the lowdown on Logan from a number of sources. He was a collaborator and a catalyst for a circle of musicians. Whereas some guys might get together on the weekend to go fishing or watch ball games, Logan and company would buy a few

---

cases of beer and spend entire weekends recording on a four-track cassette machine. The players would line up to supply Logan with music beds for him to add words and a vocal melody to, and turn them into a song. The result of all this was an enormous catalog of home recordings.

Rob Veal, the Saviors bass player, took me out to Winder, Georgia, to meet Logan. Rob and Logan were clearly close and had played a lot of music together. Though I knew Rob as a bass guitarist, he was Logan's drummer in a loose aggregation they called Liquor Cabinet. Logan himself wasn't really a musician, though he did dabble with guitar and keyboards on some of the recordings. The true musicians (Logan's "enablers") included members of Redneck Greece, the Saviors, and various other Athens bands. Besides Logan and Rob, the main cast of characters were Logan's right-hand man and best friend, Kelly Keneipp (piano/guitar), Dave Philips (guitar), Mike Gibson (guitar), Eric Sales (bass), and Todd McBride (guitar).

I told Logan I'd like to hear some of his songs. He downplayed the prolific songwriting reputation that preceded him, very much an "aw shucks" kind of guy. He was reluctant to give me any of his recordings, but he eventually said something about putting a few on tape for me. As Rob and I were leaving, I gave Logan my card and said if he had the tape done before I headed back to Minneapolis, I'd come pick it up. Otherwise, he could just mail it to me. And we left it at that.

But I never got anything from Logan. So, I asked again. And I still didn't get anything. I thought, *Now this is a novel way to get an A&R person's attention—when they ask you for music, don't give them any.* I persisted, and finally one day I received a package. I eagerly tore it open and found three *full* ninety-minute cassettes. There was something wonderfully naive about Logan overdoing it. I set the tapes aside to listen when time allowed.

That opportunity arrived the next week. Maggie and I were making the long drive to see the Big Star reunion at the University of Missouri in Columbia on April 25, 1993. Ample time to investigate at least some of the nearly 100 songs Logan had sent. At a gas stop somewhere in Iowa, I was looking through the music I'd brought along and decided to throw one of Logan's tapes into the cassette deck. Once we got on the road again, I hit play. The first song was called "15 Years in Indiana," and I heard Logan sing:

> It's after two o'clock and she walks out to her car
> Her keys are in her purse at the bottom
> The dumpsters 'round in back are giving off a scent of something cold
>   and damp, something rotten
> And she's prettier than this, it's only that she's tired
> The tips were not as good as she'd planned on
> Spent fifteen years in Indiana as a cocktail waitress

It was as much a short story as it was a song. My antenna went up, big time. Not every song was as strong as the first, but the ratio of great to not-so-great was definitely in Logan's favor. The recordings were low-fi but filled with spirit, imagination, humor, and personality. I was amazed by how many tracks made my thumbs-up pile from the first cassette alone. I couldn't stop there, and as we drove, I listened to the other two tapes one after the other. This Logan guy was the real deal.

Logan didn't have a phone, but I got his work number and called him there. I told Logan I loved the recordings and would like to talk with him about the possibility of making some records. He was surprised but said he'd be willing to meet. I played a number of tracks for Paul, who liked what he heard and totally supported bringing Logan to Medium Cool. As did Joe and my other new allies at Restless.

On my next trip to Athens in June, I met with Logan and Kelly Keneipp. The two of them were clearly the brain trust of this musical endeavor. I told them my partner and I wanted to offer them a record deal, and they were thrilled! I said I looked forward to getting them in a proper recording studio at some point, but I suggested that the first record be a compilation of the best of the four-track home recordings.

I think they were surprised and maybe a little disappointed at first, but they came around. I said I wanted to listen to everything they had on tape and pick the very best songs. Logan and Kelly looked at each other, laughed, and said, "No, you don't!" I countered with, "No, I really do. I want to listen to all the recordings you have and make an educated selection of what we all think are the best." And that's how it began. They loaded me up with tapes, and I basked in it all, listening carefully and evaluating.

Accumulating a steady stream of tapes, both given to me in Athens and arriving in Minneapolis by mail, I had to develop an inventory system. I started keeping track of all the songs on index cards. I made note of the song title, song length, tempo, how each one began and ended, and a brief description of the song's style. It was a months-long process. When all was said and done, I'd sorted through more than 600 songs.

This was timeless stuff of remarkable quality. I wanted to put out as many of the songs as we possibly could. Paul Stark and I decided on a package that was enticing, practical, and affordable: a double CD with a thirty-two-page booklet that we could sell for the price of a single disc.

So, my task now was to whittle the track list down to something in the neighborhood of seventy-ish minutes per disc, and I reveled in the process. I got it down to forty-two songs: forty-one originals and one cover, of Neil Young's haunting "On the Beach." The total running time was two hours, fifteen minutes, and forty-nine seconds. Logan, Kelly, and the other enablers approved my construct, so the opus was set. But we still needed a title. Mr. Logan, what shall we call it? He replied with one word: *Bulk*.

It was an interesting time in Twin/Tone's history. We had twenty-six releases in 1993, and only three of them were on Twin/Tone proper: Zuzu's Petals' *When No One Is Looking*, Beyond Zebra's *Mad Mad Mother*, and the music for Theatre de la Jeune Lune's adaptation of *Children of Paradise* by Chan Poling. On Medium Cool, we put out titles by Marlee

MacLeod, the Dashboard Saviors, and Slim Dunlap. Paul Stark's Twin/ Tone expansion included distributing other labels, and the other twenty releases fell into that category.

In September, I moved out of the apartment above Oar Folk and into my own one-bedroom a few blocks away. An office move was brewing as well. Paul Stark had decided to get out of the recording studio business, sold the building at 26th and Nicollet, and went on the hunt for another location. That fall, Paul purchased an old funeral home at 2217 Nicollet Avenue South, just down the street from the previous office.

I timed my next trip to LA to coincide with the Slim Dunlap Band doing a promotional appearance at the Virgin Mega-Store on November 6. With Slim being an ex-Replacement, and the combined promotional efforts of Twin/Tone and Restless, we had a good turnout of fans and music industry folks. Terry Reid came with his two young daughters, and I was especially excited to meet him. I also ran into a woman originally from Minnesota, Maria Garza. She introduced herself and her companion, Jennifer Menard. Maria did music licensing for EMI-Capitol, and Jennifer had a similar position in the film and TV department at the Warner Music Group. They were both huge Replacements fans, and we had a lovely chat.

On January 23, 1994, Paul Stark and I drove from Minneapolis to Royal Center, Indiana, to meet Terry and Jamie Rouch—or "The Roach Brothers," as they were called—the farmers who had been Logan and Kelly's four-track recording inspiration. A few years earlier, through a musician friend, Logan and Kelly had heard several crude but ingenious home recordings Terry and Jamie had made and thought, *Hey, let's try that ourselves.* Logan and band were driving up from Athens to meet us, and we planned on doing some last-minute new recordings we hoped to add to Logan's *Bulk* project. Because the Roach Brothers had been so influential, Logan wanted them properly represented on his first album. Jamie had set up an eight-track ADAT recording system in the barn studio, which he called Big as a Barn Studios. Paul was on hand to help with the technical side of things and make sure everything was up to industry standards. It was a wonderful, if rustic, environment to work in, smack-dab in the middle of acres of cornfields. We recorded a number of songs that week, two of which made it onto *Bulk*.

The project was coming together nicely and was getting some notice. The Minneapolis weekly *City Pages* mentioned it, and I was surprised to discover how far its reach went. The spring before *Bulk* was released, I was in New York having lunch with *Rolling Stone* senior writer and contributing editor Chris Mundy. I met him at the magazine's HQ, and as we were heading out to eat, we passed the office of senior editor David Fricke. I'd known David since 1986, when he was first writing for *Rolling Stone* and came to Minneapolis to interview Paul Westerberg. I waved as I went by David's open door, but he stopped me and asked, "Hey, do you have any of that Jack Logan stuff with you?" I was surprised he even knew about the project. David said he'd read about it in *City Pages* and was intrigued. I did indeed have some of Logan's recordings with me and pulled out a couple of cassettes from my backpack. He pointed to his tape deck, and I played him a handful of tracks. His reaction was more than gratifying. He pounded his fist on his desk and said something to the effect of, "This is just the kind of thing I'd love to write about!" Chris also responded enthusiastically to the music. Needless to say, I was beside myself!

On that same trip, I attended a show at Irving Plaza with my publicist friend Stacey Sanner, and we bumped into a colleague of hers, Jim Pitt, who was the talent booker for the Conan O'Brien show. As Stacey introduced us, she mentioned I was from Twin/Tone and had signed the Replacements and Soul Asylum, among others. This got Jim's attention, and he asked what I was currently working on. I filled him in on a few things and gushed at length about Jack Logan. He seemed to be listening quite intently, and I thought to myself, *Holy cow, he might be considering putting Logan on TV!*

While Logan's project was gaining momentum and taking a lot of my attention, other Twin/Tone releases were hitting the stores and airwaves in 1994. Duane Jarvis's album *D.J.'s Front Porch* came out in

March. I'd met D.J. when he was playing guitar in Lucinda Williams's band, and I knew of his previous work with John Prine and Dwight Yoakam. He'd given me a demo tape, and I loved his songs. We held the LA record-release show at the famed Palomino Club in North Hollywood on the eighth. A couple weeks later, on March 26, we had a show at the 7th Street Entry in Minneapolis. Local Twin Cities writer Jim Walsh did an advance cover story on the album and the concert for the *St. Paul Pioneer Press* entertainment section, and we had a great turnout there as well. D.J. was transitioning from sideman to front man, and he and the band put on a strong performance for the Minneapolis crowd.

In early June, the Dashboard Saviors headed to Royal Center to let the barn–studio vibe seep into album number three for them. They spent a week there getting the basic tracks recorded. Most everything, including the vocals, was captured live, which left only a handful of overdubs to do in Athens. The mixing was completed in the fall, and the album was slated for an early 1995 release. They titled it *love sorrow hatred madness*.

Finally, on June 14, 1994, Jack Logan's *Bulk* was released, and the response was pretty incredible. Just ahead of its release, *Billboard* editor Timothy White wrote a raving endorsement in a full-page story in his weekly editorial, "Music to My Ears":

> Jack Logan writes songs the way he fixes electric motors: with offhand proficiency, in the company of chums, and at a frightening clip. . . . There is gentleness in Logan's unassuming instinct, literature in its agility, and thunder in his grasp of grace among the grotesque. Marking the full-blown arrival of an exceptional commiserator, *Bulk* will stand with the most substantial rock 'n' roll of this decade.

Michelle Roche headed up the publicity department at Restless Records and was the main point person handling Logan at the time. She was from Georgia, and we knew a lot of the same people. She loved Logan's music and worked hard on his behalf. David Fricke wrote a full-page feature in *Rolling Stone* that, like Timothy White's piece, made many people in the music industry and the general public take notice.

Getting Jack Logan and Liquor Cabinet on the road took some doing, but eventually Keith Sarkisian from the William Morris Agency became their booking agent and did a remarkable job getting dates in good clubs for a virtually unknown band. We started slowly, with one showcase in LA and four on the East Coast. The LA show was at the Mint on September 29. The core of the band—Logan, Kelly Keneipp, and Dave Philips—flew out from Georgia, and we recruited LA resident Duane Jarvis to sit in on bass. There was no drummer for this gig, but it was a terrific performance nonetheless. Logan, Kelly, and Dave had never been to LA before, so it was fun to show them around. These small-town southern boys were thrilled to be in this massive city. I'll never forget driving one evening and pointing out that we were at the famous intersection of Hollywood and Vine. Kelly piped up from the back seat and said in his rural southern accent, "This month Hollywood and Vine. Next month, Times Square!"

The next month, we did, indeed, visit Times Square. The whole band made the trip this time, including bassist Eric Sales and drummer Aaron Phillips. We were invited to have lunch with Timothy White, and he took us to a private club near his *Billboard* office. He was a big fan of the *Bulk* album, and he kept showering the band with praise. Timothy must have suspected the band thought he was just being overly polite and he needed to drive the point home. In one of the most amazing moments I've witnessed in my career, Timothy raised his arms in the air and said, "I don't think you guys get it: You're like Zeppelin to me!" The band sat in stunned silence for a few seconds before thanking him profusely. They had gotten the message: He wasn't just being nice; he genuinely loved their music.

Late that October I was back in LA for work obligations. My timing was strategic, as an incredible run of events was happening that week.

Big Star was playing two shows at the House of Blues on November 1, and I was dying to see them again. In addition, there was a Brian Wilson Tribute at the Morgan-Wixson Theater, an Alex Chilton solo show at McCabe's, and Beatles producer George Martin was giving a lecture on the making of *Sgt Pepper's* at the Hollywood Palace.

Perhaps even more exciting, my new friend Jennifer Menard asked me if I wanted to see Big Star do a taping for *The Tonight Show* on Halloween. *Are you kidding me?!* I got into LA early on the thirty-first and met up with Jennifer. She had passes for the show, and we were joined by her friend Maria and former Replacements soundman Mike Bosley. Getting to see Big Star's first national TV performance in person was thrilling. Introducing the band, Jay Leno said: *"Rolling Stone* magazine called our next guests the missing link between the Beatles and the Replacements. Ladies and Gentlemen, Big Star!"

I guess we'd all missed that quote when it appeared in *Rolling Stone,* and the four of us did double takes. *What did he just say?!* Then the band launched into "In the Street" from their first album, *#1 Record.* After the taping I called Westerberg and told him about Leno's intro. He didn't jump up and down or anything, but I could tell he was flattered. Suffice to say, all the above events were much more than memorable. I was also enjoying spending all this time with Jennifer.

In early December, we received the big news: Jack Logan and Liquor Cabinet were invited to appear on *Late Night with Conan O'Brien* on January 6. Naturally, we accepted the offer and began making plans to get everyone to New York. I talked to Keith Sarkisian about booking a concert for the band while we were in Manhattan, and he got a slot at CBGB for January 7. Everything was falling into place quite nicely.

We had a 10:00 AM call at the Conan studio. The sound check went well, and the band looked so cool on camera. They were going to perform "Female Jesus." The lyric was wonderfully poetic, and the song featured an especially emotive guitar solo by Dave Philips. The taping, in front of a live audience, was nerve-racking, but it went off without a hitch.

On Saturday, everybody went their own way in the early part of the day, exploring the city, before we met back at the hotel and headed to the club for sound check. The band had never been to CBGB before and were jazzed to see the legendary place. They had an early set, so the crowd wasn't huge, but it was respectable.

We were taken by limo to Newark Airport the next morning, courtesy of the O'Brien show. I flew to Atlanta with the band, and I spent a day in Athens making plans for the year ahead with the Saviors, Marlee, and Logan. Then I flew back to Minneapolis on January 10 to clean my apartment for an impending visitor. Jennifer and I had started dating in December, and she was coming to stay for the long Presidents' Day weekend.

On February 6, I met Logan and the band in Royal Center to begin work on album number two. Once again, the players brought demos for Logan. This time I observed firsthand how it was done: Logan listening intently with pen in hand while a music bed was played, seeming to pull lyrics out of thin air. While I'd witnessed a bit of their songwriting process over the past few months, to be present at the moment of spontaneous creation for an album's worth of songs was wondrous to me. It reminded me of something Logan had said to a journalist from *Interview* magazine. When asked how he was able to write lyrics so fast, he said, "I don't know; I guess I paid attention in English class."

Logan and the Liquor Cabinet recorded for six days, getting all the basic tracks, lead vocals, and overdubs done. It was like an assembly line, with songs coming off the conveyer belt, one after the other. We wrapped the sessions on February 12 and headed back to our respective homes with an album's worth of songs in the can—seventeen of them, to be exact.

That spring, I hit the road with Logan and the band for their first substantial tour. It kicked off in Cincinnati on May 1 and ended on May 13 in Chapel Hill, North Carolina. It was a great group of people to travel with. Kelly and I split the driving, and the other four kept busy listening to their Walkmans most of the time. The last four shows were with the Saviors—a big love-fest between the two bands of old friends. They also had a healthy sense of competition, which made for some spirited performances.

Late in the evening on February 18, 1995, I received a phone call from Maggie with excruciating news: Bob Stinson had passed away. My heart sank. It came as a shock, but it was not completely unexpected. He'd been walking a high wire for a long time. We found out later that he died of organ failure, and the longtime drug and alcohol use was a contributing factor. He was only thirty-five years old.

Bob's death took a long time to process. I barely remember the funeral; it's just a series of cloudy fragments in my mind. Anita Stinson asked me to do the eulogy, but I knew there was no way I could keep my composure. Our friend Jim Walsh did it.

So many memories: Bob's habit of actually patting himself on the back after a guitar solo he thought he'd done a particularly great job on; or whenever I was worried we were going to be late for a show, no matter what day it was, he'd say, "Don't worry, it's only Tuesday"; or if someone thought they'd lost something, he'd say, "If it was up your ass you'd know where it was." When we were on the road and checking out from a hotel, often Bob was nowhere to be found; all we had to do was look for the nearest phone booth, and there he was, on the phone with his wife Carleen. We rarely did anything touristy when on tour, but one time when we were driving past Niagara Falls, we decided to stop. Everyone got out of the van to admire the spectacular site, but when we were ready to leave, Bob had disappeared. Sure enough, there he was—on the phone, somehow drinking a beer, smoking a joint, and urinating in the phone booth, all at the same time. I also fondly recall going to see the movie *This Is Spinal Tap* with Bob and some other folks, and Bob thinking it was all too real and maybe not exactly getting that it was a "mockumentary." Or Bob, Chris Mars, Monty Lee Wilkes, and me touring Graceland together. I have sweet memories of Bob too, such as when he called and broke the news to me that Ricky Nelson had died because he knew I loved Ricky.

Though he had a hard life in so many ways, and he could be difficult, most of my time with him was really fun. Bob was as unique an individual as I've ever encountered. I found him endlessly interesting. When I think of him, it always brings a smile. As his bandmate Paul used to say, Bob was a gentle giant. I loved the guy, and I know he loved me.

Things were going great with Jennifer and me, but we didn't like living so far apart. Since her job at Warner was firmly based in LA, and mine had presented the possibility of working there, it seemed the only viable option was for me to move to Los Angeles. With me in and out of town so much, she did the bulk of the work searching for a place for us to live, and she was good at it. She found us a two-bedroom duplex with an upstairs-downstairs floorplan in a 1920s-era Tudor-style structure in West Hollywood.

I finally up and moved to Los Angeles on Saturday, July 29, 1995. Most of my belongings were being shipped cross-country by truck. I had Sunday to unpack, get acclimated to the new place, and relax a bit before going in to Restless on Monday to set up my new office.

Working in the Restless building was all positive in the beginning. Though I missed Paul Stark and others back home, I was excited to be in a new environment. I felt very welcomed, and the staff seemed happy to have me in-house. The company infrastructure was more formal than at Twin/Tone, and the finances were sturdier. My strongest allies there were Liz Garo, who was transitioning from publicity to A&R; Michelle Roche in publicity; Wendy Erikson, the receptionist and later PR assistant; and Lyndsey Parker, the marketing manager.

By this time, I had four artists on Medium Cool: the Dashboard Saviors, Slim Dunlap, Marlee MacLeod, and Jack Logan. (The Leatherwoods had broken up, and Ticks and D.J. were no longer on the label.) With three of the bands based in Athens and one in Minneapolis, I was doing a lot of traveling. Label president Joe Regis referred to Restless as a "mini-major," and budgets reflected that attitude, so I was pretty free to travel as needed. I was also a thrifty traveler. I'd never had a real expense account before, so I was used to eating on the cheap, plus I didn't drink, and I was an avid user of public transportation. I mostly bunked with friends in whatever city I was working in, only staying in hotels when necessary.

Living in LA also reignited my relationship with Tommy Stinson. He had moved there in 1991, and life had been a bit up and down for him. We'd been so tight in the early 'Mats days, maybe it was inevitable that we would eventually come back together, and our newfound proximity facilitated that. His first post-Replacements band, Bash & Pop, had broken up, and he was in the process of putting a new one together. We started meeting for lunch in the fall of '95, and bygones quickly became bygones, and any hard feelings from the tempestuous 'Mats days evaporated. We talked about the new songs he was writing. Some major label folks were definitely keeping an eye on Tommy, and with the right lineup and a strong batch of songs, it seemed like a deal with one of them was possible.

A few weeks later, with a solid four-piece called Perfect in place, Tommy and band headed to Calabasas and producer Don Smith's studio. Don had produced the Bash & Pop album in 1992, and Tommy and Don were fast friends. I went out for one of the sessions and was impressed by what I heard. Tommy's plan was to record an EP to generate label interest for a full-length LP.

Besides the rockier songs, Tommy also had some fantastic material that was of a more introspective, non-rock kind. I floated the idea of him doing a solo album with Medium Cool while working on the band thing, and he was into it. He gave me a few demos, and there was one song in particular that I found very moving. It was called "Hate It," a melancholy tune with a gorgeous melody and one of the sweetest

vocals he'd ever done. A promising start for an album! When a major
label deal for Perfect began to look less promising, we opened the door
to conversations about doing the band record with Medium Cool as
well. The folks at Restless were especially excited about signing another
ex-Replacement with a tour-ready band. Perfect had finished five of
the Don Smith recordings, and we thought, *Why not stick with the EP
idea?* It would be a great way to launch the group and give them something to help promote live dates. Unfortunately, this meant the solo
album plan was shelved, though we did put "Hate It" on a Restless
Records sampler, where it got some notice.

Meanwhile, Slim was slowly working on his second album with
Minneapolis producer–engineer Tom Herbers, as well as recording at
home in his basement studio. I always found Slim's music so uniquely
him. I couldn't wait to hear the final results.

January brought the release of the second Jack Logan album, *Mood
Elevator*, featuring Liquor Cabinet. We had a solid run of dates in February starting in Boston, going down the East Coast, and finishing
at the prestigious Mountain Stage radio show in Charleston, West Virginia. Logan shared the bill with Mike Scott of the Waterboys and
Once Blue.

In March, Perfect, Logan, and the Liquor Cabinet boys did some tour
dates together, working their way to and from the South by Southwest
music festival in Austin. The two groups bonded, and after seeing some
of Logan's drawings, Tommy asked him to do the cover art for their
upcoming EP, *When Squirrels Play Chicken*. Logan obliged with a fantastic, full-color cartoon. I love that kind of incestuous behavior between
labelmates! The release date for Perfect's debut was set for July 9. It
made quite a splash at retail and in the press. One of the highlights was
a hidden, unlisted track of the band covering Elton John's "Crocodile
Rock," which had been recorded in a live session for Minneapolis radio
station Rev 105.

The second Slim Dunlap album, *Times Like This*, hit stores in October. It was a mix of rockers and some real oddball stuff; I couldn't have

loved it more. The title song is a masterpiece. The band Dramarama offered Slim a number of opening slots all around the northeast, which took him to places like the Stone Pony in Asbury Park, New Jersey, and the Iron Horse in Northampton, Massachusetts. I spent some time with Slim and his band on the road, bringing them to radio stations and record stores between the live shows. Watching Slim talk with fans is a real treat. He is so humble and free with his advice to younger musicians. It's easy to see why he's such a well-loved figure in music.

As Logan continued to garner lots of attention, we started planning a third album. He had been approached by Kosmo Vinyl, a Brit who'd worked with the Clash, the Jam, and Ian Dury. Kosmo had heard Logan's music through a mutual friend and was interested in producing a record for him. He didn't have a production track record, but Logan, Kelly, and I met with him, and we thought he had many ideas that could bring something fresh to the project; he clearly had a creative and unconventional mind. I discussed it with Paul Stark and Joe Regis, and they liked the idea too. We reserved time in January 1997 at Casino Studios in the Little Five Points neighborhood of Atlanta. Kosmo exceeded our expectations. Along with ace engineer Phil Hadaway, Kosmo helped Logan make a more polished record that took some interesting turns, implementing tape speed manipulation and reverse tape effects. It featured most of Liquor Cabinet—Kelly Keneipp on guitar and piano, Dave Philips on guitar, Aaron Phillips on drums—in addition to session man Keith Christopher on bass and special guests like Vic Chesnutt (on trombone!), the Roach Brothers, and Anne Richmond Boston of the Swimming Pool Q's.

On May 25, 1997, Jennifer and I were married—smartest thing I've ever done. Being the non-churchy type I am, Jennifer (a recovering Catholic) was cool with an alternative location for the wedding: the site of Prince's old club in downtown Minneapolis. (It was called Glam Slam when it was Prince's club, but by this time it was the Quest club.) The wedding was quite a to-do. Tommy Stinson was my best man. Steve Klemz and Dave Philips were groomsmen. Our dear friend Kevin Cole—former First Avenue disc jockey and now a programming director and on-air host at KEXP radio in Seattle—was kind enough to spin records at the wedding and reception. Several bands played at the reception, beginning with a solo set from John Critchley (of 13 Engines), followed by local pals Jim and Dave Boquist. Next was Jack Logan, featuring an ad hoc backing group of attendees: Dave Philips and Terry Rouch on guitars, Jamie Rouch on drums, and Steve Brantseg on bass. Perfect were next, and then the Slim Dunlap Band closed the festivities, with a guest appearance by Curtiss A. I'll always be proud of the fact that our party inspired Tommy Stinson to invite Dave Philips to join Perfect and move to LA. Sadly, Dave passed away in 2021. We'd grown very close over the years. He is not only one of my favorite guitar players; he's one of my all-time favorite humans.

Perfect was ready to make a full LP. When we brought up the possibility of doing the album at Ardent Studios in Memphis with Jim Dickinson producing, Restless president Joe Regis didn't balk at the higher budget it would require. Big Star drummer Jody Stephens is the vice president of production at Ardent. He and I are great friends, and it was hilarious negotiating with him on the studio budget—two not-exactly-hard-ass guys crunching numbers. Sessions were booked to start the week before Thanksgiving.

We worked on the record in two segments, before and after the holiday, and I had a ball being at Ardent for this extended period. I felt like this could be Tommy and the band's big break. Perfect were a formidable and cool-looking band, and the songs were the best Tommy had ever written. We all thought three of the songs had serious radio potential: "Better Days," "Turn It Up," and "7 Days a Week."

Besides the excitement of Tommy and the band laying down a dozen or so classic pop-rock songs, I found it illuminating getting to know Jim Dickinson and studio owner John Fry. These were men with a deep knowledge and understanding of both the artistic and the technical sides of recording. John Fry is like a rock star to me. The sound he got on the Big Star records he produced is unparalleled. To this day, when I stand between my speakers and listen to "Thirteen," I marvel at how it feels like you're in the room with Chris Bell and Alex Chilton's acoustic guitars. At Ardent I spent a lot of time in a spare office transcribing Tommy's lyrics, and from time to time John would pop in for a lengthy chat. We first bonded over our shared obsession with the Beatles, and I was delighted when I discovered he was a Sherlock Holmes devotee, like I was. Dickinson was a whole other kettle o' fish. He was one of the most intuitive musical thinkers I have ever been around. He was a master of creating a conducive vibe in the studio, and his almost shamanistic ability to pull extraordinary performances out of artists is the stuff of legend. The Perfect album was wrapped just before Christmas.

In early '98, I was busy making plans for the new Jack Logan and Perfect records. Restless had hired a new radio promotion man a few months prior. He came from the mainstream music world, and we did not see eye to eye. One day, I was called into his office to discuss the Perfect album, and he promptly told me that he didn't hear a "slam dunk at radio." It was such a record biz cliché, I nearly burst out laughing—a true *Spinal Tap* moment, if I've ever had one! I felt differently, of course, but thought it best to take a wait-and-see position. Imagine my surprise when soon after Regis told me Restless had decided not to release either the Perfect or the Jack Logan albums. After the initial Twin/Tone–Restless honeymoon period, I had slowly started to feel that our interests weren't completely aligned. But this was different. To allow us to work so long and hard on these projects and then make an eleventh-hour decision to not release them at all felt like a betrayal.

I broke the news to Logan and Tommy. Logan and the band were disappointed but rolled with it, and the orphaned album eventually found a home at Capricorn Records (thanks to Michelle Roche). Tommy, on the other hand, was pissed off. He disbanded Perfect, auditioned for the bass guitar position in Guns N' Roses, and was hired. Tommy would keep that job for the next sixteen years.

As for me, it was clear I couldn't stay at Restless. The situation with the Logan and Perfect records made things untenable, but I also had to consider that because of the perpetual license deal Restless had with Twin/Tone, if I walked away from Restless I would be leaving behind a significant portion of my life's work, including the first four Replacements albums. But I really had no choice. My time with Restless ended on May 5, 1998.

Over the next couple of months, Paul Stark and I talked at length about what to do next. Paul saw that the music business was headed in a digital direction, and he wanted to quit making CDs and vinyl altogether. I understood and trusted his instincts, but I wanted to look around and see what other kinds of music-related work might be out there for me. We decided to close down Twin/Tone as an active label. We stopped signing new artists and making new records but kept the back catalog available through digital downloads or burn-on-demand CDs.

At the time, the Restless debacle made me angry, but I've since come to terms with it. I'm still as artist-oriented and naive as they come, but I understand business decisions need to be made, that money often dictates, and that my idea of how a record company should operate doesn't always jibe with others' ideas. It's the age-old struggle between art and commerce—to be continued, dammit!

Ten

New West Records:
A New Label in a New Town

In 1998, after my business partner, Paul Stark, and I had repositioned Twin/Tone Records to a strictly back-catalog company, I wasn't sure what to do next—or what I wanted to do next. I was proud of what we'd accomplished but thought maybe it was time for me to try something else.

This transitional period was difficult for me. For twenty-five years, beginning soon after I graduated high school, I'd had three jobs, which overlapped for periods of time. I worked at a record store for ten years, helped run a record label for twenty, and managed a band for six. I'd never had to look for work before. Having moved to Los Angeles in 1995, I was still somewhat new to the city, which made the search more challenging. And being in one of the main centers of the record business, I was competing with many other people for music-related work. I figured I might have an advantage since I had helped lots of folks over the years and thought it was reasonable to expect some reciprocation. I did hear back from several of my colleagues, but I also spent a fair amount of time listening to the phone not ring. It was a tough lesson in humility.

To complicate matters, in early June 1999, my wife Jennifer, our niece Heather, and I were in a nasty car accident. Jennifer took the brunt of it. During our convalescence, Jennifer received a call from Kathleen

Day-Cohen, a photographer who'd taken pictures at our wedding. She told Jennifer she knew a man who lived in LA and had a fledgling record label and was interested in expanding. Kathleen said she thought her friend needed someone like me, and that I needed someone like him. She put us in touch. Her friend was Cameron Strang, a lawyer from Vancouver, Canada. He called and asked if I'd be interested in discussing the possibility of coming to work with him at his label, New West Records. I said I was.

My meeting with Cameron was to be the first time since the accident that Jennifer would be left alone for any length of time. I chose Barney's Beanery, a location that was a short walking distance from our house, and promised Jennifer I wouldn't be gone long.

Cameron and I talked for more than four hours. He cut a striking figure—over six feet tall, handsome, short black hair, and a smile a mile wide. Conversation was easy, and we quickly connected. He admired the work we'd done at Twin/Tone. I was impressed with his knowledge and love of music, his intelligence, and his confidence. Cameron gave me an overview of the artists he'd worked with so far. I asked him what his aim was with New West. He thought about it for a moment, then said, "I'd like to create a place where people can make a living doing what they love to do." His mission statement and what I perceived as palpable sincerity won me over. I told Cameron I was interested but needed to think about it.

When I got home, I raved to Jennifer. I told her I couldn't have been more impressed with Cameron, and only half-jokingly I said, "I'll bet that man could walk into a banker's office and walk out five minutes later with a sack full of cash. He's just the kind of person anyone would want to be in business with!" Taking the job felt right to both of us. After sleeping on it, I called Cameron and accepted his offer. He replied, "Great! Now I have to go and find the money to pay you." That would take a couple of months, but he was as good as his word, something I became accustomed to over the next decade. In the meantime, I familiarized myself with the ten albums Cameron had released so far. I was duly impressed with the quality and the varied styles.

I started working with Cam (as many call him) in September 1999. We formulated future plans for the label and mapped out what our individual roles would be. He would handle the business side of things, we'd share A&R responsibilities, and I'd shop New West's music to movies and TV shows, which would help to pay my salary. Cam's title was president and mine was vice president A&R/film & television licensing. We talked extensively about what kind of artists we'd like to bring into the fold. He asked me to make a wish list. It makes me laugh to think about it now, but I put Vic Chesnutt at the top of that list—there I go again, picking a surefire chart-topper. Cam and I also started going to see live music together. In addition, I was upfront with Cam about two things: I told him I thought it was important to improve album artwork and that the label needed an updated logo design. Luckily, Cam agreed. I felt good about working with someone I could be that candid with.

Just prior to my hire, Cam brought in a temp to help him get organized. Her name was Sharon Cohen, and she soon became our full-time office manager. New West was now a staff of three. Cam had set up an office in his house on Martel Avenue, just south of the vibrant Melrose Avenue shopping corridor, and that's where our alliance began.

In Minneapolis, I'd worked with a tremendous art director named Chuck Hermes. So, when it came time to address New West package design and label logo, he was my first call. Cam looked over Chuck's portfolio and endorsed the idea. We discussed terms, and Chuck became New West's first art director.

Over time, New West came to be known for roots music, though that wasn't planned. The label's first signing and release was punk rock: the Kelly Deal 6000. Two other artists in particular were crucial in establishing the credibility of the label in its early days.

Billy Joe Shaver had been New West's second signing. He was a charming, bona fide Texas hell-raiser and teller of tall tales—not to mention one of the finest songwriters I ever got close to. He wrote classics like "Georgia on a Fast Train," "I'm Just an Old Chunk of Coal," and "Live Forever." Bob Dylan even covered a Billy Joe song called

"Old Five and Dimers Like Me" during the sessions for his 1988 album, *Down in the Groove*. Years later Bob referenced him lyrically in his 2009 song "I Feel a Change Comin' On": "I'm listening to Billy Joe Shaver/ And I'm reading James Joyce."

Stephen Bruton was Cam's next signing. Stephen was a respected guitarist from Fort Worth who'd played with dozens of musicians, including T Bone Burnette, Bonnie Raitt, and Delbert McClinton, but he was best known as Kris Kristofferson's lead guitarist. Stephen was the best ambassador New West ever had. We'd never have been able to pull off subsequent signings like Delbert McClinton or Kris Kristofferson without Stephen vouching for the label.

I don't think I can overstate just how important it was to have two artists the caliber of Billy Joe Shaver and Stephen Bruton on the label so early in its existence. It sent a signal to the industry and fans that New West had savvy musical instincts.

The first project Cam and I worked on together was Tim Easton, a young folk-rock artist from Columbus, Ohio. One Saturday in early 2000 a package arrived with a return address that read: Damon Booth— EMI Publishing. Cam opened it to find Tim's first album, *Special 20*, which had been released on the Columbus-based indie Heathen Records. In the enclosed letter, Damon explained that EMI had signed Tim to a publishing deal and hoped someone at New West would check out his music. Cam was flattered to receive a submission from EMI. He loved what he heard on the CD, and he emailed Damon saying he'd like to talk. When I came in that Monday, Cam played the album for me, and I liked it right away. I chuckle when I think about the series of events: on a Friday, Damon sends Tim Easton packages out to a number of labels. The very next day he gets an email from one of them expressing interest. And then on Monday, he has a conversation with the label's president saying he'd like to offer Tim a recording contract. It doesn't usually work that way, or that quickly, in the record biz.

The first Tim Easton album on New West was *The Truth About Us*. We were lucky to get Joe Chiccarelli, an A-list producer, on board. We recorded basic tracks at Kingsize Sound Labs in Chicago, and through Joe's connections, Wilco's John Stirrat, Jay Bennet, and Ken Coomer came in to play on it. The whole undertaking was a blast, and the album still sounds great to me now. Cam and I helped Tim make a world-class record. We were off to a good start.

In late January, Cam announced he wanted us to move into real office space and asked me to look for something conveniently located. I found a second-floor, three-room suite in Beverly Hills above a small law firm. It was nothing fancy, but we were so dang busy, we barely noticed.

Shortly after our office move, Cam received a phone call from an associate asking for some advice. Jay Woods, who worked with indie label Doolittle Records in Austin, Texas, told Cam the company was struggling, business-wise, and they were looking for a creative solution. Cam, with his wise and fair instincts, said he'd try to help. He mulled it over and saw a way to solve the problem that could be beneficial to both Doolittle and New West. Doolittle had three things that appealed to him: an established infrastructure, solid financing, and a presence in another great music town. Cam proposed a deal whereby Doolittle could be salvaged and absorbed into New West. Doolittle's owner, George Fontaine Sr., was delighted by this unexpected opportunity, and he and Cam became business partners. Doolittle bands and staff were offered the opportunity to stay, though terms would have to change to accommodate New West's more prudent financial model. This didn't suit everyone, and some artists and staff members moved on of their own accord. We announced the new union at Austin's South by Southwest music conference in mid-March of 2000.

One of the Doolittle bands that accepted the new deal with New West was Slobberbone. Front man and primary songwriter Brent Best was a quiet fellow with a fierce talent, and we loved the band's rockin', country-ish punk style. Slobberbone's third album, *Everything You Thought Was Right Was Wrong Today*, was recorded at Ardent Studios in Memphis and released in July.

Overall, 2000 would be a terrific year for New West and in many ways a rebirth. The company was growing fast; we moved into our first formal office in LA; a new logo was unveiled; Cam had a new partner; Doolittle was smoothly merged in; we upped the ante in our artist pursuits; and we hired Georgia-based Jeff Cook to be our radio promotion man.

It was an exciting time. New West had vast potential, like Twin/Tone with sturdier financing. I had twenty years of experience with an indie label while Cam was just beginning, and I was constantly astounded at his ambition. One day he walked into my office and said, "I think we should try to sign Delbert McClinton." It was the first time I doubted Cam. I said, "What a great idea!" while inside I was thinking, *That'll never happen.* But damn if Cam didn't pull it off. Stephen Bruton put Cam in touch with Wendy Goldstein, Delbert's wife and manager. They met in Nashville. Cam's knowledge of Delbert's music, his vision for the potential partnership, and his plans for the label won Delbert and Wendy over. Delbert's first album for New West, *Nothing Personal*, went on to sell 200,000 copies and win the label its first Grammy.

Although working at New West had many great aspects to it, I found getting New West's music into films and TV programs to be a difficult task. My wife, Jennifer, had worked in that field for years and schooled me well. But even with her help, the hurdles I came up against were daunting. Everyone was trying to place their songs into movies and TV shows, so the competition was intense. In addition, most film and TV people told me firmly they couldn't use music with a "twang," and that was something New West had plenty of. We eventually had better luck when we outsourced the work to a company that specialized in song placement. Truth be told, keeping up with A&R was a job and a half in itself. My title eventually shifted to VP of A&R and production.

Doolittle founder George Fontaine Sr. (or "Senior," as he was called) had long championed the Georgia artist Randall Bramblett. Randall's

CV sported names of acts he'd played with like Steve Winwood, Traffic, and Greg Allman. In early 2001, Randall was signed to New West and we released his third solo album, *No More Mr. Lucky*. I loved working with Randall, and I would assist him with five more albums over the next fifteen years.

Yet another bold A&R move on Cam's part was his decision to pursue the Texas trio the Flatlanders. The band was made up of friends from Lubbock: Joe Ely, Jimmie Dale Gilmore, and Butch Hancock. In today's world, they'd be called Americana, but back when they started in the early 1970s, their brainy hybrid of folk, country, and rock was hard to categorize. They'd been offered a contract in 1972 by a small Nashville label, only to have the label back out after an album had been recorded. Bootlegged tapes made the rounds in collector's circles. In 1980, UK label Charly put out seventeen tracks under the title *One More Road*. In 1990, US label Rounder released a thirteen-song version under the header *More a Legend than a Band*. A small cult developed around them. The Flatlanders performed together occasionally over the years, though they always chafed at being referred to as "the legendary Flatlanders."

In 1998, the Flatlanders' most famous fan, Robert Redford, wooed them to record a song for his film *The Horse Whisperer*. This recognition stirred the guys into renewed activity—more frequent live performances, a little recording, and even seeking out management. Word of the band recording again circulated, and when they scheduled a small run of dates in 2001, including the House of Blues in LA, Cam saw an opportunity. He arranged a dinner with the group's new manager, Mark Hartley, at the club before the show. After dinner, Mark walked us into the band's dressing room, introduced us to Joe, Jimmie, and Butch, and left the room. We had a friendly talk and stated our case to the band. Apparently we made a good impression. After a few weeks of discussion and negotiation, the Flatlanders signed to New West. We made five albums with the band over the next decade.

In the summer of 2001 I found myself in an exciting but emotional A&R situation. I was talking to Paul Westerberg on the phone. He mentioned he'd written a large batch of new songs. Then, out of the blue, he said, "You're gonna have to help me sort through them." I was caught off guard. After all, it'd been sixteen years since I'd done that kind of work with Paul. I told him I'd be happy to help. At some point the possibility of working on a record together for New West came up, and we decided the best course of action was for me to speak to Paul's longtime manager, Darren Hill. Paul is generally not a patient man, so things began to move quickly. Darren thought we should meet in person as soon as possible. Cam and I hopped on a plane with less than twenty-four hours' notice to meet Darren at his Rhode Island home.

I enjoyed traveling with Cam. Away from the office our conversations were more free-flowing and allowed us to brainstorm and get to know each other better. When we arrived at Darren's, we quickly got down to business. Darren pulled out Paul's new recordings, separated into acoustic and electric tracks. He proceeded to play us the best new songs I'd heard from Paul in years.

I have to admit, I was a little spooked about the idea of working with Paul again. Regardless of the problems we had in the past, though, we'd always circled back to being friends, and my hopes were high. Cam and I left Rhode Island with twenty-five new Paul Westerberg songs.

Back in LA, we started making plans: giving Paul and Darren our suggestions as to which songs should go on the album; thinking about art directors; working on descriptive copy for the publicity, marketing, sales, and distribution people, etc.

Alas, it wasn't meant to be. Paul and I had been talking regularly during the day, when I was at the New West offices. But one night when I got home from work, Jennifer had a grim look on her face. She said I'd better listen to a voice-mail message. It was from Paul. As it turned out, he had some reservations. He admitted he was calling me at home knowing I wouldn't be there. He said he'd felt some pressure from us that didn't sit well. I immediately flashed on a phone conversation Cam and I had with Darren a day or two before. We'd asked some pertinent questions. Would Paul tour? Would he do press interviews? Would he be willing to perform a song or two at radio stations around the country? We weren't insisting he do any of it; we just needed to know what he would and wouldn't do. Perhaps this was why Paul got cold feet. Or perhaps he just preferred another label's offer. Either way, a deal with New West did not happen. I was disappointed but not brokenhearted.

The fall of 2001 brought another impassioned artist pursuit, and resulted in one of my career highlights. From the moment I first connected with Vic Chesnutt's music, I had dreamed of being his A&R man.

My introduction to Vic was in 1991 on a trip to Athens, Georgia, to visit Peter Buck. One day we were out record shopping and Peter told me that if I bought only one record by a local artist, it had to be Vic's debut album, *Little*. I added it to my stack. It took two or three plays before Vic's highly unconventional freak-folk began to click with me. Specifically, it was a song called "Mr. Reilly." Vic's roughshod voice sang:

Have you heard the news about Joan our ex-newspaper girl?
They found her swinging from a tree and idle
Just a week ago she was beautiful
But now she's rather vile
They found her by the frozen lake
But it wasn't froze enough to skate
But by the look on her face, it must have been awful tempting
They found her in her skates
She was the coldest cadaver in the state
And look at the lake
Not even the ducks are risking it

I think I gasped, teared up, and laughed simultaneously. This was radical stuff. The severe and unvarnished language stopped me in my tracks.

Peter told me that when Vic was eighteen he had been partially paralyzed from a car accident and was confined to a wheelchair for the rest of his life. It was taxing to relearn how to play guitar with limited use of his hands. As Vic described himself, "I'm a quadriplegic from the neck down." As I got to know him, his staunch refusal to be defined by this tragedy made me admire him all the more.

In October 1991, Vic came to Minneapolis for the first time, opening for Bob Mould at First Avenue. Knowing I often housed traveling musicians, my Athens buddy Len Hoffman, manager of the Dashboard Saviors, called and asked if I might be able to provide lodging for Vic and his wife, Tina. They hadn't planned ahead. The Minnesota Twins were playing a World Series home game that night (against the Atlanta Braves), and there wasn't a hotel room to be found within a hundred-mile radius. I told Len I'd be honored to put Vic and Tina up, but reminded him about the steep stairway to my apartment above Oar Folk. Len assured me Vic was very adaptable and that it would be no problem for Tina and me to scoot him up and down the stairs.

Thinking about meeting Vic for the first time still makes me smile. I went to the club a little early, figuring it would be a good idea to say hello before the show. I had just walked into the dressing room and was about to introduce myself when Conrad Sverkerson, First Avenue's long-suffering stage manager, came in to tell the Georgia natives that the Braves had just tied with the Twins. Vic's response? "Fuck the Braves!" I laughed, Vic looked at me and grinned, and there began our close, nearly twenty-year friendship.

Intros taken care of, I exited the backstage area and went out front to watch Vic perform live. The lights were dimmed, and the big video screen that doubled as a curtain went up. There was Vic, alone in the middle of that big stage with a gut-string guitar in his lap and a glove with a pick glued into it on his right hand. He opened with a song from *Little* called "Speed Racer." A minute or so into it he sang:

The idea of divine order is essentially crazy
The laws of action and reaction are the closest thing to truth in the
   universe

So don't try to spray me with your archaic rites of soul
Your vision is a biological one. I can dodge the thunderbolts
And scratch out an existence on this glorious but simple plane
I'm not a victim!
I'm not a victim!
I am intelligent, I am intelligent!
I'm not a victim!
I'm not a victim!
I am an atheist, I am an atheist!

I had heard the song before, but seeing him do it live made me feel like I was hearing it for the first time. It was the first of many, many times Vic left me speechless. He was a provocateur of the first order. And it increased my appreciation for his art to see that he was as powerful live as he was on record.

Len Hoffman had been right—it was no problem to get Vic up the stairs when we got back to my apartment. I can still hear Vic's voice as he wheeled himself into my music room. Seeing a picture of Leonard Cohen pinned to my wall, he shouted, "Lenny! Lenny! Oh, I love Lenny!" Surprise, surprise—we stayed up till dawn talking and listening to music.

Over the next few years I was in Athens often working with other musicians, and that proximity allowed me to spend a lot of time with Vic. In 1995, as he worked on what would become his masterpiece, *Is the Actor Happy?*, I attended several of the recording sessions at producer John Keane's studio. And we spent many nights at Vic's house, talking into the wee hours about music and books and life and watching the fireflies from the screened-in porch in his backyard. I was ecstatic to discover that he seemed as interested in working with me as I was in working with him. For a number of reasons, though, it would take some time for that to happen. For one thing, he was under contract to an indie label out of Santa Monica, California, called Texas Hotel Records, which put out Vic's first three records and would release *Actor* later in the year.

In our initial New West planning meeting in 1999, I told Cam the first artist I thought we should go after was Vic Chesnutt. Cam was game. Early the next year I approached Vic expressing our interest. Vic was unsure about going with a company that had such a short track record. This was too bad, because his next album was *Left to His Own Devices*, a career high point. I didn't give up, and a year later we resumed our talks. This time it was different. We had expanded our company to include an office in Austin, Texas; we had made an acclaimed Tim Easton album with venerable producer Joe Chiccarelli and members of Wilco; and we'd won a Grammy for our first release by Delbert McClinton. I could tell Vic had revised his thinking. So, Cam and I flew to Atlanta and spent two days in Athens with Vic, discussing the possibilities and sharing a few meals. It was especially fun for me to show Cam around the town that meant so much to me, and one that has spawned so much extraordinary music.

Over the next few months, we ironed out the details, and in January 2002 we signed Vic to New West. It was a big month for me. My son, Autry, was born on the twelfth. Becoming a father for the first time and signing Vic Chesnutt—life was pretty dang good!

Then began the process of choosing the songs Vic would record. I'd known for years that he was a prolific writer, but experiencing it up close was overwhelming. He actually said to me, "I have about a hundred songs ready to go, but if you don't like any of those, I'll write you some more."

After considering producer options, we approached Mark Howard, a protégé of Daniel Lanois, and he leapt at the opportunity. Mark recorded Vic's album in LA with his studio installation set up inside the grand ballroom at the Paramour, a stunning, twenty-three-room mansion built in 1923 atop the hills of what became the album's namesake, Silver Lake. Mark is an inspirational man to work with. Technically he's a mastermind, but he also puts a lot of heart into his approach. Mark recruited several amazing musicians to back Vic: drummer/percussionists Mike Stinson and Don Heffington, keyboard ace Patrick

Where it began: my music room in the basement of my parents' house in Minnetonka, Minnesota, 1973. *Photo by the author*

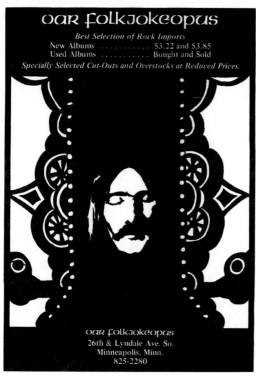

Oar Folkjokeopus record store at Lyndale Avenue and 26th Street in Minneapolis was a destination for music fans of all stripes. *Photo and print ad from the author's collection*

At Oar Folk soon after I started working there in 1973. *Author's collection*

Former New York Dolls front man David Johansen at Oar Folk, July 2, 1978. Left to right: employee Mike Morris, me, Johansen, employee Dan Fults, and store owner Vern Sanden. *Author's collection*

In the DJ booth at Jay's Longhorn, 1978. *Photo by Jay Nolan*

Backstage at the Longhorn with Peter Perrett (right) of the Only Ones,
October 1979. *Photo by Jay Nolan*

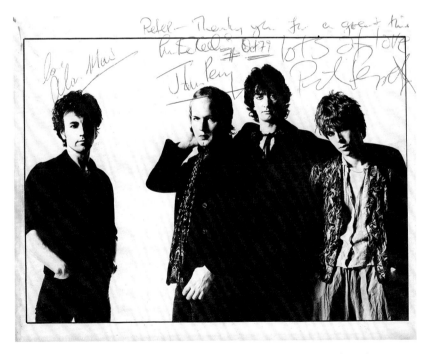

Autographed promo photo of the Only Ones, 1978. Left to right: Alan Mair,
John Perry, Mike Kellie, Peter Perrett. *Author's collection*

The Suburbs performing at the Longhorn, 1978. Left to right: Chan Poling, Michael Halliday, Hugo Klaers, Beej Chaney, Bruce Allen. *Photo by Michael Markos*

Flamingo at the Longhorn, 1978. Left to right: Joseph Behrend (partially cut off), Jody Ray, Robert Wilkinson, Bob Meide, Johnny Rey. *Photo by Paul Lundgren*

The Longhorn marquee for the Suicide Commandos' farewell concerts in 1978. *Author's collection*

At the record-release party for the Suicide Commandos' *Time Bomb* at Treehouse Records in Minneapolis, May 2017. Left to right: me, Chris Osgood, Curt Almsted, Dave Ahl, Steve Almaas. *Photo by Paul Lundgren*

With Paul Stark in Twin/Tone's first office in Minneapolis, 1982. *Photo by Julia Stark*

Poster for the Twin/ Tone compilation *Big Hits of Mid-America Volume Three*

The first demo tape I received from the Replacements in May 1980. *Photo by Kevin Scanlon*

The Replacements onstage at the 7th Street Entry, 1981. *Photo by Laurie Schendel Lane*

With three of the Replacements at my apartment in the Modesto, 1982. Left to right: Paul Westerberg, Tommy Stinson, me, Chris Mars. *Photo by Tim Schuck, courtesy of Dave Carroll*

In Paul Stark's mobile recording truck during the Replacements' *Hootenanny* sessions. Left to right: Paul Westerberg, me, Tommy Stinson. *Author's collection*

Calendar listing for the Replacements' show at Irving Plaza in New York, December 1984. *Author's collection*

Celebrating the Replacements signing with Sire Records, spring 1985. Left to right: lawyer George Regis, Tommy Stinson, Bob Stinson, me, Chris Mars, Paul Westerberg. *Photo by Peter Kohlsaat*

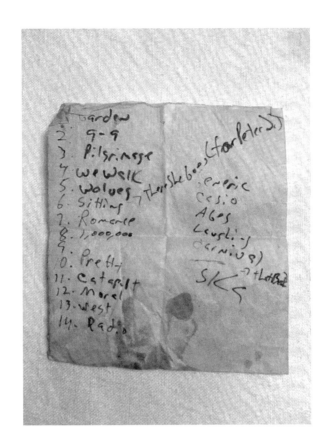

R.E.M.'s set
list—written on
a napkin—from
their April 1982
show at First
Avenue. *Author's
collection*

R.E.M. at Shea Stadium in New York, August 18, 1983, with Peter Buck (left) and Michael Stipe (right). *Photo by Michael Plen, michaelplenphotography .bigcartel.com*

The Dashboard Saviors in my apartment above Oar Folkjokeopus in Minneapolis, 1993. Clockwise from left: Todd McBride, John Crist, Rob Veal, Mike Gibson, and Sage. *Photo by Jay Smiley*

photo by: Jill McLean

THE LEATHERWOODS
Todd Newman - Tim O'Reagan

Medium Cool Records

Medium Cool is manufactured and distributed by Twin/Tone Records

A Medium Cool promo photo for the Leatherwoods, 1992. *Photo by Jill McLean*

At the Rykodisc office in Minneapolis during a Ticks recording session, 1992. Left to right: me, coproducer Brian Paulson, Erick Hubbard, Tom Hicks, session man Slim Dunlap, and Eric Fisher. *Photo by Jay Smiley*

The mighty Slim Dunlap, 1993. *Photo by Dave Biljan*

Jack Logan performing with Perfect at Jennifer and my wedding reception at the Quest Club in Minneapolis, May 25, 1997. Left to right: Marc Solomon, Jack Logan, Tommy Stinson. *Author's collection*

New West Records founder Cameron Strang at the Austin, Texas, offices in 2001. *Photo by the author*

With Daniel Romano and the Trilliums at Joshua Tree National Park, October 2015. Left to right: Daniel Romano, Ian Romano, me, Kay Berkel, Kenny Meehan, and Roddy Kuester. *Photo by Roddy Kuester*

With Terry Katzman at
Hi-Fi Hair & Records
in Minneapolis, 2017.
Author's collection

With my wife, Jennifer,
in North Hollywood,
May 2023. *Photo by
Jennifer Jesperson*

With my son, Autry, in
Tulsa, Oklahoma,
during our pilgrimage
to the Bob Dylan
Center in March 2023.
Photo by Tate Wittenberg

Warren, bassist Daryl Johnson, and guitarist Doug Pettibone. Vic and Tina lived on the estate while recording, and it was an incredible place to work for a couple of weeks. And in the bigger picture: holy crap, I was doing A&R for Vic Chesnutt!

The *Silver Lake* album came together well. All of the players connected with Vic in a way that inspired strong performances. Many of Mark's suggestions for the songs' arrangements—multi-voice backing vocals, offbeat instrumentation, and epic buildups—added a production value to the tracks that hadn't been present on Vic's previous albums. Vic also worked harder than ever before on his lead vocals, which brought an uncharacteristic polish to *Silver Lake*.

Working on new material with Vic was my dream, but I couldn't stop thinking about how unfortunate it was that his first four albums had gone out of print. The label, Texas Hotel, had closed, but the owners were very protective of the masters. They had turned down a number of suitors who wanted to buy or license the recordings. Through Vic, I'd gotten to know label co-owner Susan Farrell, and she knew I cared deeply for Vic and those records. I asked her about the possibility of New West purchasing the masters. I gave her my word that New West would take good care of them. In the end, she trusted me, and the deal was done. Vic and I then spent the better part of a year digging through all the demos, outtakes, and other related recordings for a set of expanded reissues, ending up with twenty-six extra tracks in all. The four albums were released simultaneously in June 2004. I couldn't be more proud of the result.

In 2005 we did a new studio album with Vic entitled *Ghetto Bells*. It was recorded at Don Heffington's home studio in the Los Feliz Hills of LA. Produced by John Chelew, it featured the immense talents of Van Dyke Parks (piano, accordion, organ, arrangements) and Bill Frisell (guitar, thumb piano). *Ghetto Bells* is darker and sparser than *Silver Lake*, and I consider it one of Vic's best.

The following year Vic began working on his next album, *North Star Deserter*, with producer–engineer–musician Howard Bilerman and a consort of Montreal musicians revolving around the experimental ensemble God Speed You Black Emperor. But for the previous few months I'd had a nagging feeling. New West had gotten so busy it couldn't give an outlier like Vic Chesnutt enough attention. And not everyone at the label connected with his challenging and often blatantly uncommercial music. In early 2007 I called Vic and told him I no longer thought New West was the right home for him. I explained he would be better off with a smaller, boutique label that could devote more attention to his music. Vic had sensed it himself but said he needed some time to think it over. On January 19, I received an email from him saying he agreed with me and that "Our noble experiment at New West has run its course." Sometimes the business of music can be heartbreaking.

Less than three years later, on Christmas Day 2009, Vic died after taking an overdose of muscle relaxants. He'd attempted to take his own life more than once in the past, so as devastating as the news was, it was not a complete surprise. Earlier that month, we had hung out when he was in LA on tour, and he seemed in good spirits. But I knew he'd long been despondent over his medical bills and his essentially being "uninsurable" due to his quadriplegia. I loved him like a brother, and his music had a profound effect on me. I miss him dearly.

In early 2002, new recruit Mary Jurey joined us in New West's LA office. Mary was a terrific addition to the company, and we quickly became great friends. She was a real go-getter and joined the label as our LA office manager, but she would go on to do so much more.

It wasn't easy to get New West to sign the artists I championed. Among those I was unable to get Cam to agree to were A. A. Bondy, the Walkmen, Nathaniel Rateliff, Bahamas, Hurray for the Riff Raff, Dan Kelly, Leslie and the Badgers, and the Parson Red Heads. Cam kept a very tight lid on A&R and had a very fixed idea of what would be successful. Even George Fontaine Sr. had trouble signing acts he thought worthy, and he was funding the label! Our release schedule was full with artists Cam had signed. The production work on those albums kept me plenty busy, and since I loved most of them and the whole record-making process, I was okay with that.

Of course, I did manage to get some artists added to New West's roster that made strong albums artistically and were successful in a business sense. Top among them were San Francisco's Chuck Prophet, who, in 2002, hit the top ten on the Triple-A (adult album alternative) radio format with his song "Summertime Thing," a first for Chuck and the label; and Australian Ben Lee, who at one time was New West's highest-grossing artist in film and TV licensing.

A significant new acquisition for New West occurred in early 2003. Drive-By Truckers came to us via Ken Levitan and his company, Vector Management in Nashville. DBT had been hard at it since 1998. The band self-released the epic, double concept album *Southern Rock Opera* in 2001, but when it garnered a landslide of positive press and public reaction, they found it hard to keep up with demand, and so they signed with the Nashville-based Lost Highway Records to take over production and distribution. Later the next year, after starting a follow-up album, DBT parted ways with Lost Highway. Ken then reached out to Cam regarding DBT's availability in early 2003. Coincidentally, I had just caught a raucous performance by the band at the Troubadour and raved about it to Cam.

After signing DBT, New West did a deal with Lost Highway for the masters of the album *Decoration Day* and released it in June 2003. This album was particularly significant for the band because it was the first with new member Jason Isbell. To have a frontline as strong as Patterson Hood, Mike Cooley, and Isbell made the group more substantial than ever. We did many projects together: three more albums; reissues of the band's first two albums; two live DVD projects; a rarities set; a double best-of compilation; and solo albums from Hood and Isbell. Part of the fun was working with their forever-producer, David Barbe, one of the true good guys in rock 'n' roll. Sadly, the business side of the relationship between band and label became strained, and the Drive-By

Truckers left New West in 2009. They're a hardworking band, I liked their music, and I was proud to support the political and social activism of their lyrics. I was sorry to see them go.

Cam had shocked me in the past with his ability to bring artists with the stature of Delbert McClinton and the Flatlanders to New West, and when he told me that we were signing John Hiatt, I was ecstatic. I had been a fan of Hiatt's work for many years, and this meant a lot to me. Artist, management, and label had an uncommonly symbiotic connection, and it's gratifying to know that New West's work with Hiatt continues to this day.

Midway through 2003, New West pulled off one of its greatest coups. We acquired the rights to commercially release the *Austin City Limits* TV shows. Many companies had tried to license or buy ACL's catalog over the years, but leave it to Cam to close the deal. They'd been on the air for thirty seasons and had more than 400 shows in their archive. Most of the concerts ran roughly ninety minutes but had been edited into half-hour programs for television, which meant New West could present them in their entirety for the first time on DVD, CD, and vinyl and digitally. The ACL archive featured a treasure trove of artists ranging from Johnny Cash to Willie Nelson to Norah Jones. The series was very successful and a large feather in New West's cap.

The ACL deal required expansion for New West, both in additional staff and a larger office to house us all. Cam negotiated to buy a 4,000-square-foot building in Beverly Hills, just a few blocks west of where our current office was. We had it remodeled to suit our needs and moved in in the spring of 2004. It was an inspiring office space with high ceilings and a light, airy feel. We had a small recording studio built in the back, which allowed us to cut demos with artists and do various types of audio production work without incurring the costs of a separate recording facility elsewhere.

Basic sales and distribution duties were handled by Jay Woods and his team in Austin. Cam felt that a formal head of sales, based in the LA office, was in order, and he hired former DreamWorks marketing man

Steve Rosenblatt as director of sales and marketing. Since the beginning, New West's publicity had been outsourced to Mark Pucci Media in Atlanta. Mark was like family to us, but Cam wanted to bring the job in-house. Mark chose not to make the move to LA, so we parted ways. In his place we hired Traci Thomas, who had run her own publicity firm in Nashville.

Our relationship with manager Ken Levitan continued to bear fruit. The next group he pitched to us was the rockin' country outfit Old 97's. Those guys were a joy to make records with. They're still together, with the same lineup they've had for thirty years. Why they haven't had a hit record yet is a complete mystery to me. Also thanks to Mr. Levitan, we signed Buddy and Julie Miller. Julie was reclusive and not always directly involved with the records we made with Buddy, but she always contributed material, and her songwriting had a big impact on me. And what can one say about Buddy? His boundless musicality is matched by his noble character. I handled his A&R, and we had a great rapport.

I guess I was getting used to it by 2005, but in yet another canny move, Cam signed Dwight Yoakam. Being the vocal-centric music fan that I am, I was thrilled—what a singer that man is! He is also a die-hard music nut, of many different genres. New West did two studio albums with Dwight—an album of originals called *Blame the Vain* and a collection of Buck Owens songs titled *Dwight Sings Buck*—as well as a greatest hits album, and we reissued two of his older albums that had gone out of print.

I mentioned earlier what a terrific ambassador Stephen Bruton was for New West over the years. In 2005, he pulled his trump card and told his former boss, Kris Kristofferson, that New West would love to make records with him. A deal was struck. Don Was produced. I'll never forget the first meeting we had with Kris. Cam, Don, and I were sitting in New West's conference room. I had my back to the door when Kris walked in. Before I laid eyes on him, I heard his voice and completely lost whatever cool facade I'd been trying to muster. All I could think about were those transcendent songs he'd written for Monument Records in the early '70s—"Help Me Make It Through the Night," "Me and Bobby McGee," "Sunday Mornin' Comin' Down." We sold so many of Kris's albums at Oar Folk I still remember their catalog numbers. And there he was, standing tall in faded denim and well-worn boots. When he and I were introduced, I said something like, "I gotta thank you for helping us pay the rent at our record store in Minneapolis back in the day." He laughed heartily, shook my hand, and said, "You're welcome, Peter!"

After the final mixes of Kris's first recordings for New West, *This Old Road*, were delivered, I came up with an idea for a song sequence for the album, and Cam thought it was "the one." We ran it by Kris and Don, and they liked it too. That's the running order on the finished album—a small deed, but something I'm very proud of. We did a second album with Kris in 2009, *Closer to the Bone*, and it was another collection of beautiful and poetic folk ruminations. Kris was in his seventies by this time, but damn if he didn't tour hard. His wife, Lisa, managed him, and they were both gracious and a pleasure to deal with.

By 2006, we had a fairly sturdy staff in place at New West but still had some growing to do. Herb Agner came in to take over marketing and operations, and he brought in Mike Ruthig to be marketing director. Herb was a great addition to the staff but left after two years. Mike stayed for nearly nine. David Lessoff came in as VP of business affairs. He'd been a longtime supporter of New West and was a perfect fit. David was also a music fanatic, and he and I became fast friends.

In 2007, we finally took the plunge into vinyl, which was essentially my department. Getting vinyl right is not a simple task, but I'd been at it since 1977 when it was the primary format in the music industry, so I had a leg up. Of all the various elements in record label work, I never feel more qualified than when I'm dealing with the vinyl medium.

Jason Isbell provided our maiden vinyl voyage with his solo debut, *Sirens of the Ditch*. To my ears, the first test pressing came back sounding substandard. Correcting it meant missing our planned release date. But in doing so we set a high standard for New West vinyl right from the start. Jason chose to move to another label for his next solo record, which surprised me. We'd done a good job with *Sirens*, and I felt he and I had a strong working relationship. I can only guess that his leaving had something to do with New West's bumpy relationship with Drive-By Truckers.

Speaking of bumpy relationships, Cam and I experienced a bit of that as well. Some of it was procedural and occurred because of the relentless pace at which we worked. Mostly, though, we clashed over our different approaches to A&R, and I was beginning to feel marginalized.

The way I see it, music is art, and it should be treated it as such. I've always winced whenever I hear label representatives refer to music as "product," or when they see themselves as an artist's boss. I consider it the greatest of privileges to represent an artist and their work.

To me, modern-day A&R is an umbrella term, under which falls several responsibilities. Generally speaking, it includes finding an artist you feel is extraordinarily talented and convincing them your label is the best home for them; supporting them through the process of preparing their music for release; helping with song selection; deciding where to record, mix, and master the music, and with whom; discussing design possibilities for the accompanying artwork; compiling text such as credits, liner notes, acknowledgments, and other pieces for the record; monitoring the budget; and getting it all done on deadline.

My A&R interest always starts with hearing a song I'm so knocked out by that I can't stop myself from pursuing its creator. From there, it's a matter of sorting through a checklist: Are there more songs where that one came from? Is there a solid band in place? What sort of fan base have they built up? Is the artist capable of putting on a knockout live show? Can they handle and commit to a steady touring schedule? Is their vision compatible with mine and the label's? Is the artist in it for the long haul? Can they weather the shitstorm that working in the music business can sometimes be?

As for the talent-scouting part of the process, there's no rule book, of course, and there are many ways to approach it. In basic terms, I'd say it's a combination of instinct and developed skills. I admire A&R people who can pull off some form of objectivity, but I'm not one of them and I don't aspire to be. For me, A&R is purely subjective. I can't not work with my heart. I've spent my life obsessively listening to music—studying it, if you will—and I strongly believe that if I'm over the moon about an artist, a reasonable number of others will be too. I can do exceptional A&R work, but it needs to be with a label where the business serves the art, not the other way around—and I know that not all labels operate that way, nor do I think all labels should.

Those were the guidelines I'd learned and developed over the years. I'd worked with them at Twin/Tone, and from our conversations, I believed Cam was supportive of me continuing to use them at New West. But it ultimately led to conflict.

In the big picture, we made a great team, and he and I complemented each other well. It wasn't a hard-fast rule, but generally Cam would seek out the more established, upper-echelon artists, while I would search for the up-and-comers, the diamonds in the rough, to create a balance whereby sales of the known artists would help to fund the growth of the new ones.

Then, in 2004 or 2005, Cam changed the A&R mandate at New West. It wasn't stated out loud, but the message was clear: We had to find artists that would sell. That's when things got problematic for me. As soon as a dollar sign was put at the top of the list of prerequisites, it was as if my A&R ability had been neutered. Every time I started thinking too much about sales numbers, or whether a band would be profitable, it was like a jinx. I lost my mojo.

What perplexed me most was that I thought the selling was supposed to be done by the sellers—meaning the staff that handles sales, marketing, publicity, and promotion. Why encumber the creative arm of the company with demanding sales concerns? New West wasn't a mainstream top-40 label, and it seemed wrong to me. The A&R person's role is to be the liaison between artist and label. It's important to shield the artist and the A&R person from the business side to some degree. It's a deep-seated belief I share with many who have gone before me. I think Paul Westerberg summed it up best in a May 2013 opinion piece for the *New York Times*: "Aim for the audience's pockets and you'll miss their hearts by a mile."

To my way of thinking, truer words have never been spoken. As I see it, when an artist is signed, the sales and marketing people should take it as a challenge to get the music into the ears of as many people as possible. I'm reminded of an anecdote I heard Tony Bennett tell an interviewer at SXSW:

> My favorite story of all time was the one about Duke Ellington, when he got let go from Columbia. [Columbia Records president] Clive Davis invited Duke into his office one day. "Mr. Ellington, I have some bad news for you," he said. "We are going to have to drop you from the label." "How come?" Duke asked. "Well, you're not selling enough records," Davis replied. Duke said, "I thought I was supposed to make the records, and you were supposed to sell them."

Don't get me wrong though. I understand that a project needs to be financially viable, and I have never suggested signing an artist that I didn't think had the potential to sell.

The shift in Cam's attitude confused me, but I wasn't angry about it. Although we have different mindsets, I have great respect for the man, and I sympathized with the position he was in. I suspected that managing the finances of an independent record label for over a decade had worn Cam down. His whole demeanor around the office changed. Some days there seemed to be a dark cloud over his head. My perception was that much of Cam's unhappiness and frustration stemmed

from the weight of responsibility he was carrying for New West's artists and staff. Cam was up to his neck in something beyond his control:
the turbulence in the music industry brought about by declining sales
of physical music formats, the easy duplication and free sharing of digital music, and the lawlessness of the internet.

Nevertheless, I began to question my position at New West, worrying
I was being asked to do something I couldn't deliver. I was an indie-rock
guy who found himself having to deal with a major label's bottom line.
As if to hammer the point home, around this time I read a quote in
an industry trade magazine: "These days A&R is 80 percent marketing." I started looking for another job.

Then one day, I got a call from Jennifer. She'd just been laid off after
seventeen years as director of film & TV in the Warner Music Group's
licensing department. She wasn't alone—400 other employees were
cut that day—but nonetheless it stung. Suddenly, the thought of me
leaving New West and looking for another job, or going back to school,
was impractical. As I only half-jokingly said at the time, I made the first
adult decision of my life: I had a wife, a son, and a mortgage, and I
needed to hang on to this job.

Though Cam and I didn't always see eye to eye, and the company's
A&R priorities were shifting, Cam gave no explicit indication that he
wanted me to leave New West. More than once in the previous few
years, I'd come right out and asked him if his dark moods had anything
to do with me or my work, but he'd always assured me that was not
the case, and I trusted he was being honest with me. I decided the best
course of action was to keep my nose down, do my job to the best of
my ability, and hope whatever was bothering Cam would be resolved
soon. This continued for the next three and a half years.

In 2007, New West made a huge signing: Steve Earle. Steve's first album
for New West was *Washington Square Serenade*. It was recorded at Electric Lady Studios in New York City and was produced by John King

(Beastie Boys, Beck). The record won the Grammy for Best Contemporary Folk/Americana album. We were incredibly fortunate to have Steve on the label. I'm not sure what appeals to me more about Steve: his music or his intellect. He is one brilliant man.

Earle's manager, Danny Goldberg, soon pitched another interesting project to us. In the early 2000s, Danny's label Artemis Records had released Warren Zevon's final three albums. In the process Danny had gotten close not only with Warren but also with his son, Jordan. After Warren died, Jordan was cleaning out one of his dad's storage lockers and came across something that, Jordan said, "sent a jolt of electricity through my spine": a box containing demos by his dad, including sketches for some of his most iconic songs. There were dozens of reel-to-reel tapes, as well as a huge stack of acetates and test pressings. Danny asked if New West was interested in releasing a selection of them. For Cam and me, that was an easy decision. The result was a sixteen-song CD called *Preludes*, containing what may be the first versions ever committed to tape of classic Zevon songs like "Poor Poor Pitiful Me," "Carmelita," "Hasten Down the Wind," and "Werewolves of London."

Another unexpected windfall came our way in September when I received a call from my friend Michael Nieves. Michael managed Mark Olson, founder of the Jayhawks. He asked if New West was interested in releasing a newly recorded collaboration between Mark and Gary Louris, the other lead singer of the 'Hawks. Mark and Gary hadn't sung together since 1995, when Mark left the band. I'd had a history with these guys in Minneapolis, both because they were regulars of Oar Folk and because Twin/Tone released the Jayhawks' second album, *The Blue Earth*. I told Michael we were interested, hung up, and literally ran into Cam's office with the news. The wheels were quickly set into motion, and New West released the album, *Ready for the Flood*. It's a beautiful record, and it was wonderful to work with old friends.

One of the greatest achievements in New West's history was when we acquired the soundtrack rights for the film *Crazy Heart*. Knowing of

Stephen Bruton and T Bone Burnett's involvement, and of the roots-centric music that would be featured in the movie, Cam doggedly pursued Fox Searchlight Pictures and ultimately convinced them New West was the right home for the project. It was a true feat of diplomacy, and it was well worth the effort. The soundtrack is New West's all-time biggest selling title (more than 600,000 sold). It was also the label's first audio-only release to receive a Gold Record sales award from the Recording Industry Association of America. (Note, nineteen of New West's ACL DVDs have gone Gold or Platinum.)

One of the last projects I brought to New West came to my attention through our old friend Damon Booth, formerly of EMI Publishing. He was now running another publishing company called Notable Music, which had been founded by popular music composer Cy Coleman in 1962. In January 2009, Damon called and asked if I'd listen to some tracks for an all-female-sung Coleman tribute album. I had always loved Broadway/Tin Pan Alley–type songwriting, and I certainly knew a few of the iconic songs Cy had written, like "Witchcraft" (Frank Sinatra), "I'm Gonna Laugh You Right Out of My Life" (Nat King Cole), and "Big Spender" (Peggy Lee). I also loved the idea of New West pushing our boundaries. With vocalists the caliber of Patty Griffin, Madeleine Peyroux, Perla Batalla, and Jill Sobule, not to mention the first recordings by Fiona Apple in five years, the collection sure looked good. When I listened to the tracks Damon sent, I was impressed. But what convinced me was a live show he put together with several of the artists at the intimate Largo club in LA. New West signed the project, called *The Best Is Yet to Come: The Songs of Cy Coleman*. Unfortunately, for reasons I never understood, New West just wasn't able to get behind the album, and it did not do well.

One day near the end of 2010, a truly unexpected thing happened. Cam came into my office, shut the door, and told me he'd been offered a job.

"A job?" I asked. "What do you mean? You're the owner and president of New West. Who offered you a job?"

"Warner Chappell Publishing," he replied.

"Wow! What position are they offering you?" I asked.

"Chairman and CEO."

Warner Chappell is one of the three or four largest music publishing companies in the world. It took me a moment to process this information, but then I thought, *This actually makes total sense.* On top of founding a record label and building a formidable catalog, Cam was involved in successful publishing investments with the likes of Bruno Mars, Brody Brown, and Kings of Leon. It made sense that a company of Warner Chappell's stature would have Cam on its radar. I knew this was an opportunity he couldn't decline. Cam left New West in January 2011, George Sr. became president, and Mike Ruthig was appointed general manager.

Although I would miss Cam on a personal level, I wasn't sure what his departure would mean in terms of my position in the company. George Sr. and I were similar as people, and we'd always gotten along well. Maybe this was for the best.

It was pretty much business as usual for the first Cam-less six months of 2011. I'd long felt that New West needed a GM, and Mike Ruthig fit the bill well. He was smart, I admired his work ethic, and he was a good team leader. He had a way of identifying each staff member's personal strengths and emphasizing them, which invigorated the whole team. Mike also took the initiative of moving the LA office. Cam and I had originally chosen a location in Beverly Hills because it was midway between where he and I lived. Now, most of the staff lived on the east side, so the Media District in Burbank became our new home. We moved into a building near Disney, Universal, Warner Records, and the Warner film lot, which was directly across the street.

It was going to be a busy year. Quickly putting his stamp on the label as president, Senior brought in three new Texas artists: Robert Ellis, Wild Moccasins, and Buxton. We also released new albums from southern rockers Ponderosa; an eclectic Buddy Miller project called the Majestic Silver Strings; Steve Earle's T Bone Burnett–produced *Never*

Get Out of This World Alive; and a Drive-By Truckers greatest hits album. The Old 97's were finishing up volume two of their sizeable *Grand Theater* undertaking. In an interesting twist for the label, Tom Morello, of Rage Against the Machine fame, joined the roster, and we released three albums by his folk alter ego, the Nightwatchman. John Hiatt made an incredible new album called *Dirty Jeans and Mudslide Hymns*, and we were prepping to reissue two of his earlier records that we had licensed. Plus, we were sorting through more than 100 titles from the Texas Music Group that New West had acquired in a bankruptcy court purchase Cam had engineered. The acquisition included the labels Antone's, Watermelon, and Lone Star Records and albums by Doug Sahm, James Cotton, and Alejandro Escovedo.

Following New West's annual company meeting in September 2011, Mike Ruthig informed me that a decision had been made regarding my position. I would not handle A&R anymore. I would remain VP of production, and in addition, I would mine New West's considerable catalog for reissue opportunities. Hence, I received a new title: VP production & catalog.

Thinking back on this bombshell, I'm amazed I took it so calmly. I'd been doing A&R for thirty-four years. It was part of my identity. But in the back of my mind I had an inkling that a change like this had been brewing for me at the company for a while. Again, I thought it might be time to look elsewhere for work. The problem: I was fifty-seven years old, and other opportunities in A&R, or in the record biz in general, were hardly plentiful.

So, after some serious soul-searching, I decided I was going to make this job revision work to the best of my ability. I still felt loyal to the label, but I'll admit, part of my resolve came from a sense of giving up. I'd been pitching what I believed were strong artists for over a decade, and only a small percentage of them were getting signed. My work had primarily been doing the day-to-day A&R for artists that Cam, and later Senior, brought in. Going forward, I'd still be handling the production process for all New West releases, which I liked doing and was good at. And, in some ways, swapping A&R for catalog development was a welcome relief.

Over the years, I've spent a lot of time comparing my experiences at the two labels I worked for. Of course, at Twin/Tone, I was part-owner of the company, which gave me an authority I never had at New West. But I also felt Twin/Tone had a sense of staff unity that New West lacked. At Twin/Tone, regardless of an employee's personal feelings, once an artist was signed and an album was put on the release schedule, everyone got behind it. There was an implicit trust in all A&R decisions, and the entire staff pulled in the same direction. At New West, that didn't always seem to be the case.

The quality of New West's releases over the years has been remarkably high, and I have many favorites, but there is one album and artist I must address: *Mosey* by Canadian artist Daniel Romano. We have George Fontaine Jr. to thank for signing Daniel.

In 2012, Junior received some recordings from Daniel's booking agent, who was looking to generate US label interest. Junior liked what he heard and let the agent know. The agent then sent Junior a plane ticket to see Daniel and his band live at the Horseshoe Tavern in Toronto. According to Junior, "the club was packed and there was a line down the street. The show was pretty straight country/folk. The band was awesome. I was instantly sold." He quickly signed Daniel, and on January 22, 2013, we released a collection of original compositions called *Come Cry With Me* on Junior's brand-new New West imprint, Normaltown Records.

I was initially wary of Daniel. Maybe it was the album cover that put me off—Daniel decked out in classic country garb, cowboy hat, Nudie Suit, and all. I was worried it was a gimmick and that more thought had gone into the image than the music. Soon after *Come Cry With Me* came out, I saw Daniel and a stripped-down version of his band play a few songs in the lobby of our Burbank office. I was impressed with his confidence and brainy vibe, and the songs began to click with me. In March, I saw him perform at SXSW and was further intrigued. When I heard demos for his next album, another country project, his music started to sound even better to me. I was warming to him, but I still hadn't drunk the Kool-Aid.

My moment of Romano-clarity came at SXSW in 2015. It was at the annual New West party on the outdoor stage at Threadgill's on a Thursday afternoon. He performed with a truncated version of the band: Kay Berkel on acoustic guitar and harmony vocals, Aaron Goldstein on pedal steel, and Daniel on vocals and acoustic guitar. A couple of songs into the set, they kicked into a new one I hadn't heard—I found out later it was "Valerie Leon," which opens his 2016 album *Mosey*. In rapid-fire delivery, Daniel sang:

> I really shouldn't oughta
> But I think I kinda gotta
> Since the second that I saw ya
> I've been weak'nin' in the knees
> There's a reason for my misery
> But my baby's off and busy
> And you probably shouldn't oughta
> Come-a-walkin' by the wata
> Just to talk and get ta know ya
> For the sake ta make ya fa-la-la-la-love me
> But it's been stayin' dark, past dawn

My brain was scrambling to keep up with the words. Then it was like a scene in a movie where the clouds parted and rays of sunshine beamed down on me alone. I might have actually been tingling.

I can now unreservedly gush: After eighteen more studio albums over the next six years (think about that for a second), plus two live albums, an EP, assorted singles, hundreds of live shows, not to mention producing other artists, painting, and doing leatherwork, Daniel Romano is one of the most gifted artists I have ever come across. His writing consistently astounds me; he can sing in a wide variety of voices; he plays many instruments ridiculously well; the musicians he surrounds himself with are always top-shelf; he's stylistically uncategorizable (my favorite kind), doing country, folk, and rock equally well; and he blends the serious with the mischievous in equal measure. His creativity seems limitless. Daniel has studied the masters, yet his originality is always apparent. Recent live performances have been very rock 'n' roll, like an intense fusion of Dylan's Rolling Thunder Revue and the Who. In my opinion, Daniel's album *Mosey* is the best thing New West Records has ever released.

On February 19, 2012, veteran Minneapolis musician and former Replacements lead guitar player Bob "Slim" Dunlap suffered a massive stroke. It was exacerbated by him falling and hitting his head, causing a hemorrhage in his brain. He was left paralyzed and bedridden. His recovery and future were uncertain. He would require around-the-clock care, and the medical expenses were going to be astronomical. Slim had been a close friend and musical inspiration for nearly four decades. I was heartbroken.

Three days later I received an email from Brian Balleria, a close friend of the Dunlaps, asking if I'd considered doing a Slim tribute/benefit record. I hadn't, but I started to right then. After discussing it with Slim's wife, Chrissie, and getting her blessing, I began sketching out a plan.

The idea of doing some type of benefit was good, but I was wary of tribute albums. They'd become ubiquitous, and most of them didn't sell. I couldn't bear the thought of doing something for Slim that might fail. I needed to come up with a way we could raise money that would be creative and compelling. I decided to reach out to musicians who

knew and admired Slim to see if they'd be interested in recording songs
he'd written. If I could persuade enough of them to lend a hand, and
we could release the recordings in some novel fashion, maybe we'd at
least generate income for Slim from the publishing rights. I wondered
about the possibility of New West being involved, and when I brought it
up to Mike Ruthig, he was excited. We did some brainstorming. What
if we did a limited-edition series of 7-inch 45s with a different artist on
each side and, instead of going through normal retail channels, we
auctioned them on eBay? I could ask Chris Mars if he'd do the cover
art. If the auctions were successful, we could release a CD compilation
of all the tracks.

Without hesitation, George Sr. gave us the go-ahead. We decided
to call the project *Songs for Slim*. From tragic circumstances, we saw a
remarkable outpouring of musical love. Artists who stepped up to
donate their time to do recordings of Slim's songs included Steve Earle,
Craig Finn, Lucinda Williams, Tommy Keene, The Minus 5 with Curtiss A, Tim O'Reagan and Jim Boquist, Jakob Dylan, Joe Henry, John
Doe, Deer Tick with Scott Lucas and Vanessa Carlton, Frank Black and
the Suicide Commandos, You Am I, Patterson Hood and the Downtown Rumblers, the Young Fresh Fellows, Jeff Tweedy, Lucero, Chris
Mars, and a reformed, rejiggered Replacements.

Leave it to the Replacements to throw a wrench in the works—in a
good way this time. They were among the first artists to record a song
for the project, and Tommy Stinson called me after their session. He told
me that once they'd recorded Slim's "Busted Up" they kept the tape rolling and laid down three more cover songs: "Lost Highway," written by
Leon Payne and made popular by Hank Williams; Gordon Lightfoot's
"I'm Not Sayin'"; and "Everything's Coming Up Roses," from the 1959
Broadway musical *Gypsy*. Tommy said: "I know the plan was for us to
do just the one song, but how about an EP?" I told him I'd have to hear
the tracks first. But if he thought they were good, I figured I would too.

For personal reasons, drummer Chris Mars had chosen to sit out the
sessions with his former bandmates but contributed his own terrific

Slim cover, "Radio Hook Word Hit," handling all instruments and vocals himself. For the new Replacements recordings, Tommy and Paul had tapped old friend and former Dads' guitarist Kevin Bowe to play lead guitar, and on drums was the versatile Peter Anderson.

Tommy sent me rough mixes of the four songs, and I loved them. Even though it wasn't the original band, I thought the recordings had a classic 'Mats feel—loose, full of spunk, and rockin'. In particular, I was knocked out by "I'm Not Sayin'," a recording I'd include on any Replacements best-of compilation.

With four recordings from a Paul and Tommy–fronted version of the 'Mats, and one from Chris, we decided to combine them onto a five-song 10-inch EP. Launching the series with the closest thing we could get to a new Replacements record gave us something to really shout about.

A big part of the credit for the success of the series goes to associate producers Ben Perlstein and Chris Trovero. Ben figured out how to make the eBay procedure work and expertly handled all the auctions. Together, Ben and Chris put the packages together and shipped the records out to the winning bidders. On Ben's recommendation, I called San Diego–based designer Mike Buchmiller of Hand Carved Graphics and asked if he would design a logo for us. Within an hour of hanging up the phone, Mike sent me an idea: a 45 adapter with a heart in the center. Not only was it some of the fastest design work I ever encountered, the concept couldn't have been more perfect!

Each record in the series was packaged in a picture sleeve, and Chris Mars—now an accomplished painter—did the cover art. His beautiful and macabre paintings gave the series a spooky yet elegant look. New West art director Paul Moore's design for the Replacements' 10-inch lent an air of class to the project too—a black faux-suede jacket with embossed lettering and a die-cut window, through which peered a haunting pair of eyes from one of Chris's paintings on the inner sleeve. It blew everyone away. To make the package even more appealing, we included four glossy prints of never-before-seen band photos, a poster of Slim, and a digital download card.

The auctions kicked off with a bang in January 2013. The Replacements EP was a limited release of 250 numbered copies, each one signed by Tommy Stinson, Chris Mars, and Paul Westerberg. The bidding lasted ten days. A Replacements fanatic from New York was determined to get copy #1, and they did, with a bid of $10,000! By the end of the auction, we'd sold all 250 copies and raised $106,750. And that was just the beginning.

Each month from February through September, we auctioned one 7-inch 45. The jacket of each single was autographed by the artists. They were all pressed and numbered in limited editions of 100, with two exceptions: the April single—by the Minus 5 featuring Curtiss A backed with Tim O'Reagan and Jim Boquist—was released for Record Store Day in a limited edition of 1,000; and for the grand finale, the September single—Jeff Tweedy backed with Lucero—was upped to 250 copies.

The Replacements five-song EP was later made commercially available, first in digital form on March 5 and then as a 12-inch vinyl on April 16. On November 12, after all the auctions were done, we released a double CD entitled *Rockin' Here Tonight: A Benefit Compilation for Slim Dunlap*. Disc one featured the Replacements' and Chris Mars' Slim covers from the EP and all sixteen sides from the eight 45s. Disc two contained ten bonus tracks: eight additional covers of Slim songs, plus two new songs written for Slim. The contributors were Peter Holsapple; Jon Eller; Soul Asylum; a second Young Fresh Fellows track; Bee, Louie & Brien, consisting of Slim's oldest daughter, son, and longtime drummer, respectively; a second Chris Mars track; Chan Poling of the Suburbs; Frankie Lee; LP.ORG (the Jayhawks under a pseudonym); and the West Saugerties Ale & Quail Club, featuring Steve Almaas and John Sebastian of the Lovin' Spoonful.

By the end of the year, the *Songs for Slim* series brought in over $200,000, with all proceeds going to the Slim Dunlap Fund. The success of the project wouldn't have been possible without the dedicated teamwork of artists, managers, musicians, studios, engineers, producers, pressing plants, printers, radio promotion and marketing people, publicists, and so many others who either donated their time or gave us a generous discount. Showers of praise are due to Joe Henry and Ed Ackerson, both of whom produced multiple tracks; as well as Golden Mastering in Ventura, California, which knocked all twenty-eight tracks into shape. I still get choked up thinking about it. It was a gargantuan amount of work, but I'd do it all over again in a second. And I am eternally indebted to New West for supporting the cause.

In 2015, we folded one more Slim Dunlap project into the benefit series: Slim's two solo albums, *The Old New Me* (1993) and *Times Like This* (1996). New West licensed both titles from Medium Cool–Twin/ Tone and released them on Record Store Day as a double vinyl package. World-class recording engineer and restoration expert Jim Wilson did the remastering. Slim's longtime musical partner, Curtiss A, created an intricate collage for the inside of the gatefold jacket. Slim's drummer of many years, Brien Lilja, wrote heartwarming and funny liner notes. And former New West art director Chuck Hermes put together a beautiful package, which also included a Slim guitar pick, 45 adapter, and poster. Having his albums out on vinyl had been a dream of Slim's for many years, and through some dark days following his stroke, it quite literally gave him something to live for.

Meanwhile, things were going swimmingly in New West's Burbank office. I'll always have a soft spot for the Cam years, but I think we got better at being a label as the company continued to grow under George Fontaine Sr. There was a fresh feeling of efficiency, of getting the job done and done well, that I think made us all feel good.

Senior had held the position of president since Cam left at the start of 2011. I liked having him in the role of leading the label and thought he'd done a great job, but I also understood him wanting to bring in someone with more business experience. In the late fall of 2014, Senior announced that he was appointing John Allen to take his place. John had been in the music publishing sector for years, as a vice president at

Bug Music and then at BMG. He was based in Nashville, and expanding the office there was clearly in the cards. I knew Senior had never been fond of LA, but I always had the impression he believed it was important to have a presence there.

In the spring of 2015, the West Coast staff was informed that management had decided to vacate the LA office and officially move New West's HQ to Nashville. The details were vague, and naturally it put everyone on edge. Several key employees quit. Mike Ruthig, Tim Plumley, and I were left as the lone remaining LA employees. We moved into offices just down the street in the Pinnacle Building, which was home to several other labels, including Atlantic, Elektra, and Rhino, plus our distributor, A.D.A. It wasn't long before Mike left to take a job with Universal. And then there were two. I always loved working with Tim, and we made the best of it.

Then, in April 2016, John Allen came to the LA offices. He told me he was doing some restructuring and my position was being terminated. It was a shocker, no question. It took a day or two for me to wrap my head around what had happened, but once I did, I accepted it and quickly began to feel better. I'd already had one foot out the door on a number of occasions, and deep down I was ready to go. My good friend Josh Troy offered the best perspective of all. When I told him I'd been laid off, without a moment's hesitation he exclaimed, "Freedom!" It made me laugh out loud, and I'll be forever grateful to Josh for that. He was right. I did feel a certain liberation.

Tim stuck around until July, when he left for a position at Universal. The LA office of New West was officially closed. C'est la vie.

Epilogue

Since the spring of 2016 I've kept quite busy. Initially, I explored full-time employment opportunities at two of the larger music companies: first, at BMG regarding the possibility of working with a new in-house label they'd started; then at the ever-expanding Concord Records. Neither one worked out, but ultimately I was glad they didn't, much as I respect both companies. The culture at BMG and Concord wouldn't have allowed the kind of "elbow room" I'd been accustomed to at Twin/Tone and New West. Plus, the whole idea of starting over at another label just didn't seem like the right move for me at the age of sixty-two. Going freelance was more up my alley.

As a freelancer, I continued to do much of what I'd been doing at labels over the previous forty years: A&R–related work. I acted as a sounding board for LA's Christopher Pappas and his groups Elle Belle and the Everyday Visuals; Criminal Hygiene, also LA–based; Brisbane, Australia, octet Halfway; and Austria's Son of the Velvet Rat. I did some writing as well, including liner notes for Blackberry Way Records and bios for Pappas, the Criminal Hygiene boys, and artist–producer Butch Walker. I listened to demos by dozens of other artists and gave them feedback. I still receive music from young musicians who like the work I've done and are looking for advice. Helping out in the early stages of an artist's development is one of the most rewarding aspects of the work I do.

A lot of music is being made these days by musicians who don't even consider aiming for the corporate conglomerates. I find it especially satisfying to interface with artists who aren't reaching for the brass ring of a major label, the artists who are driven to make music because it's in their blood. In many cases, musicians aren't looking for a label at all. We have entered a new era. The internet has allowed for a new kind of DIY. Circulating and promoting your own music has become a viable option. Though the competition is staggering and streaming revenue is obscenely unjust, with proper organization, consistent hard work, including steady touring, and a bit of luck, it's more possible than ever for artists to make at least a decent living.

In the spring of 2017, my pal Kevin Cole rang me up with an irresistible proposal. We were both jazzed that Peter Perrett, former front man for the Only Ones, was about to release his first solo album, *How the West Was Won*. Kevin asked if I'd interview Peter for the website of KEXP, the Seattle radio station where Kevin was and still is a program director. I leapt at the opportunity. Since Peter and I first met in Chicago in 1979, we have kept in touch, and when I ran the interview idea by him, he was all for it. We spoke by phone for nearly two hours. I'd done my homework and painstakingly organized my questions, and our conversation went swimmingly. After I transcribed and edited the piece, I was struck by how warm it felt, like two old friends talking. I'm proud to say that Peter told me he thought it was the best interview he'd ever done. It's one of my most treasured experiences (and it's still available on KEXP's website).

Another work opportunity came my way when longtime friend Cheryl Pawelski at Omnivore Recordings extended an invitation for me to produce archival releases for her company. This resulted in an expanded reissue of Tommy Stinson's first Bash & Pop album in 2017 and a series of reissues for Soul Asylum in 2018 and 2019. In a thrilling pursuit for me personally, I tracked down Mike McCartney and made a pitch to him to do an expanded reissue of his *McGear* album. Mike and I emailed back and forth for a spell, but he ended up taking the project to the London-based label Cherry Red. They did a fine job, but all due respect, I thought we could've done better. Not much has changed as far as Slim's health, sadly. Though still partially paralyzed and confined to a hospital bed at home, he has his wits about him, and his will to live remains as strong as ever.

Slim's former bandmate Tommy Stinson has been busy touring and writing and recording his own music, as well as producing other groups. He has always bounced his demos and studio recordings off of me, and to my ears he just keeps getting better. Tommy put together a new Bash & Pop lineup in 2016 and made the album *Anything Could Happen*, released by Fat Possum the following year. Tour dates took them around the United States, with select dates overseas. I saw the LA show at the Troubadour, and the place was packed; the band was in top form.

More recently, Tommy's been focusing on Cowboys in the Campfire, a rootsy duo with his friend and guitar player Chip Roberts. They recently put together their first album, *Wronger*. Not only did Tommy ask for my input on the tracks-in-progress, he also invited my son to get involved in offering feedback. Autry has always been a music kid and, since hitting his late teens, has begun working in the field and has developed a genuinely professional ear. We gave Tommy detailed critiques of performances and mixes and sequenced the songs, which earned father and son executive producer credits on the album.

The Replacements camp has also seen substantial activity for the first time since 1991, and I believe their contribution to the *Songs for Slim* project is partly responsible. Though the Replacements had attempted to record new material over the years following the band's breakup, they didn't catch a real spark until motivated to aid their ailing friend. The strength of the recordings, and the fervor generated when those recordings were auctioned, gave them confidence, a *we can do this again* feeling, which surely was a factor in the band reuniting (with a modified lineup) and performing live again in 2013–15. Doing thirty-five-some shows, from Toronto to LA, London to Barcelona, the Replacements pulled off something they had rarely done before: They played consistently well every night, including a so-great-it-was-almost-hard-to-believe television appearance on *The Tonight Show with Jimmy Fallon*.

In March 2016, *Trouble Boys*, an exhaustively researched biography of the Replacements by journalist/author Bob Mehr, hit the shelves. It's a tough, not always happy story, but it told the truth. The book was widely well received and made it onto the *New York Times* bestseller list. I participated in promo events for the book in Seattle and Portland (with special guest Scott McCaughey of the Young Fresh Fellows, Minus 5, etc.!).The experience of signing books alongside Mehr and meeting so many die-hard fans of the Replacements all these years later was incredibly gratifying. I've never been thanked so much in my life.

This flurry of activity perked up Rhino Entertainment's interest in the Replacements' recorded catalog. In a circuitous trail of label purchases, the titles that Twin/Tone had licensed to Restless in 1992 first went to Rykodisc, then ended up at the Warner Music Group, Rhino's parent company. This means that the Replacements' four Twin/Tone albums and the four they made for Sire now all reside under one roof. Along with Rhino's director of A&R, Jason Jones, Mehr spearheaded a series of Replacements reissues. I coproduced the 100-track *Sorry Ma, Forgot to Take Out the Trash* fortieth anniversary set with Bob and Jason, and I consulted on the others. The Replacements seem to be more popular than ever before.

I keep in touch with Chris Mars and visit him whenever I'm back in Minneapolis. Communication between Paul Westerberg and me is sporadic.

Though the Twin/Tone Records Group was active through 1998, the Twin/Tone label's last release was *The Suburbs: Live at First Avenue* in 1994. That is, until 2017.

Chris Osgood approached Paul Stark and me in mid-2016 with an enticing idea. The Suicide Commandos had decided to make a new album—their first in thirty-nine years—and wondered if we'd be interested in reviving Twin/Tone to release it. The Commandos had periodically reformed to do shows, and all three members were still musically active with their own projects, so it wasn't as if they'd been entirely absent from performing. In July 2014, the death of Tommy Erdelyi, the last surviving original member of the Ramones, was like a call to action, inspiring the Commandos to get into the studio while the gettin' was good. The band produced, Kevin Bowe engineered, and Mitch Easter mixed the album *Time Bomb*. Twin/Tone released it in May 2017 in a limited edition of 1,000 numbered vinyl copies, the label's first new offspring in twenty-three years. The band had planned to do a number of national live dates but, unfortunately, day jobs got in the way. We did have a rockin' album release weekend in the Twin Cities, including in-stores at Treehouse Records (formerly Oar Folkjokeopus) and Hi-Fi Hair & Records in Minneapolis and a blowout party at the Turf Club in St. Paul.

This got me to thinking: *What if we resurrected Twin/Tone to work with new artists again?* Paul Stark is semiretired but supported my idea and was willing to help on an as-needed basis. This meant I had to find a new partner, someone to oversee the business side of things so I could concentrate on creative matters. Enter Stephen Judge, an industry hero of mine. Among many other things, he was the former general manager of Redeye Distribution, and he is now the owner of the Schoolkids Record Stores in North Carolina. I told Stephen I'd like to start with just four releases per year in order to give each one sufficient attention. He was as excited about the concept as I was. We formed a partnership, Stephen put together an attractive and modest business plan, and we sought financial backing. Over the next few months, we secured tentative commitments from investors for three-quarters of the necessary start-up capital. We were close! I reached out to Daniel Romano, the Tulsa band Broncho, and Jayhawks founding member Mark Olson, and they all expressed interest in the possibility of working with us, if and when we got the label off the ground again. We also began sketching out a plan for a multi-artist, fortieth-anniversary Twin/Tone box set. Then on April 9, 2018, I received an offer to write a memoir.

The flood of emotions was intense. Daily, hourly, I lurched from *Yes, I can do it!* to *Who am I kidding?* But the one thing I kept coming back to was this: The timing was remarkable. It was the right point in my life to write a book. I'd been working in music for nearly fifty years and had reached a stage where looking back and reflecting was an appealing prospect. I accepted the offer. It took me a few months to finish the projects I already had in motion, and label resurrection was moved to the back burner.

My appetite for music remains insatiable. I still have a new favorite artist or album or song weekly. The artists who have inspired me the most in recent years include Dan Kelly, Broncho, Angus & Julia Stone, Eisley, the Unthanks, Daniel Romano, Fontaines D.C., and maybe the most immense talent I've encountered in the last decade, Phoebe Bridgers. And the list doesn't end there. Other recommendations include new works from Wet Leg, Julianna Riolino, Carson McHone, Michigander, Rayland Baxter, Ian Hunter, Luluc, Tristen, Robert Forster, Taylor Swift, and solo offerings from Supergrass's Gaz Coombes and Danny Goffey.

Two other moments stand out in my ongoing musical mania. First, in 2013, David Bowie snuck up on us and unleashed one of the finest albums of his career, *The Next Day*, a towering achievement of art in rock, and my personal favorite record of the twenty-first century so far; second, Peter Jackson's 2021 Beatles documentary, *Get Back*, was eight of the best hours of my life.

Inevitably, many stories I hoped to include in the book didn't make it: my pilgrimage to see David Bowie's first American tour in Chicago and Detroit in October 1972; meeting Paul McCartney at the Capitol Tower in LA in April 1989; the "fly-in series" I hosted with Steve McClellan, and later Maggie Macpherson, at the 7th Street Entry and the Uptown Bar to bring in the likes of Ted Hawkins, Lucinda Williams, and Freedy Johnston for their Twin Cities debuts; Kevin Cole providing me with the opportunity to host a weekly show on his Rev 105 radio station and the resulting 150 programs I did under the moniker Shakin Street; my trips to Australia and New Zealand for music conferences and so much more; or my lunch with Grace Slick at her publisher's office in 2016. There are also many more people I intended to name-check, but when the text started looking like an attendance roster, revisions were required. But for the most part, I think I covered the ground I wanted to.

When I was a teenager, I believed that as I grew older the ways of the world would make more sense to me. That hasn't happened. While I've gained wisdom, I'm still as mixed up as ever. Do I have regrets? Yes, loads of them. Somewhere along the way, though, I came to a realization: we don't get to where we're going just by the good choices we make; we get there by a combination of the good and the bad choices. I had to learn to accept it all. And overall, I'm happy with where I'm at, and I'm happy with the work I've done. All my life I have seen the world through a musical prism, and I've been steadfast in my belief that the art of music improves people's lives and makes the world a better place. That's why I do the work I do. To quote author Ottessa Moshfegh: "I think art is the thing that fixes culture, moment by moment."

Over the course of writing this book, my son, Autry, has grown into adulthood and is now pursuing his own musical path. To share the wonders of music with him is one of life's greatest gifts. During the pandemic lockdown, Jennifer, Autry, and I spent endless hours watching music documentaries about artists ranging from Frank Sinatra to the Clash. The one that resonated the most with Autry, though, was *No Direction Home*, Martin Scorsese's 2005 documentary about Bob Dylan. When the film was over, Autry stood up and exclaimed, "That was the closest I've ever come to a religious experience."

The long and the short of it is: We can't explain it in words, but somehow, music gives us a feeling we don't get from anything else.

"Single Slices" cartoon by Peter Kohlsaat. *Courtesy of the artist*

Acknowledgments

With immense amounts of gratitude to my family (blood and extended): Chet and Carolyn Jesperson (who instilled the love of the written word in me), Alan Jesperson (whom I've looked up to all my life), Janine Kemmer, Elise and Richard Balderrama, Ryan and Brett Ebhardt, Wendy and Michael James, Debbie and Charly Murray, Heather Murray and Willo Morales, Steve Klemz and Janet Scott, Dan Fults and Richard John, Tommy Stinson, Tom and Anita Kurth, Lonnie Stinson, Lisa Stinson; Dave, Kathleen, and Marlowe Philips; and Sarah, Josh, Willa, and Talia Troy.

To my first musical mentors: Tony Glover and Duncan Hannah.

Linda Hultquist, who reminded me that books are as essential a safety net in this life as music, and so much more.

Peter Bystol and Dave Postlethwaite for taking the bull by its horns and saving my life.

Jim Proefrock and Mark Engebretson (it's all your fault!).

Blake Gumprecht for his no-nonsense literary guidance along the way.

Slim-Bob, Chrissie, Delia, and Louie Dunlap; and Emily Bee, Chuck, Eloise, and Audrey Boigenzahn for decades of friendship and inspiration.

Steve and Merrie Brantseg for their immeasurable warmth.

Curt Almsted, Chris Osgood, Robert Wilkinson, and Chan Poling for leading the bands that provided liftoff for a glorious era in Twin Cities rock 'n' roll.

Minnetonka friends: Bill "Frondo" Gamec, Jon Siegel, Paul Sylvestre, Kevin Glynn, Steve Carlson, David Aiken, Robb Henry, Bob Ivers, Mike and Terri Owens, Melanie Bitz Tinkham, Tom Mohr, Julie Abeln, Libby Johnson.

Guthrie compadres: Rod Gordon, Pam Williams, Beth Segal, Michael Markos, Duncan Hannah, Kurt Thometz, Reid Papke, Nelson King, David Hawkinson.

Oar Folk-ers: Vern and Donna Sanden, Barry Margolis, Terry, Ben, and Nick Katzman and Penny Myers; Andy Schwartz, Mitch Griffin, Jim Peterson, Bill Melton, Mike Lehecka, Rich Blomme, Reid Matko; and Wayne Klayman for starting it all with North Country Music.

The Longhorn mob: Jay Berine, Margaret Duvall, Al Wodtke, Erik Hanson, Dale, Janine, Cindy Bergquist, Gypsy, Anita, Jacque Horsch; Charlie Burton, Dave Robel, and band; Kenny Vaughan, Leroy X, and the Jonny III; Bob Mould, Grant Hart, and Greg Norton; the Hypstrz, Jim Skafish, and Yipes, among so many others.

The Twin/Tone (and related) crew: Paul and Julia Stark, Charley Hallman and clan, Curt Almsted and Gini Dodds, Roz Ferguson, Ellen Stewart, Dave Ayers, Jill (McLean) and Davin Odegaard, Sarah (Brace) and John Beggs, Jill Fonaas, Abbie Kane, Amy Silvers, Jake Wisely.

The Replacements and adherents: Paul Westerberg ("Morgan The Pirate" still resonates), Chris Mars (who overfloweth with artistry and kindness), Bob Stinson (guitar savant; singular human being), and Tommy Stinson (my best man for good reason): the long arm of the Replacements never ceases to amaze; Lou Santacroce, Tom Carlson, Bill Sullivan, Bill Mack, Mike Bosley, Monty Lee Wilkes, Michael Hill, Seymour Stein, Bill Holdship, Lilli Dennison, Frank Riley, Curt Schieber, Darren Hill, Matt Wallace, Harpo Wilkes, Tommy Erdelyi and Claudia Tienan, George Regis, Peter Kohlsaat. And to Bob Mehr for his conviction and thorough work in cementing the Replacements' legacy.

R.E.M.: Berry, Buck, Mills, Stipe, Jefferson Holt, Bertis Downs, Gevin Lindsey, Kevin O'Neill.

Medium Cool-ers: Tim O'Reagan, Todd Newman; Jack Logan, Kelly and Nikki Keneipp, Aaron Phillips; Eric, Anita, and Jarrett Sales; Marc

Solomon, Gersh, Robert Cooper; Todd and Shayne Jordan McBride, Rob Veal, Mike Gibson, John Crist, Len Hoffman; Buck Hazlett, John Hazlett, Jim Thompson, Brien Lilja; Tom Hicks, Erick Hubbard, Eric Fisher, Todd Dare; Duane Jarvis, Kevin Jarvis, Marlee MacLeod, William Tonks, Ben Mize, John "Strawberry" Fields, Chuck Hermes, Stacey (Sanner) Fils-Aime, Liz Garo, Wendy Erikson, Michelle Roche, and Chris Richards.

My home-away-from-home, Athens, Georgia, and denizens: Vic and Tina Chesnutt, John Keane, Dave Barbe, William and Debbie Tonks, Sharon Neff, Barrie Buck, Velena Vego, Sharon Camp, Tony Eubanks, DeWitt Burton, and the Taco Stand!

New West-ers: Cameron and Tory Strang, Sharon Cohen Masters, Stephen Bruton, Mark Pucci, Kelly Ellis, Tim Easton, Jeff Cook, Jon Gomez, Mary Jurey, David Lessoff and Cynthia Sanchez, Paul Moore, Tommy Robinson, Clare Surgeson, Traci Thomas, Steve Rosenblatt, Chris Fagot, Steve Nice, Kat Delaney, Amanda Hale, Nic Armstrong and all Thieves, the Old 97's and Salim Nourallah; Herb Agner, Mike Ruthig, Mike Mauro, Katelyn Craig LaBrel; Tim, Anna, and Miles Plumley; Joel Habbeshaw, Hope Selevan, Hillary Riley, Billy Smith, George Fontaine Sr., George Fontaine Jr., Jay Woods, Matt Etgen, John Allen, and all the artists we were so fortunate to work with.

All who toiled in front of and behind the scenes, and those who answered my endless questions: Steve Almaas, Dave Ahl, Karen Haglof, Jody Kurilla, Steve Fjelstad, Hugo and Debbie Klaers, Bruce Allen, Beej Chaney, Michael Halliday, Casey Macpherson, Jack Brisley, Maggie Macpherson, PD Larson and Jody Wahl, Mark Freeman and Cindy Blum, Dick Champ, Jim Tollefsrud, Jeff Waryan, Jay Peck, Tom Herbers, Lori Barbero, Laurie Lindeen, John Freeman, Grant Johnson, Jeff Buswell, Mary Beth Mueller, Danny Amis, Tim Carr, Lori Bizer Leighton, Kevin Bowe, Danny Murphy, Dave Pirner, Pat Morley, Tim Schuck, Dave Carroll, Jeneen Anderson, Roy and Dawn Freid, Ken Abdo, Chris Morris, Curt Scheiber, Will Rigby, Jon Bream, Marty Keller, Jim Walsh, Chris Riemenschneider, Greg Helgeson, Mike Hoeger, Mark Trehus and Treehouse Records, Mark Leviton, Ryan Cameron and Nancy

Bachrach, Danny Goldberg, Jack Rabid, Peter Davis, Jim Boquist, Dave Boquist, Martin Zellar, Allison Locey, Peter Perrett, Kelly Bell, Shannon Welch, Mary Anne Welch, Tom "Chuck Fred" Taylor, Greg Faulds, Phil Caruso, Eric Martin; the Philly contingent: Tom Moon, Dan DeLuca, Bruce Warren, David Dye, Frank Brown, Pat Feeney, and Main Street Music; Terry Currier and Music Millennium, Mark Howard, Michelle and Anthony Aquilato, Evan Way and the Parson Red Heads, Leslie Stevens and the Badgers, Dan Kelly, Paul Kelly, Bernadette Ryan, John Busby and Halfway, Robert Forster, Graham "Asho" Ashton, Alistair Cranney, Dave Laing, Damon Booth, Tom DeSavia, Andy Freeman, Ben Perlstein, Chris Trovero, Mike Buchmiller, Tim Schuck, Johnny Buzzerio, Steve Tagliere, Stephen Judge, Christopher Pappas and Mary Beth Sullivan, Cheryl Pawelski and Audrey Bilger, Jim Merlis, Larry White, Tate Wittenberg, David Fricke, Glenn Morrow, Danny Fields, Monte Melnick, Darin Harmon, Tony Berg, Josh Grier, Jac Holzman.

Daniel Romano and Carson McHone, Ian Romano, Roddy Kuester, and Julianna Riolino for reams of excellence.

John Perry, Alex Chilton, and Jody Stephens, who turned "fear of meeting your heroes" on its head and became true friends.

To the photographers: Jay Smiley, Dave Biljan, Michael Plen, Jay Nolan, Greg Allen, Paul Lundgren, Laurie Schendel Lane, Michael Markos, Kevin Scanlon, Peter Kohlsaat, Julia Stark, Dan Corrigan, and all the others we couldn't track down.

Josh Leventhal, Shannon Pennefeather, freelance editor Jennifer Gehlhar, and all at the MNHS for expert editing and transforming this thing into a book.

Keith Covart, Dan Foley, and Ron Korsh for inventing the Electric Fetus, the first *real* record store I frequented.

And the Big Four: the Beatles, Bob Dylan, the Rolling Stones, and David Bowie.

Discography

A select discography of projects I was involved in over the last forty-five years, edited for brevity. My roles often overlapped, ranging from finding and signing an artist, to helping guide them through the record-making process by providing advice and general creative input, to writing promotional content, to in some instances producing. I always did my best to facilitate, encourage, and promote all the artists I worked with. In the case of Twin/Tone, I also helped set up the distribution of our music.

All titles listed from 1978 to 1998 are full-length albums on Twin/Tone Records, unless otherwise noted. All titles listed from 2000 through 2016 are full-length albums on New West Records, unless otherwise noted.

1978
The Suburbs (EP), self-titled
1980–1990 (EP), Spooks/Curtiss A
Fingerprints (EP), self-titled
Hypstrz Live (EP), The Hypstrz, Bogus–Twin/Tone Records

1979
The Commandos Commit Suicide Dance Concert (live), The Suicide
   Commandos

Big Hits of Mid-America Volume III (two-record set), various artists
Flea Pasts Ape Elf, Orchid Spangiafora

1980
In Combo, The Suburbs
Courtesy, Curtiss A

1981
"I'm in Trouble" b/w "If Only You Were Lonely" (7-inch 45), The
    Replacements
Sorry Ma, Forgot to Take Out the Trash, The Replacements
Flight 581, The Pistons
Credit in Heaven (two-record set), The Suburbs
Sir Crackers (12-inch EP), The Crackers
Safety Last (12-inch EP), self-titled

1982
"Music for Boys" (12-inch 45), The Suburbs
The Replacements Stink (12-inch 45 mini-album), The Replacements
"Waiting" (12-inch 45), The Suburbs
Dream Hog (12-inch EP), The Suburbs

1983
Changing Minds, The Phones
Hootenanny, The Replacements
Figures, Jeff Waryan
Struck by Love, Safety Last
Damage Is Done, Curtiss A
Cybernetic Dreams of Pi, The Slickee Boys

1984
Blind Impulse, The Phones
Say What You Will Clarence ... Karl Sold the Truck (mini-album),
    Soul Asylum

"I Will Dare" (12-inch 45), The Replacements
Let It Be, The Replacements

1985
The Shit Hits the Fans (cassette), The Replacements
Tim, The Replacements, Sire Records
Uh Oh . . . No Brakes!, The Slickee Boys
In a Chalk Circle, Figures

1986
Big Hits of Mid-America Volume IV, various artists

1990
Blur to Me Now, 13 Engines, SBK Records

1992
Topeka Oratorio, The Leatherwoods, Medium Cool–Twin/Tone
    Records
Kitty, The Dashboard Saviors, Medium Cool–Twin/Tone Records
Ladies and Gentlemen, The Suburbs Have Left the Building (compilation),
    The Suburbs

1993
sun shinin on your rain, Ticks, Medium Cool–Twin/Tone Records
The Old New Me, Slim Dunlap, Medium Cool–Twin/Tone Records
Drive Too Fast, Marlee MacLeod, Medium Cool–Twin/Tone Records
Spinnin' on Down, The Dashboard Saviors, Medium Cool–Twin/
    Tone Records

1994
DJ's Front Porch, Duane Jarvis, Medium Cool–Twin/Tone Records
Bulk (double CD), Jack Logan, Medium Cool–Twin/Tone Records
Viva! Suburbs! (Live at First Avenue), The Suburbs

1995

love, sorrow, hatred, madness, The Dashboard Saviors, Medium
   Cool–Twin / Tone Records
Favorite Ball and Chain, Marlee MacLeod, Medium Cool–Twin /
   Tone Records

1996

Mood Elevator, Jack Logan, Medium Cool–Twin / Tone Records
When Squirrels Play Chicken (EP), Perfect, Medium Cool–Twin /
   Tone Records
Times Like This, Slim Dunlap, Medium Cool–Twin / Tone Records

1998

7 Days a Week (unreleased), Perfect

1999

Buzz Me In, Jack Logan, Capricorn Records

2000

Lunette, Jim Roll
Everything You Thought Was Right Was Wrong Today, Slobberbone

2001

The Truth About Us, Tim Easton
Nothing Personal, Delbert McClinton
The Earth Rolls On, Billy Joe Shaver
No More Mr. Lucky, Randall Bramblett

2002

Hooray for the Moon, Jon Dee Graham
Holiday in Dirt, Stan Ridgway
Spirit World, Stephen Bruton
Music for Courage and Confidence, Mark Eitzel

Now Again, The Flatlanders
No Other Love, Chuck Prophet
Slippage, Slobberbone
Room to Breathe, Delbert McClinton

2003
Break Your Mother's Heart, Tim Easton
Silver Lake, Vic Chesnutt
Beneath This Gruff Exterior, John Hiatt
Decoration Day, Drive-By Truckers
Live, Delbert McClinton

2004
Wheels of Fortune, The Flatlanders
Thin Places, Randall Bramblett
Killers and Stars, Patterson Hood
Drag It Up, Old 97's,
Village Gorilla Head, Tommy Stinson, Sanctuary Records
The Dirty South, Drive-By Truckers
Age of Miracles, Chuck Prophet
Once, Twice, Three Times a Maybe, Perfect, Rykodisc
Universal United House of Prayer, Buddy Miller

2005
Awake Is the New Sleep, Ben Lee
Exploration, Sarah Lee Guthrie and Johnny Irion
Greatest White Liar, Nic Armstrong & The Thieves
Ghetto Bells, Vic Chesnutt
Master of Disaster, John Hiatt
From the Five, Stephen Bruton
Dirty Diamonds, Alice Cooper
Cost of Living, Delbert McClinton
Alive and Wired (double CD), Old 97's

2006

This Old Road, Kris Kristofferson
A Blessing and a Curse, Drive-By Truckers
Ammunition, Tim Easton
Rich Someday, Randall Bramblett
Jubilee Dive, The Drams
If We Can't Escape My Pretty, IV Thieves

2007

Black Snake Moan (soundtrack), various artists
Sermon on Expedition Boulevard, Rickie Lee Jones
Preludes (double CD), Warren Zevon
Sirens of the Ditch, Jason Isbell
Ripe, Ben Lee
Washington Square Serenade, Steve Earle
Dwight Sings Buck, Dwight Yoakam

2008

Brighter Than Creation's Dark, Drive-By Truckers
Working Man's Café, Ray Davies
Live at Twist & Shout (EP), Jason Isbell & The 400 Unit
Insides Out, Jordan Zevon
Sorry Ma, Forgot to Take Out the Trash; The Replacements Stink;
    Hootenanny; Let It Be; Tim; Pleased to Meet Me; Don't Tell a Soul;
    All Shook Down (expanded CD reissues), The Replacements,
    Rhino Records
Blame It on Gravity, Old 97's
Same Old Man, John Hiatt
A Love Extreme (double CD), Benji Hughes
Now It's Tomorrow, Randall Bramblett
The Imus Ranch Record, various artists

2009

Ready for the Flood, Mark Olson and Gary Louris
Written in Chalk, Buddy and Julie Miller
Hills and Valleys, The Flatlanders
The Rebirth of Venus, Ben Lee
Porcupine, Tim Easton
Townes, Steve Earle
Man Overboard, Ian Hunter
Acquired Taste, Delbert McClinton
The Best Is Yet to Come: Songs of Cy Coleman, various artists
Closer to the Bone, Kris Kristofferson
Losin' Lately Gambler, Corb Lund

2010

Crazy Heart (soundtrack), various artists
The Open Road, John Hiatt
Mimeograph (EP), Old 97's
The Grand Theatre, Volume One, Old 97's
The Imus Ranch Record II, various artists

2011

Moonlight Revival, Ponderosa
skin collision past, Wild Moccasins
The Majestic Silver Strings, Buddy Miller with Bill Frisell, Marc Ribot,
    Greg Leisz, and others
I'll Never Get Out of This World Alive, Steve Earle
Photographs, Robert Ellis
The Grand Theatre Vol. 2, Old 97's
Union Songs (EP), Tom Morello: The Nightwatchman
Dirty Jeans and Mudslide Hymns, John Hiatt
Ugly Buildings, Whores, and Politicians: Greatest Hits, 1998–2009,
    Drive-By Truckers
World Wide Rebel Songs, Tom Morello: The Nightwatchman

2012

Nothing Here Seems Strange, Buxton
Birds Fly South, The Mastersons
Ukred, Kalen Nash, Normaltown Records
Pool Party, Ponderosa
Cabin Fever, Corb Lund
Hiding, Mingling, White Violet, Normaltown Records
Grandfather Child, self-titled
The Odessa Tapes, The Flatlanders
Enjoy the Company, The Whigs
Mystic Pinball, John Hiatt
I Am the Man You Know I'm Not, Ronnie Fauss, Normaltown
    Records
Let Down, Lilly Hiatt and the Dropped Ponies, Normaltown
    Records
Buddy & Jim, Buddy Miller and Jim Lauderdale

2013

Rule the World, Max Gomez
Come Cry with Me, Daniel Romano, Normaltown Records
Before the Revolution: The Best of, 1998–2011, Tim Easton
Electric, Richard Thompson
"Songs for Slim" benefit series (45s, plus full-length vinyl and
    CD compilation), various artists
The Low Highway, Steve Earle & The Dukes (& Duchesses)
American Kid, Patty Griffin
The Bright Spots, Randall Bramblett
Blind, Crippled, and Crazy, Delbert & Glen
Stay Reckless, Austin Lucas
I Am a Stranger Here, The Devil Makes Three
Shaver's Jewels: The Best of Shaver, Shaver
The Coincidentalist, Howe Gelb

2014

88 92, Wild Moccasins

Any Old Love, Halfway, +1 Records

The Lights from the Chemical Plant, Robert Ellis

Sunswimmer, New Madrid, Normaltown Records

The Happiest Man in the World, Hamell On Trial

New As Dew, Ruby the Rabbitfoot, Normaltown Records

Rock 'n' Roll Blues, Luther Dickinson

Tarpaper Sky, Rodney Crowell

Modern Creation, The Whigs

All or Nothin', Nikki Lane

Counterfeit Blues, Corb Lund

Good Luck Charm, The Mastersons

Terms of My Surrender, John Hiatt

Any Way, Shape or Form, Ben Miller Band

Body Question, Floating Action

The Shipwreck from the Shore, Anthony D'Amato

Crocodile, Young Rebel Set

Stay Lost, White Violet, Normaltown Records

An Americana Christmas, various artists

Lonely in a Crowded Room, Pegi Young & The Survivors

Built to Break, Ronnie Fauss, Normaltown Records

2015

Terraplane, Steve Earle & The Dukes

Royal Blue, Lilly Hiatt, Normaltown Records

Half a Native, Buxton

The Old New Me / Times Like This (double vinyl), Slim Dunlap

Terraplane Blues (10-inch vinyl), Steve Earle / Robert Johnson

Dawn Teeth Rattling (12-inch EP), New Madrid, Normaltown
    Records

Heartbreak Pass, Giant Sand

The Deslondes, self-titled
If I've Only One Time Askin', Daniel Romano
The Whistles & The Bells, self-titled
Jason James, self-titled
So There, Ben Folds
Devil Music, Randall Bramblett
Things That Can't be Undone, Corb Lund
YPD (CD-EP), Yip Deceiver
Cicada Rhythm, self-titled, Normaltown Records
Dying Surfer Meets His Maker, All Them Witches

2016
Cayamo Sessions at Sea, Buddy Miller & Friends
Blues & Ballads: A Folksinger's Songbook, Volumes I & II,
    Luther Dickinson
The Golden Halfway Record, Halfway, +1 Records
Keep It Together, Lily & Madeleine
Bees and Seas: The Best of, Slobberbone
magnetkingmagnetqueen, New Madrid, Normaltown Records
Strange Country, Kacy & Clayton
Mosey, Daniel Romano
Robert Ellis, self-titled
Cold Snap, Anthony D'Amato
Young in All the Wrong Ways, Sara Watkins
Divorce Party, Ruby the Rabbitfoot, Normaltown Records
Redemption & Ruin, The Devil Makes Three

2017
Time Bomb, The Suicide Commandos, Twin/Tone Records
Friday Night Is Killing Me (two-CD expanded reissue), Bash & Pop,
    Omnivore Recordings

2018

Rain Lover, Halfway, +1 Records

Say What You Will . . . Everything Can Happen and *Made to Be Broken*
(expanded CD reissues) and *The Twin/Tone Years* (five-LP vinyl box
set), Soul Asylum, Omnivore Recordings

Sprezzatura, The Literary Vagabond, self-released

The Man in the Rainbow Suspenders, Lou Santacroce, self-released

All You Get, Andras Jones, self-released

2019

While You Were Out/Clam Dip & Other Delights (expanded CD reissue),
Soul Asylum, Omnivore Recordings

Run It Again, Criminal Hygiene, Dangerbird Records

Stowaway Among the Surf (unreleased), The Everyday Visuals

Dead Man's Pop (deluxe-edition box set), The Replacements,
Rhino Records

2021

Sorry Ma, Forgot to Take Out the Trash (deluxe-edition box set),
The Replacements, Rhino Records

Where the Beat Goes On, Fingerprints, Blackberry Way Records

2023

Wronger, Tommy Stinson's Cowboys in the Campfire, Cobraside

Tim: Let It Bleed Edition (deluxe-edition box set), The Replacements,
Rhino Records

Credits for Song Lyrics Quoted

"Sixteen Blue"

"Nowhere Is My Home"

"15 Years in Indiana"

"Mr. Reilly"

Index

system" for major labels, 56; first groups signed, 45, 48–50; first releases, 51; formation of, 46–47; and Hüsker Dü, 53, 59; and Jonny III, 40–41; labels added to, 60; movement from EPs to LPs, 55; name and logo, 45–46; new headquarters, 58–59; new label under author, 176; 1993 releases, 184–85; partners, 45; releases by, 40, 46, 51, 59, 60–61, 186–88, 190, 221, 236–37; Replacements as preferred group, 70; Replacements releases with, 56, 66, 67, 68–69, 74–77; roster of bands after two years, 53; staff, 61, 177, 225; Suburbs' *In Combo*, 53; success of, 57; Suicide Commandos' releases, 51, 52; Tunes concert, 52. *See also* Medium Cool Records

Uncle Sam's, 33, 42
Uptown Bar, 133, 158, 168
Urban Guerillas, 32

"Valerie Leon" (Romano), 226
Vaughan, Kenny, 40
Veal, Rob, 170, 182
Vector Management, 213
Village Voice, 53, 119, 126–27
Violent Femmes, 90–91

Wagner, Rick, 125
"Waiting" (Suburbs), 56
Walker, Butch, 233
Walker Art Center, 7, 52
Walkmen, 212
Wallets, 8, 32
Walsh, Jim, 187

Warner Bros./Warner Music Group, 137, 150, 179, 185, 220, 236. *See also* Sire Records
Warner Chappell Publishing, 222–23
Warren, Patrick, 210–11
Waryan, Jeff, 6, 56, 57
Was, Don, 215
Washington Square Serenade (Earle), 220–21
Waterboys, 176
Watermelon, 214
Welch, Skip, 88, 89
Westerberg, Paul: on artists' aiming for profits, 219; author and solos by, 72–73, 76–77, 79–80, 84, 116, 143, 158; and author as Replacements manager, 158–59; and author's first exposure to Replacements, 54; author's relationship with, 70; career dissatisfaction of, 147; and Dunlap, 180; guitar smashing episode, 71–72; health of, 82; and Hultquist, 71; and "I Will Dare," 113; and Leatherwoods, 168, 169; and New West, 205–7; and Palomino gig headgear, 138–39; and Replacements, 64, 66, 67, 68; single from Replacements' first album, 76–77; solo career, 168–69; song about Tommy, 111; and song lyrics, 74; *Songs for Slim*, 230
When No One Is Looking (Zuzu's Petals), 183
When Squirrels Play Chicken (Perfect), 194
When the Shit Hits the Fans (Replacements), 124–25
While You Were Out (Soul Asylum), 61